Privacy Engineering

A Data Flow and Ontological Approach

©2014 by Ian Oliver

ALL RIGHTS RESERVED.

No part of this publication may be reproduced, stored in or introduced into a retrieval system, or transmitted, in any form or by any means (electronic, mechanical, photocopying, recording or otherwise), without the prior written permission of the copyright owner, except by a reviewer who may quote brief passages in a review.

This book is sold subject to the condition that it shall not, by way of trade or otherwise, be lent, re-sold, hired out or otherwise circulated without the author's prior consent in any form of binding or cover other than that in which it is published and without a similar condition including this condition being imposed on the subsequent purchaser.

First Printing: 2014

ISBN-13: 978-1497569713

ISBN-10: 1497569710

Further information at *www.privacyengineeringbook.net*

10 9 8 7 6 5 4 3 2

I fy nheulu, Perheelleni

APPROACHING PRIVACY FROM AN engineering perspective rather than legal or advocacy has been enlightening in the extreme. What appeared to an (over) eager scientist to be simple information filtering and an application of semantics turned out to be a fantastically complex interaction of laws, regulations, software engineering, risk management, safety-critical systems design, ethics, metrics, economics and information theory - a veritable, unexplored netherworld of practice and theory - and I think that's merely just scratching the surface of this area. I've found myself exploring ideas from aviation, medicine, surgery, anaesthesia and even chemical plant design which gives an idea of how vast an area of experience we might have to draw upon in order to fully develop the tools and techniques we require to make privacy and inherent property of our systems just as safety is in other domains.

The maxim of 'code is law' has never been truer as whatever we decide in some high-level policy **must** be engineered into the code that runs our information systems. Turning privacy laws and user expectations into meaningful information systems is going to take a major unification of legal and engineering disciplines, making it one of the most exciting, difficult and inclusive areas to work in.

I'd like to thank the following for reviewing, contributing to and participating in the development of this work: Marja Marttinen, Markus Salminen, Sergey Boldyrev, Tomi Kulmala, Antti Lappeteläinen, Jari Karjala, Kimmo Syrjänen, Dan Swartwood, John Howse, Aidan Delaney, Gem Stapleton, Jim Burton and my colleagues in the Legal and Markets Privacy teams at Nokia and Here; and especially Here's diverse and talented Security, Privacy and Continuity Team. Finally a special thanks goes to my good friend Ora Lassila with whom countless hours working on the foundational aspects of information systems, ontologies, Semantic Web and many, *many* other ideas were made,

Ian Oliver, Sipoo, July 2014

Contents

Introduction   21

    From Where Comes Privacy?   22

    Privacy By Design   23

    Importance of Privacy   25

    Structures for Privacy   27

    Summary   29

Case Study   31

    The Social Camera Application   32

    Data Flow Models   33

    Data Collection from the Data Subject's Perspective   38

    Categorising the Purpose of Data Collection   41

    Traffic Data   43

Data Stores   46

Notices, Consents and Control Points   47

Data Breaches   51

Summary   53

Privacy Engineering Process Structure   55

'The' Process   56

Auditing Processes   59

Terminology and a Structure   61

Ontology and Classification   62

Summary   66

Data Flow Modelling   67

Basic Notation   67

Annotating Data Flow Models   72

Partitioning   76

Decomposition   81

Refinement   84

Channels and Data Flows   86

Documenting APIs   87

Analysing and Checking the Model   89

Summary   91

Security and Information Type Classifications   93

Security Classification   94

Information Type   98

Personal Characteristics   100

Location   101

Financial   103

Health   103

Identifier   104

Quasi-Identifier   106

Temporal   107

Content   107

Summary   109

Additional Classification Structures   111

Data Transformation   111

Provenance 113

Jurisdiction 115

Purpose 117

Usage 118

Data Subject, Controller and Processor 121

Identification and Authority 123

Personal Information and Personally Identifiable Information 126

Traffic Data 135

Risk and Vulnerability Taxonomies 135

Summary 142

Requirements 143

Types of Requirements 144

Example Security Requirements 149

Example Information Type Requirements 152

Example Requirements for Further Classification Systems 154

Personal Data and Requirements 154

Applying Requirements to a Model 159

Summary 162

Risk and Assessment   165

The Privacy Impact Assessment   167

Failure Mode and Effects Analysis   171

Root Cause Analysis   174

Threat Assessment   177

Gap Analysis   178

Risk Register   179

Summary   180

Notice and Consent   183

Notice   184

Consent   187

Implementation of an Agreement   191

Clients and Servers   196

Summary   197

Privacy Enhancing Techniques   199

Hashing   200

Encryption   203

Dataset Partitioning   205

Tokenisation and Randomisation   206

κ-Anonymity   209

Summary   212

Auditing and Inspection   213

The Audit Process   214

Contents of an Audit   215

Checklists for Auditing Activities   220

Metrics for Audits   225

Summary   227

Developing a Privacy Programme   229

The Reporting System   230

The Information Distribution System   233

The Privacy Committee   235

Education and Training   236

Accident Preparation and Investigation   238

The Knowledge Base   240

Summary   241

Conclusions   243

Bibliography   245

List of Figures

1   Sources and Foundations of Privacy   23

2   PbD, The Manifesto and Privacy Engineering   24

3   DIKW Pyramid   27

4   The Privacy Stack   28

5   User Interface Flow of the Social Camera App   33

6   Starting Model of the Social Camera App   34

7   Initial Architectural Partitioning   34

8   External Flows from Selected Partitions and Processes   35

9   Controller, Processor Partitioning   35

10   Decomposition and Refinement of the Product Improvement Data Flow   36

11   Complete High-Level Data Flow with Architectural Partitioning   37

12   Example Partial EXIF Information Contained in a Picture   39

13   Data Flow Information Content   41

14   Data Flow Information Content (Protocols)   43

15	MSC Showing the Upload to Server Functionality	43
16	Uses of Data in the Social Camera System	45
17	Refinement of the Device Storage	46
18	Data Flows with No Marketing Consent Given	50
19	Refinement Data Flows with No Marketing Consent Given	50
20	Privacy Engineering Process Flow	56
21	Model Structure, Aspects and Layers	58
22	A Generic or Template Data Flow Diagram	61
23	Relationships Between the Ontologies of Information	63
24	Aspect Structure in an Object Oriented System	64
25	Aspect Structure in a File Oriented System	64
26	Aspect Structure in a Relational Database Structure	65
27	Processes, User, Environments, Stores and Leaks	68
28	Data Flow Between Two Processes	69
29	Multiple Data Flows Between Two Processes	69
30	Return Flow Notation	70
31	Example Prototypical Initial Data Flow	70
32	Example Leak to an Unknown Entity	70
33	Example Leak to a Known Entity	71
34	Annotating Data Flow Transport Protocols	73
35	Annotating Data Flow Contents	74

36	Example Annotation of Processes	76
37	An 'Over Annotated' Process	76
38	Example Simple Partitioning	78
39	Example Hierarchical Partitioning	79
40	Example Overlapping Partitioning	79
41	Example Annotated Partitioning	80
42	Data Flow Decomposition: Initial Model	82
43	Data Flow Decomposition: Decomposed Model	82
44	Node Decomposition: Initial Model	83
45	Node Decomposition: Decomposed Model	84
46	Refinement Example: Initial Model	85
47	Refinement Example: Refined Model	85
48	A Security Classification Meta-Model	94
49	Security Hierarchy	95
50	Top Level Information Type Classes	99
51	Characteristic Hierarchy	100
52	Location Hierarchy	102
53	Financial Class Hierarchy	103
54	Health Class Hierarchy	104
55	Identity Hierarchy	104
56	Quasi-Identifier Construction	106
57	Denoting Quasi-Identifier Fields in a Data Flow Model	106

58	Content Hierarchy	108
59	Content Transformation Example	108
60	Data Transformation Hierarchy	112
61	W3C PROV-O Provenance Ontology Core	114
62	The Provenance Classification	114
63	Annotating Provenance in Data Flow Diagrams and Use Cases	115
64	Example Annotating a DFD with Jurisdiction Information	117
65	Purpose Ontology	117
66	Annotating Purpose in a DFD	118
67	Usage Ontology	119
68	Example Usage Annotation in a DFD	120
69	Data Subject, Controller and Processor Classification	121
70	Identification Annotations in a Data Flow Diagram	125
71	Personal Data, PII and Subclasses	126
72	Derivation of the Personal Data Terminology	127
73	Measuring the information content of different information types	133
74	Solove's Taxonomy for the Conceptualisation of Privacy	136
75	The Antón-Earp Taxonomy of Privacy Vulnerabilities and Protection Goals	136
76	Human Factors Analysis and Classification System Taxonomy	137

77	Risk Area Classification	139
78	The Derivation of Requirements	144
79	System, Requirements and Audits	144
80	Three Dimensions of Requirements	145
81	Classification of Requirement Aspects	146
82	The Release of Personal Data	159
83	Refined Design for the Release of Personal Data	161
84	Cost vs Risk and Privacy	165
85	Location Sharing vs EXIF Removal	166
86	The Chosen Data Flow for FMEA of Location Data via Social Media Provider	172
87	3rd Party Backup Data Flow for STRIDE Analysis	178
88	Structure of an Agreement	183
89	Examples Notices over the Usage Life of an Application	185
90	Example System and Service Provisioning Data Flows	186
91	Agreement Limits and Humans	187
92	First Time Usage Consent Data Flow Model	189
93	Cross-referencing First Time Usage Consent Information	189
94	Social Camera First Time Usage Screen with Notice	191
95	Control Flow for Modal Notices and Consent	192
96	Control Flow for Modeless Notices and Consent	192

97 Marketing Consent Example   192

98 Consent Data Flow   193

99 Marketing Data Flow   194

100 Simplified Client-Server Data Flows For Agreement Calculation   197

101 Two Clients, One Database   205

102 Two Clients, One Partitioned Database   206

103 Data Flow for an Example κ-Anonymisation of a Data Set   210

104 One Method of Organising Audits in the Software Development Process   214

105 Audit Team Checklist   221

106 Development Team Pre-Review Checklist   222

107 Development Team Post-Review Checklist   224

108 Development Team Checklist   225

109 Audit Complexity Metric   226

110 Information Privacy Programme Structure   229

111 Dataflow in a Reporting System   231

112 Reporting System Ticket Process   233

113 Dataflow in an Information Distribution System   234

114 Privacy Committee Skills Continuum   235

115 Accident Investigation Timeline   239

List of Tables

1	High Level API Specification	88
2	API Specification with Protocol Details	89
3	Identity Classification Levels	124
4	Example Anonymised Data set	129
5	Example Security Classification Requirements	150
6	Example Information Type Classification Requirements	153
7	Example Policy Level Provenance Classification Requirements	155
8	Example Policy Level Purpose and Usage Classification Requirements	156
9	Example Policy Level Requirements for Personal Data	157
10	Example Policy Level Requirements for Storage and Declassification of Personal Data and Specific Information Types	158
11	Example FMEA for Location Sharing	172
12	Example FMEA Recommended Actions for Location Sharing	173

13 Example FMEA for High-Level Risk Categories   174

14 Example RCA Summary Report   176

15 Example STRIDE Analysis   178

16 Raw Example Marketing Data Set   209

17 κ-anonymised Example Marketing Data Set   210

Introduction

AS USERS BECOME MORE aware of what data about them is being collected and how it is being used and often sold onwards, they are becoming more critical and more vocal about applications and services that do not respect their wishes regarding their data [1]. While efforts to protect users are being enacted through laws it is still the responsibility of software engineers to ensure that information systems are architected, designed and coded with privacy as an inherent property [2,3].

Privacy has developed sufficiently to be a distinct discipline from information system security and is *primarily concerned* with the content and usage of *personal data*; while security is concerned with the protection and integrity of data[4] in more general terms. The two together however exist in symbiosis: without security you do not get privacy and a requirement for privacy is a requirement for security [5].

It is all too easy to create software and systems which collect massive amounts of data that can be correlated and therefore provide a detailed profile of a user. While in most part users are accepting of this as we see with store cards, credit cards, air miles, etc., there are limits to what is considered ethical and acceptable from a user's perspective.

Legislation and regulations are enforcing privacy obligations upon anyone who collects, uses or processes personal data in any way. From a business perspective, respecting privacy is therefore not just avoidance of legal punishment but becoming a mechanism for engaging the consumer and building brand value and trust. Non-compliance will result in increasingly severe legal punishments and a potentially massive loss in

[1] Helen Nissenbaum. A contextual approach to privacy online. *Daedalus*, 140 (4):32–48, Fall 2011

[2] Lawrence Lessig. Code is law: On liberty in cyberspace. *Harvard Magazine*, Jan-Feb 2000

[3] Lawrence Lessig. *Code and other laws of cyberspace*. Basic, New York, 1999

[4] R. Wacks. *Privacy: A Very Short Introduction*. Very Short Introductions. OUP Oxford, 2010. ISBN 9780191609626

[5] Helen Nissenbaum. Will security enhance trust online, or supplant it? In R. Kramer and K. Cook, editors, *Trust and Distrust Within Organizations: Emerging Perspectives, Enduring Questions*, pages 155–188. Russell Sage Publications, 2004

consumer trust and confidence.

The weak point of privacy is that it has not sufficiently penetrated to the software engineering level as a discipline as aspects such as performance and security have, yet the tools for understanding our systems from an information content and information already exist and just need to be applied in this context. In order to successfully implement privacy engineering we must move on from vague principles, high-level policies and grand statements and *understand* the fundamental software and system engineering aspects and how these are applied and implemented by engineers.

Privacy in information systems needs to be *engineered* and not dictated through policy and high-level requirements without reference to the fundamentals of creating and developing software[6] and the human factors that lie underneath[7]; thus privacy can be promoted into engineering discipline. To do that we need to understand how information systems behave with respect to the information they are carrying, how to classify that information, how to reason about it, how to measure it and how to manage it. The aim of this book is to present a set of tools that can be used during the engineering process to better understand information and its flow around and between systems.

[6] Bruce Schneier. Architecture of privacy. *IEEE Security & Privacy*, 7(1):88, 2009. ISSN 1540-7993

[7] James Reason. *Human Error*. Cambridge [England] ; New York : Cambridge University Press, 1990. xv, 302 p., 1990

From Where Comes Privacy?

THE NOTION OF PRIVACY is in embedded in the human psyche and an innate desire to be able to performs one's life without interference. This concept is enshrined in various laws with the European Convention on Human Rights and certain articles of the US Constitution being canonical examples. The notions of personal privacy and freedom however are dictated by custom, convention, morals, ethics and social norms [8]. The more modern concept of information system privacy has developed from these beginnings. Figure 1 shows the three major sources of the modern definition of privacy.

[8] D. K. Lewis. *Convention: A Philosophical Study*. Oxford: Blackwell, 1969

We additionally have the economic component of privacy[9] from business needs and the basis for these models is fairly well understood[10]. What is less understood is how the consumer actually interacts with services in terms of whether privacy is

[9] Alessandro Acquisti. The economics of personal data and the economics of privacy, 2010

[10] Shah Mahmood and Yvo Desmedt. Two new economic models for privacy. *SIGMETRICS Performance Evaluation Review*, 40(4):84–89, 2013

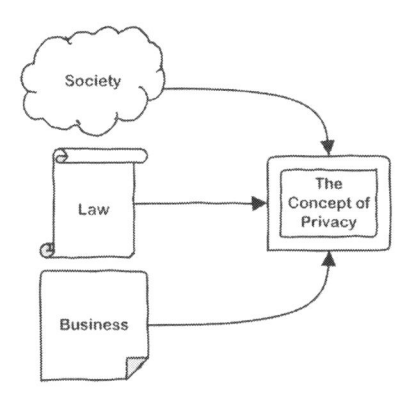

Figure 1: Sources and Foundations of Privacy

a, so called, zero-sum or non-zero-sum game. It is likely that due to the information asymmetry on how consumers' data are being used and passed between many partners that from the consumers' perspective this is more like buying a used car rather than a fair exchange of personal data for a service[11]. Even in the cases where the trade of personal data actually *is* a positive-sum or win-win game between the consumer and service provider then the balance is usually extremely off-set and certainly not in the favour of the consumer.

[11] George A. Akerlof. The market for lemons: Quality uncertainty and the market mechanism. *The Quarterly Journal of Economics*, 3(84):488–500, 1970

The value of privacy being developed at this level of detail, rather than being 'just' a compliance activity run in isolation, is bound with the overall value of privacy to the business, stock holder value, customer trust, brand value, etc.

Privacy By Design

THE SEVEN *foundational* PRINCIPLES of Privacy by Design[12] (PbD) are well known throughout the privacy community and together they stand as an idealised focus for the development of privacy in information systems as the Agile Manifesto[13] did for the software development processes.

[12] Ann Cavoukian. Privacy by Design: A Primer, September 2013

[13] Kent Beck, Mike Beedle, Arie van Bennekum, Alistair Cockburn, Ward Cunningham, Martin Fowler, James Grenning, Jim Highsmith, Andrew Hunt, Ron Jeffries, Jon Kern, Brian Marick, Robert C. Martin, Steve Mellor, Ken Schwaber, Jeff Sutherland, and Dave Thomas. Manifesto for agile software development, 2001

1. Proactive not Reactive; Preventative not Remedial
2. Privacy as the Default Setting
3. Privacy Embedded into Design
4. Full Functionality - Positive-Sum, not Zero-Sum

5. End-to-End Security - Full life cycle Protection
6. Visibility and Transparency - Keep it Open
7. Respect for User Privacy - Keep it User-Centric

As time has shown misunderstanding and incorrectly applying the principles of the Agile Manifesto has led to severe development problems and 'technical debt'[14]. One only needs to look at the modern application of the term 'agile' to understand that its original meaning in many cases has been lost if not wholly corrupted. Such is the danger facing the principles of Privacy By Design and even now statements such as 'We Follow PbD Principles' are abound in policies without any underpinning or engineering understanding of those principles in either code or process.

To move forward we must precisely understand how these principles can be integrated not just into policies, but engineering requirements, design requirements, test cases, software development processes, analysis tools, development tools and even the very psyche of software engineering. Efforts such as the Privacy Engineer's Manifesto[15] take the first step in addressing these aspects. The relationship between PbD, the Privacy Engineer's Manifesto and Privacy Engineering can be visualised in figure 2. For example, one of the principles states that privacy must be embedded into the design of a system:

> Privacy is embedded into the design and architecture of IT systems and business practices. It is not bolted on as an add-on, after the fact. The result is that it becomes an essential component of the core functionality being delivered. Privacy is integral to the system, without diminishing functionality.

Stating how this is achieved is beyond the PbD principles[16] and therein lies the problem often seen in that adherence to these principles is through a dogmatic top-down process, platitudes and policy rather than any real engineering effort. Ultimately Privacy by Design provides a number of focus points, it does not provide us with any engineering or foundational basis of privacy from which we can effectively develop our software and systems without a huge effort made in their implementation[17].

One must work simultaneously bottom-up from basic engineering and deeper theoretical perspectives to ensure that both

[14] Philippe Kruchten, Robert L Nord, Ipek Ozkaya, and Davide Falessi. Technical debt: towards a crisper definition report on the 4th international workshop on managing technical debt. *ACM SIGSOFT Software Engineering Notes*, 38(5):51–54, 2013

Figure 2: PbD, The Manifesto and Privacy Engineering

[15] Thomas Finneran Michelle Finneran Dennedy, Jonathan Fox. *The Privacy Engineer's Manifesto: Getting from Policy to Code to QA to Value*. Apress, 2014

[16] Seda Gürses, Carmela Troncoso, and Claudia Diaz. Engineering privacy by design. In *Conference on Computers, Privacy and Data Protection (CPDP)*, 2011

[17] Sarah Spiekermann. The challenges of privacy by design. *Communications of the ACM*, 55(7):38–40, July 2012

directions of thought on how to implement and engineer privacy are developed. Here we primarily take the bottom-up approach and do not attempt to define precise processes but rather present ontologies, structures and tools which can be adapted as local development practices require and dictate.

We can also talk about the ideas of privacy-by-policy and privacy-by-architecture[18], which are in effect pseudonyms for the top-down and bottom-up approaches; or possibly another way to look at this is that a privacy-by-policy approach is driven from the compliance and legal side, whilst a privacy-by-architecture is driven from a technical or engineering side. Neither can exist without the other and should be seen as mutually beneficial or symbiotic rather than two opposing mechanisms for achieving inherent privacy.

[18] Sarah Spiekermann and Lorrie Faith Cranor. Engineering privacy. *Software Engineering, IEEE Transactions on*, 35(1): 67–82, 2009

Importance of Privacy

WE MIGHT NOW ASK the question 'why is this important?'. Surely, privacy no longer exists in a connected, shared information world? Indeed this is true to a point, though as users of such information sharing systems (for example, Facebook and Google being prime examples) come to be more educated over the worth of their personal information and the amount of information that can be derived from this, as we have seen in the economic argument, this forces the consumer to become more proactive in their view of their information. This is one of the major drivers from a user's perspective: the value of that user's information.

Any interaction with and sharing information via any computer system leaves a trail of information of various kinds:

- log information generated as part of the necessary workings of the services

- log information generated by the user's interaction with the services and applications interfacing with those services

- the user's information stored within the system

- the information derived from a combination of the above

All this information can be used for various and numerous purposes: generally either for gaining information about how the provided services are being used (product improvement) or for some form of advertising; not including subversive or devious uses[19] depending upon your point of view. The accuracy of the targeting of advertisements depends upon the quality of the information used to generate the advertisement. This may be achieved in a number of ways: the first being simple random deployment of advertisements, albeit somewhat tailored for the typical demographic using that service. Secondly and more commonly, the user or consumer of a service is identified (through a log-in or cookie mechanism) and profile constructed through interaction over time, geographical information, etc, through which more 'relevant' and targeted advertising can be made.

[19] J.K. Petersen. *Understanding Surveillance Technologies: Spy Devices, Their Origins & Applications*. Taylor & Francis, 2000. ISBN 9781420038811

Privacy laws enforce a number rules over this usage of information:

- Who is the data subject?

- How the data subject's permission/consent is sought for the use their data or information

- The amount and relevancy of data or information collected and processed

- A clear identification of those architectural or logical system parts which fall under the definitions of controller and or processor

The data subject (user or consumer) is the source of the information that is going to be processed, transported, stored and transferred in various ways. The controller is the body who takes responsibility for the processing of this information and who might contract out some of this to 'processors' who are wholly under the control of the controller.

Permission for data collection is achieved using some consent (opt-in/out) mechanism(s), typically presented as an acceptance of some privacy policy or the general terms and conditions for some service. This must provide details of all collection and processing that the controller will make over that data and actually sets out the maximal criteria of the processing of data.

It is specifically worth noting how much or more accurately how little interaction and control the user has in this process and how little the user actually receives back; though it is often argued that the very provision of the service in the first place is ample payback to the user for use of their information.

This then leads to a more detailed evaluation of the feedback loop between the consumer of information and the supplier. In order to build a business based upon the collection and usage of a user's information we must simply gain the trust of that user both in terms of responsible storage, collection and usage of that user's information and in terms of the worth of that information as presented back to the user.

For the user, the most important thing here is not whether data is or isn't collected or even how it is used to support a service, but rather that the data is being used *appropriately*[20]. This notion of *appropriateness* and its connection with what data flows to where is the key to understanding the engineering aspects of privacy and therefore to construct information systems that conform with the user expectations of privacy.

[20] Helen Nissenbaum. *Privacy in Context: Technology, Policy, and the Integrity of Social Life*. Stanford University Press, 2010. 9780804752367

Structures for Privacy

To UNDERSTAND BETTER PRIVACY we can use a model or suite of models for expressing the relationship(s) between data and information. This can be taken further to include noise, knowledge and wisdom through the so-named DIKW pyramid[21] shown in figure 3. Each layer in the pyramid, or hierarchy adds structure and meaning (semantics) to the elements layer below[22].

[21] Jennifer Rowley. The wisdom hierarchy: representations of the DIKW hierarchy. *J. Information Science*, 33(2):163–180, 2007

[22] Chaim Zins. Conceptual approaches for defining data, information, and knowledge. *JASIST*, 58(4):479–493, 2007

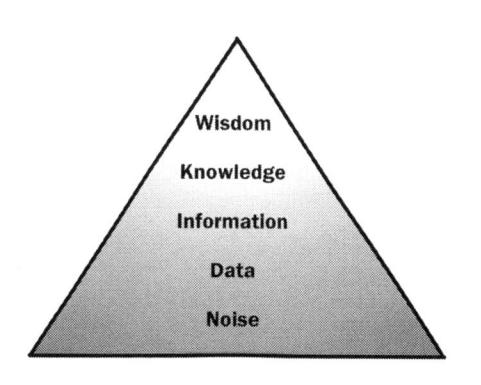

Figure 3: DIKW Pyramid

Noise is just a random collection of symbols without form nor meaning. Data is a structuring of this collection into parts to which we can ascribe meaning or semantics giving us information. A corpus of items of information provides us with knowledge over which we can reason to produce wisdom.

This model has its problems [23], but it does serve well to explain the relationships between these terms, especially the terms **data** and **information** which we use extensively. Indeed in information systems we pass data between systems and it is only the knowledge encoded in our algorithms or our viewing of that data that ascribes any meaning to that data making it information. In the software context data is just the bits and bytes that make up a message and the information is ascribed by understanding what that data represents.

[23] Martin Frické. The knowledge pyramid: a critique of the DIKW hierarchy. *J. Information Science*, 35(2):131–142, 2009

We can also place privacy into an extended ISO 7-layer model[24] which in a manner similar to the DIKW model also provides some scope of what privacy means and where it lies in relation to other aspects.

[24] International Organisation for Standardisation. Open systems interconnection - basic reference model: ISO/IEC 7498-1, November 1994

- Data

- Ontology

- Security

- Privacy

- Trust

- Belief

The layering to a point is arbitrary in that in the implementation various aspects can and are interspersed over other layers. For example, layers 5 to 7 - session, presentation and application - are often mixed; similarly transport protocols are often spread over layers 3 and 4. Indeed proposals for layers 8 and above are quite diverse but in general take into consideration the more 'human' related qualities of a system[25,26]. But again, the point here is not to define privacy but to provide us a mechanism for understanding its scope and where it 'lies' within a system when looking from differing perspectives and contexts.

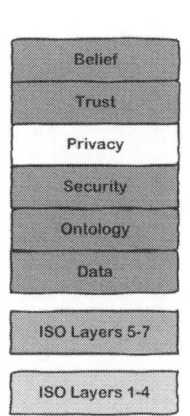

Figure 4: The Privacy Stack

[25] Ian Farquhar. Engineering security solutions at layer 8 and above. *RSA Speaking of Security Blog*, 7 December 2010

[26] Michael Gregg. OSI: Securing the Stack, Layer 8 – Social engineering and security policy. *TechTarget*, 1 May 2007

Summary

THE FORMALISATION OF PRIVACY, at least in the context of information systems is therefore embedded in law and the various jurisdictions in which those laws are applied[27]. These laws in turn form the aforementioned moral and ethical structures. Much of what is meant by *privacy* actually refers to the conformance of systems, procedures, programmes, software, etc. to the rules laid down in those in those laws.

[27] Eduardo Ustaran, editor. *European Privacy: Law and Practice for Data Protection Professionals*. An IAPP Publication, 2012. 978-0-9795901-5-3

Privacy is ultimately about the collection, processing and usage of data and specifically how that data becomes personal information. Even seemingly innocuous systems which appear not to collect anything have the potential to fall foul of the now extensive legislation and rules in this area. Therefore the key to understanding the privacy related aspects of any information system is to understand where the data, and thus information, flows: its sources, where it is processed, where it is stored and its destinations and so on.

In this book we will present by way of a case study of a simple application how various modelling techniques and ontological structures we can select and generate suitable requirements, notices, consents and control points to our information systems. Then from the "reverse" direction we show how what is required to audit a system, make a privacy impact assessment and conduct additional checks through techniques such as Failure Mode and Effects Analysis (FMEA) and Root Cause Analysis (RCA).

We do not prescribe any process but rather describe tools and techniques; the specific application is always best left to the users of these to decide how and what to deploy in this respect and that there exist a large number of fairly descriptive processes and methods[28,29] for organising aspects of software development.

[28] Bart De Win, Riccardo Scandariato, Koen Buyens, Johan Grégoire, and Wouter Joosen. On the secure software development process: CLASP, SDL and Touchpoints compared. *Information and software technology*, 51(7):1152–1171, 2009

[29] Adam Shostack. Experiences of threat modeling at Microsoft. In *Modeling Security Workshop. Dept. of Computing, Lancaster University, UK*, 2008

Case Study

EVEN THE MOST APPARENTLY benign applications can have very complex data flows and interactions of architectural and legal aspects associated with them. In this chapter we present a case study of a simple camera and photo sharing application. The act of simply taking a picture and sharing it involves data such as dates, times, device details, locations and user identities; not to mention the data generated by the infrastructure and many routes of that data to persons both friendly and unknown. Furthermore, this is all within a larger ecosystem involving marketing, advertising, user profiling and all the trappings of an application's life on the Internet.

We will model our application by describing the overall data flow from the end-user of the application, known in this context as the data subject. We then proceed by layering over this data flow aspects such as:

1. the architectural partitioning, both logical and physical
2. the various controller-processor distinctions
3. the geographical jurisdiction

As well as annotating further aspects such as identity, provenance, usage, purpose and then specific use cases and refinements as necessary. Use of this case study will also continue in other chapters to demonstrate specific features being discussed there.

A development environment's processes dictate which models need to be constructed; the data flow along with the three aspects above *and* user interface flows should be considered a minimum for privacy engineering. Specific use cases and refinements can be constructed as necessary to explain particular situations. When making a privacy impact assessment or privacy audit these models will be essential to the successful outcome these activities.

The Social Camera Application

THE APPLICATION IS DOWNLOADED by the user from an 'app store' on to a user's mobile device. The user has access to a number of settings local to the application and also the ability to log in to the application provider's services using an account provided there. Once logged in, automated backup of the photographs taken are made on that social camera application's service provider's machines. The application has facilities to enable sharing to various social media sites along with the capability to store the username, password combinations locally for convenience.

The application is partially supported by advertisements displayed to the user while the application is running. These advertisements are location specific but do not require the latitude-longitude from the device but rather via some geolocation based upon the devices reported address.

The application service provider also request information about the application's behaviour through an application improvement programme. Additionally the service provider also has targeted marketing opportunities to users who opt-in to this facility.

Other services on the device that can access the photographs locally include 3rd party backup software, which may be of dubious origin - or at least some aspects of its functionality are not clear.

As is typical for nearly all applications upon first use the user is presented with a screen detailing the relevant terms and conditions, privacy policy and options to opt in and out of product improvement and marketing options. The first time usage user interface flow is shown in figure 5.

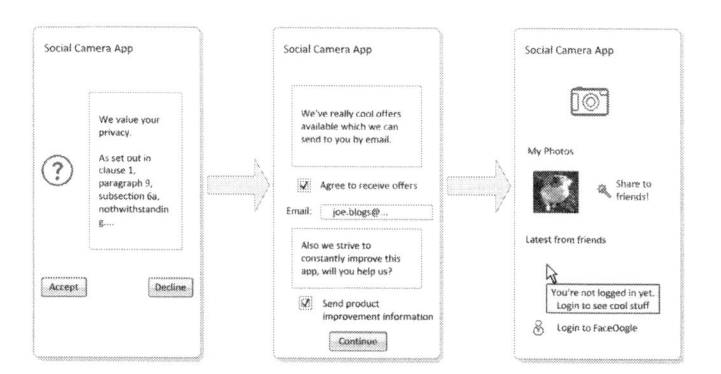

Figure 5: User Interface Flow of the Social Camera App

Once started waits for the user to press the shutter button and takes a photo. All photographs can be shared to selected social media providers simply by selecting the icon next to them.

Data Flow Models

THE SIMPLEST MODEL OF the system we can create is shown in figure 6. This consists of just the user providing information to the application and the flows of the user's information to the components listed earlier. From this point we can start scoping our system and decomposing the processing nodes as necessary to reveal the structures we require to analyse. It may also seem a little odd that the flow of data is from the user (via the social camera application) to the advertiser when ostensibly adverts are *received*. The reasoning here is that we are modelling in the context of the user and the user's data is being provided to the advertiser.

Architectural Partitioning

ONCE WE HAVE ESTABLISHED an idea of where the user's data is flowing and its direction we can turn our attention to the logical and physical architectural partitioning of the system. The level of granularity can be increased through multiple refinements so that we can vary between devices, servers and down

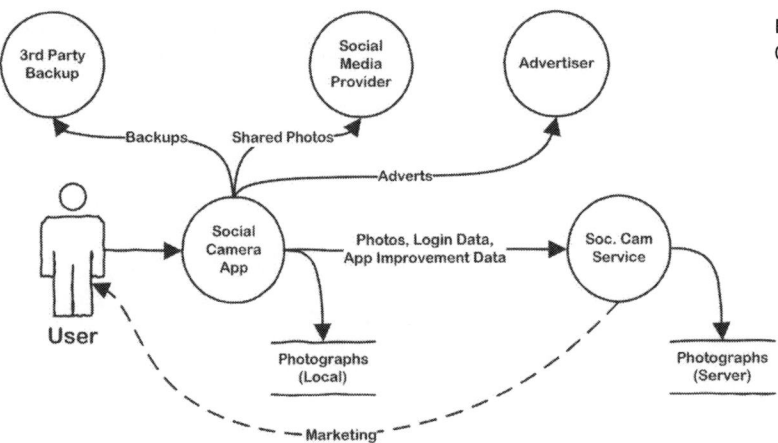

Figure 6: Starting Model of the Social Camera App

to processes if required. Figure 7 shows an initial architectural decomposition.

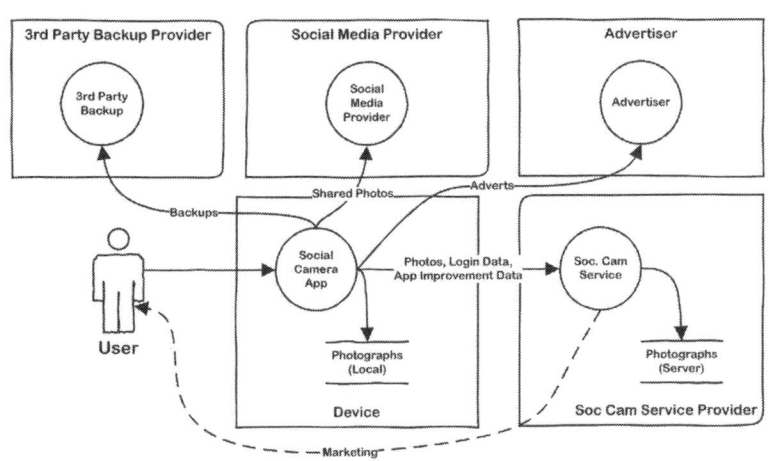

Figure 7: Initial Architectural Partitioning

Note that further data flows out of the system might exist as well as additional parties such as marketing and advertising within one of the existing partitions and of course further processes on device the outside of the scope of the local process or even services just not specified yet. All models must be considered incomplete in this respect and in figure 8 we show how we might notate this for the 3rd party backup provider which we have hinted that we can not fully trust.

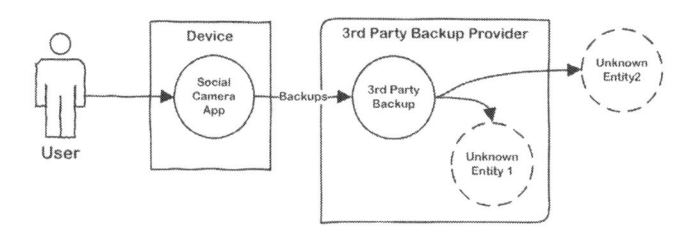

Figure 8: External Flows from Selected Partitions and Processes

Controller, Processor and Data Subject

ONCE WE HAVE SET out the architectural aspects of the data flow we must then model where the boundaries of the controllers and processors of the information. Additionally we take this opportunity to specifically denote the data subject. Figure 9 shows these legally defined boundaries.

The source of the data is marked as the data subject - this shows the initial reading point of any data flow diagram. The flows from the data subject are controlled through policies and consent defined by the controllers to which they flow into. Processors of data are always under the control of some host controller which supplies this policy and consent mechanism.

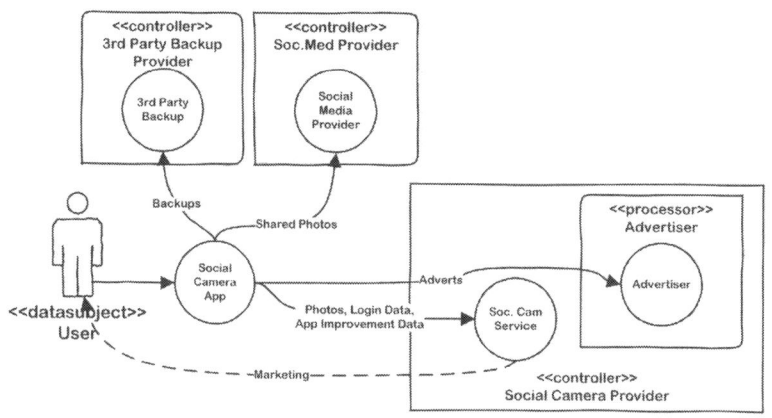

Figure 9: Controller, Processor Partitioning

The data subject defines the context of the model, that is the entity about which the model is expressing the data flows. The interactions between the data flow and the elements within particular controller and processor boundaries define the points at which the contents of data flows need to be controller and agreements between the data subject, controller and processors need to be defined. Processors are always within the bounds of a controller and it should be clear from the data flow model and partitioning here that any agreement between the data subject and the advertiser in this case is within the agreement between the data subject and the social camera provider controller.

Process Decomposition and Refinement

THE MODELS WE HAVE shown so far as fairly high-level in nature and the processes therein represent more large-scale architectural or component entities rather than functions over a stream of data. We can of course show the models at any level of abstraction as we require and for most discussions it is advantageous to abstract away many of the details, or, to show only a partial model to concentrate on one or two specific details. In figure 10 we show how the data flow for one of the analytics processes might be decomposed and refined.

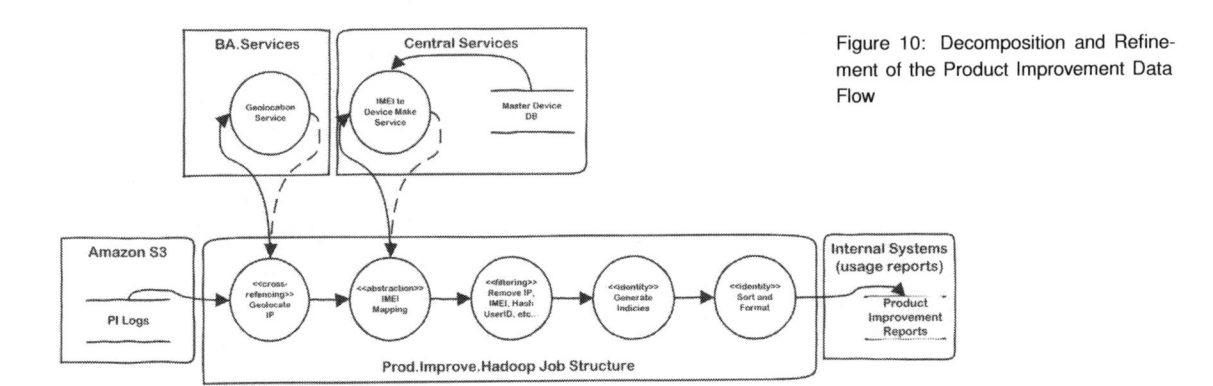

Figure 10: Decomposition and Refinement of the Product Improvement Data Flow

As we can see we are free to mix the partitioning of the model however we choose: in this case we have groupings of storage mechanisms, a process structure and two external architectural or component partitions. The main thing here is that we wish to show how a particular process is broken down into its constituent parts and how it interacts at a data flow level with other processes.

Complete High-Level Data Flow

RATHER THAN WORK THROUGH some arbitrary development flow, we at this point now show in figure 11 what we will consider here to be a 'complete' data flow model and architectural partitioning to demonstrate the possible extent of the scope of the modelling beyond the initial, seemingly simple application. Note that this model now contains a number of data flows and processes not previously mentioned - this again is to show how the complexity of such models increases.

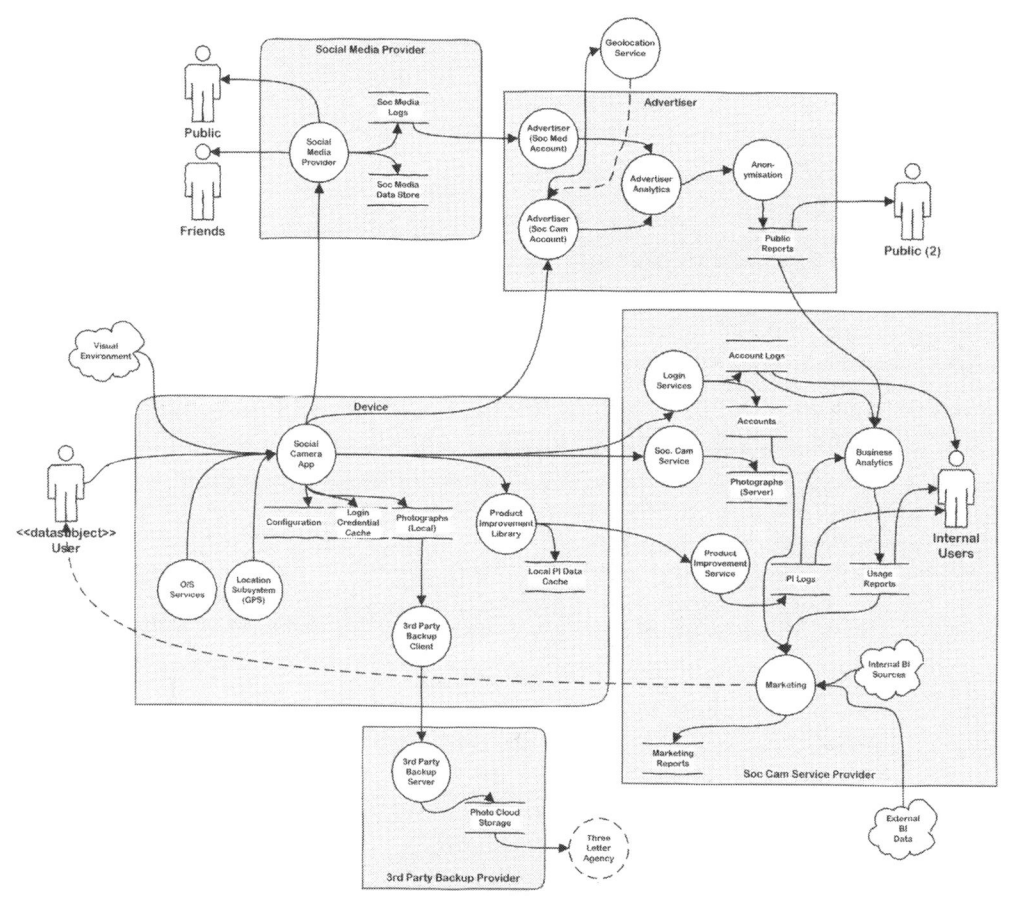

Figure 11: Complete High-Level Data Flow with Architectural Partitioning

Data Collection from the Data Subject's Perspective

LET US FIRST START following the data flow diagram in figure 11 through from the initial user's perspective. We have not annotated that particular model with the data collected over the data flows nor in the stores at this point. There are four flows that we must initially consider:

1. The data collected when a picture is taken by the user
2. The data collected when the user logs into the social camera service provider's account service
3. The data continually collected by the product improvement library
4. The data continually sent to the advertiser to obtain a new advertisement

When a picture is taken a data stream from the camera ostensibly from the visual environment is combined with data from the operating system services and location subsystem to form the picture that is stored by the social camera application. This picture contains much meta-data as partially shown in figure 12. Furthermore it is also highly likely that static data such as the user's copyright message and identity be included too. Over this flow then we can state that we are collecting data of the following kinds: Photo (which includes much meta-data), User Identity, Device Identity, Location and Temporal Data.

This data flows via various routes, either to the server-side photograph storage provided by the social camera provider and also to the 3rd party backup software via the internal storage in the device. We have also hinted that it might flow further from this latter provider.

The second flow comes into play when the user submits his or her login credentials to the login services. The data collected here is fairly simple in that at minimum it requires a user identity and password. There may be additional data such as keys and timestamps depending upon the particular protocol used for log in. Whatever data is sent via this route is going to be logged which will include most likely a machine address

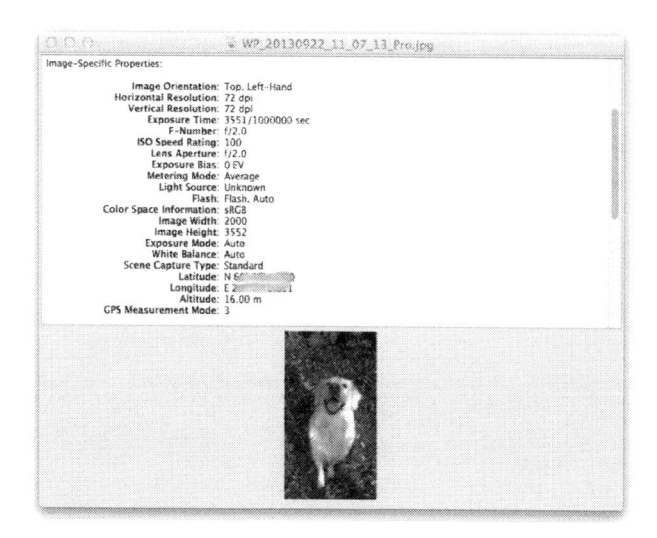

Figure 12: Example Partial EXIF Information Contained in a Picture

- an IP address usually - and some temporal data along with necessary data about the action performed and its outcome. The account database - the creation of which we have not discussed - at minimum would have a user identifier and password in some secure form.

Product improvement data can be collected from any instrumented part of the application. Mostly this is collected to understand how the user uses the user-interface and which features are being used. Additionally we can collect crash data and other data about the context and status of the device here as we see fit. For the purposes here we will state that we collect a user identifier, application identifier, device identifier, location, event (app start, stop, crash, UI action) and temporal data. For anonymity purposes some of these fields, such as the user identifier might 'anonymised' through hashing or tokenisation. Such data collection is termed secondary data collection and is typically opted-into by the user.

The flow of this data along with the user account log data eventually finds its way to the business analytics and marketing processes and their reports.

The final flow of immediate interest is the data being sent to the advertiser. It is a common technique for an application provider to create an account with an advertiser and use some form of session or application identifier such that the advertiser can provide tracking over time. In our case here we have stated that there isn't much in the way of tracking but we can assume some identifier - a session identifier - that exists for an extended period of time, say 3 months, so that the advertiser can generate reports and provide 'more relevant' adverts. Other than this no data is sent directly other than traffic data provided by the underlying protocols.

Authority and User Provenance

ONE POINT TO CONSIDER here is the degree of authority under which the data was collected. If the user uses this application without logging in then we can not be sure that it is the user using that application - or at least the data which we are collecting is not associated through any deliberate, identifying or authorising action by the user. If the user does login then they have made a deliberate choice to provide us with their authority and therefore we can with confidence use this fact when processing their information.

Complications arise here because one person might give their device to another to use on their behalf, or if a device is stolen and used without authority as one might see in identity fraud cases. The common situation here is where a user, an adult, gives the device to a child. Who are we now collecting data about? By the above statements it is the authority, that is the original user. But now consider the case where an adult has given access to a child, but the child has shared information or bought a product 'accidentally'. Many applications are not written specifically for child usage - adherence to Children's Online Privacy Protection Act (COPPA) regulations are often too difficult and time consuming even for larger corporations.

In this latter case, if we wished to make the distinction between child and adult[30] then the implications on our data flows are quite dramatic as we now have to take into consideration the provenance and authority - who have the permission to the child and when the handover between child and adult data occurs. While child related aspects typify the extreme case of data collection, more commonly we see authority related to the data use. For example, if the user is not logged in and we are collecting secondary data, can we cross-reference that data back to *a* user? Can we correlate historical data collected under the

[30] Parent or legal guardian

varying levels of authority back together? Much now depends upon what the user's expectations of privacy are? Would the user be disturbed if their historical browsing and usage were taken into consideration? From the business point of view, this would be advantageous as we would have effectively a ready-built consumer profile but at what cost[31]?

[31] Gus Lubin. The incredible story of how Target exposed a teen girl's pregnancy. *Business Insider*, February 16 2012

Categorising the Purpose of Data Collection

IN THE ABOVE SECTION we outlined the flows from the data subject. We must now turn our attention to the purpose of those flows from the data subject's perspective and answer the question of whether the data is necessary or not for the functionality of the application. This actually turns out to be one of the major concerns regarding data collection and it is here that the principle of data minimisation needs to be applied. The information available to an application on any device is far greater than the application would actually need and even be reasonable for that application's core functionality[32].

[32] Jennifer M. Urban, Chris J. Hoofnagle, and Su Li. Mobile phones and privacy. *Social Science Research Network Working Paper Series*, 12 July 2012

There are two classes of purpose of data collection: primary and secondary. Primary pertaining to that information which is required by the application to perform its service and secondary pertaining to that information which is collected to understand the application's behaviour. We will also consider a third under a different categorisation of traffic data - that data that is inherent to the underlying protocols transporting data. Figure 13 shows this distinction from a protocol stack type of view.

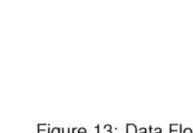

Figure 13: Data Flow Information Content

As described earlier from the data subject and various other inputs we receive the following kinds of information into our application: User Identity, Device Identity, Application Identity, Session identifiers, Photo and related meta-data content,

Location and Temporal Data. All of this data is collected for the primary purpose of providing the functionality of the application. However, data minimisation requires us to further decide what the limits on the functionality are and therefore what is the minimal set of data we should be collection versus what we are or would like to collect.

The second set of data points we may collect are those which are termed secondary data[33] - that is data which is *about* the application's behaviour and is typically collected for the purposes of understanding how a user is using the application.

[33] ChristopherJ. Cowton. The use of secondary data in business ethics research. *Journal of Business Ethics*, 17(4):423–434, 1998

Usually this is data in the form of events over time; these events containing information about the device's status, application usage etc and from which we can infer how a user uses the application, or when an application crashes what were the sequence of events leading to this within the context of the device's current status, for example, memory consumption, disk or storage usage, etc.

Again data minimisation requires use to understand for what usages this data is going to be put and whether the collection of such data is relevant to the overall service that is being provided. For example, does the set of data collect really assist in product improvement or is this more related with behavioural profiling and marketing?

There are some very specific cases which we need also to consider such as when applications crash we might collect a memory dump. This can contain passwords and other sensitive information about the user. Other cases here include the stack trace from a process, which even if this does not contain parameter values will contain details about how the software was constructed, the libraries used and potential attack vectors into the code.

Furthermore, how anonymous does the user need to be amongst this data? We will likely collect application and session identifiers, and then also consider it to be potentially reasonable to collect a user identifier additionally. Secondary data comes with many issues regarding how well the user is to be identified and many cross-referencing and fingerprinting possibilities remain.

Traffic Data

ALL INFORMATION IS TRANSFERRED over a suite of transport protocols as depicted in figure 14. In an intranet environment this typically tends to mean the HTTP suite of protocols over the ubiquitous TCP/IP protocol. In a device environment we can extend this to include various interprocess communication protocols, etc. We can even specify mechanisms of transport including using the postal service in its various forms[34].

[34] IETF RFCs 1149, 2549 and 6214 notwithstanding

We can assume that communication between the social camera app and the social camera service provider is by some call over HTTP for the purposes of this discussion. In figure 15 we show the sequence of interactions for the use case where a user takes a picture and it is automatically uploaded to the social camera service provider's storage. The following trace shows the kinds of content within the HTTP protocol:

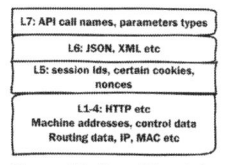

Figure 14: Data Flow Information Content (Protocols)

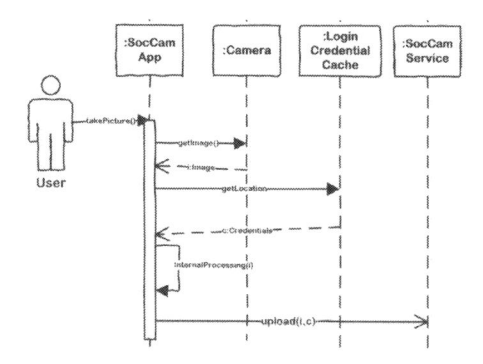

Figure 15: MSC Showing the Upload to Server Functionality

```
GET / HTTP/1.1
Host: www.socialcameraapp.xyz
User-Agent: Mozilla/5.0 (X11; OpenVMS hp_AlphaServer_ES47 ; rv:17.0)
    Gecko/20131030 Firefox/17.0
Accept: text/html,application/xhtml+xml,application/xml; q=0.9,*/*;q=0.8
Accept-Language: en-gb,en;q=0.5
Accept-Encoding: gzip, deflate
Connection: keep-alive

HTTP/1.1 200 OK
Server: Apache
Expires: Mon, 03 Feb 2014 11:54:08 GMT
Etag: "YYYYYYYYYYYYYYYYYYYYYYYYYYYYYYYY"
Content-Type: text/html
```

```
Content-Length: 114501
Date: Mon, 03 Feb 2014 11:53:08 GMT
Connection: keep-alive
Set-Cookie: SCA-UID=XXXXXXXXXXXXXXXXXXXXXXXXXXXXXXXXXX
  Mozilla/5.0 (X11; OpenVMS hp_AlphaServer_ES47 ; rv:17.0)
   Gecko/20131030 Firefox/17.0
  expires=Fri, 02-Feb-18 11:53:08 GMT;
  path=/; domain=.socialcameraapp.xyz
X-Cache-Action: MISS
X-Cache-Age: 0
Cache-Control: private, max-age=0, must-revalidate
X-LB-NoCache: true
Vary: X-CDN
```

This gives a very clear idea of what can and probably is being logged and notice that despite that we have been explicitly talking about credentials and images in MSC in figure 15 these do not appear in the above sequence which should demonstrate that we are working with two different levels of information. Even without the actual content or payload of the message, we can already know the properties of the calling application: Firefox 17, with the 2013-10-30 Gecko engine running under X11 on an OpenVMS HP AlphaServer. We know the language of the application and various aspects of the supported features of the protocol.

Also note in the response we obtain a cookie and an ETag[35] containing some kinds of identifiers. Whether these are session based or held over a number of sessions is only knowable after a number of other requests. Furthermore information from other layers of the transport protocol stack will further reveal the IP address at a minimum - proxies and other obfuscation mechanisms notwithstanding.

[35] Both obscured!

Traffic data obtained by virtue of the infrastructure is often overlooked in privacy. While efforts are made to obscure and prevent collection of identifiers and location, this can nearly always be revealed, recreated and tracked by examining the infrastructure's traffic data for such information.

Usage of Data

As a distinct concept from the purpose of collection, the usage of data pertains to the specific scenarios in which the data is to be used. We have introduced a number here such as that data which is required for the application to provide its functionality and similarly for the system, and we have also mentioned marketing and hinted at behavioural profiling. We might annotate our model of the social camera system to specifically denote which collections of data are being used for what usages as in figure 16.

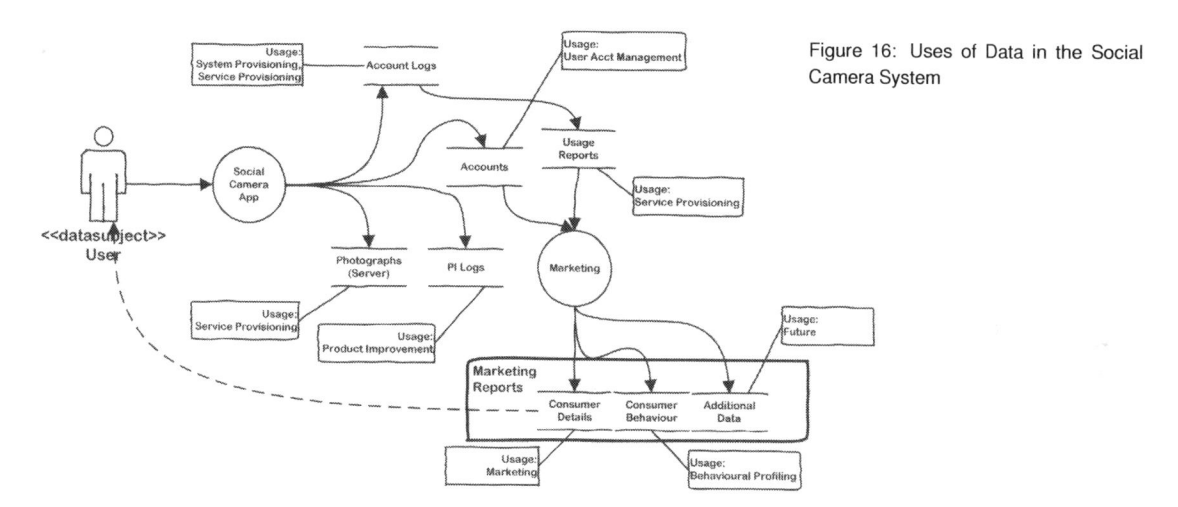

Figure 16: Uses of Data in the Social Camera System

Note that we have refined the marketing reports store now into three components with specific usages for the data inside. This does not mean that the datasets are separate in terms of their content - it is likely that there is much overlap between these. Indeed the usage distinctions here might even represent different versions of the API to access this data, or differing security levels and so on.

The terminology here will vary between businesses but we can always identify data for broad usages such as being necessary for the provisioning of the system, provisioning of the service, marketing, etc.

Understanding the usage of data is critical when constructing any agreement and presenting notices back to the data subject - these will be discussed later - but we can now calculate by tracing the usages back over the data flows to get a complete picture of the sum of usages that the user's data will be put to.

Data Stores

WE NOW TURN OUR attention to the storage of data and in particular we discuss the nature of storage on the device as this makes a good canonical example for the partitioning and security aspects we need to consider.

We have modelled the device storage as four separate stores each with a particular kind or usage of data. We have not expressed how the physical storage is constructed, the internal structures of the data nor any security protections that might be in place. It also must be noted that the layout of the diagram expressing this does not necessary convey any information about this other than by the reader's interpretation that two diagram elements placed closely together *might* mean something.

We can refine the model to show the physical storage, (operating system) processes and security domains that might exist over this as in figure 17.

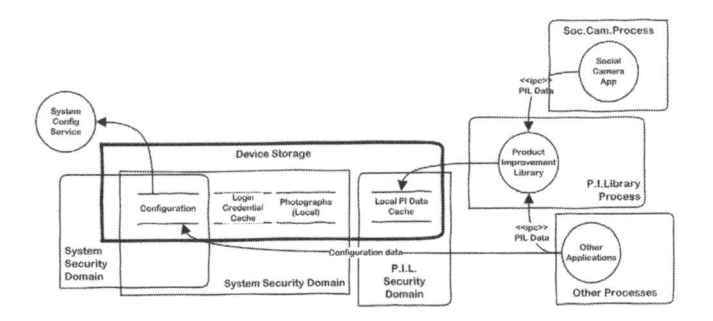

Figure 17: Refinement of the Device Storage

As we proceed with the refinement of the model we turn our attention to further aspects. The first being relatively simple in that the two stores: login credential cache and photographs may be further refined down to the actual database tables or similar structures in a 'schema-free' database being stored which might give further indication of the security issues and privacy threats here.

The second point of more concern is the nature of the product improvement library and how this runs on the device. Here we have explicitly shown that in this case this is some daemon which can be connected to over some interprocess communication form any (authorised) process. The alternative might be that this process is statically bound and each host process having their own product improvement data storage as required.

Thirdly we have an interesting overlapping of security domains between some configuration system and the social camera process itself. It is not infeasible that other applications might additionally have access to this as we have modelled and so there is an opportunity for data to be transferred via this route between seemingly separate processes.

Similar kinds of refinement and analysis can be made for the six stores of data within the social camera service provider's architectural partitioning with the amount of detail probably being significantly more as we take into consideration storage providers, cloudification, geographical location, etc.

In other cases we do not show any partitioning of the stores as obtaining this information would be impossible. For example the 3rd party backup provider's storage is modelled as just a store within that architectural domain. This in itself is perfectly acceptable from a modelling perspective, but from an analysis perspective the risks of not known the structure of from aspect such as security, location etc need to be now taken into account.

Finally we note that when constructing diagrams for particular situations or use cases it is not always necessary show all data flows, processes and other elements. This is done for reasons of simplicity of reading and understanding the diagram.

Notices, Consents and Control Points

NOW THAT WE HAVE constructed a good overall picture of what data is flowing, for what use and importantly who has responsibility for informing the data subject, we can now turn to deciding what notices must be provided to the user and what kind of consent should be obtained[36]. contain or whether even consents are valid mechanism here at all. Agreement for

[36] Daniel Solove. Privacy Self-Management and the Consent Paradox. *Harvard Law Review*, 126, 2013

collection of (personal) must be provided through a suitable notice and a consent in some form obtained either explicit or implicitly[37].

[37] EU. Opinion 15/2011 on the definition of consent. article 29 data protection working party, 2011

Returning to the data flow diagram in figure 9 there are four flows of interest corresponding to controller and processor boundaries:

- Data Subject to Controller (Social Media Application)
- Controller (Social Media Application) to Processor (Advertiser)
- Data Subject to Social Media Provider (via Social Media Application)
- Data Subject to 3rd Party Backup (via Social Media Application)

Data passing into the control of any of these controllers, and by implication to any processors via given controller must be accompanied by some agreement between the data subject and controller, or controller and processor.

There are many kinds of agreement required in differing situations, for example:

- Terms and Conditions
- Privacy Policy
- Secondary Data Collection Consent
- Marketing Consent
- 3rd Party Consent and Disclosure
- Minor or additional consents (annexes), e.g.: location collection

We can also consider the decision to download an application as a consent as well. The user here makes an informed decision regarding whether the application is wanted or not based upon the information presented, i.e.: what operating services the application requires and so on.

The data flow models do not address the positioning nor nature of the agreements and notices - this is left for legal discussion and user-interface/experience. The results of consents can appear in data flow models when explicitly annotating data flows, stores and other elements to show the movement and storage of data.

By control point we refer to the placement of the control over the flow of data at particular points in the system. For example, the choice of whether the application can collect location data or not can occur in many places in the user-interface including informing the user of such collection when the application is downloaded, when the application is first run and even outside of the application content in the operating system settings which turn on or off the GPS subsystem. The control point associated with this consent for location collection can be implemented on the data flow from the GPS subsystem to the social camera application.

As the terms and conditions and privacy policy tend to be presented together with a wholesale acceptance or not, it is imperative that the data collected, purpose and usages are in compliance with these. This is achieved by ensuring that for each item or combination of data collected, the routes that data follows, its purpose and usage are in agreement or a *refinement* of what is allowed by the (privacy) policy(ies).

The options we have when the system is not compliant are:

- alter the terms and conditions and privacy policy to make them weaker

- modify the data collection and processing over the system as a whole

- add additional content, often known as annexes

with the latter two cases being the most preferable as these can be specifically tailored to the application in question rather than alter globally (or business-wide) standard policies.

For example, in the case of a marketing consent, the application must present to the user an option[38] for whether he/she wishes to be marketed to - primarily meaning, direct or profiled marketing. The choice here however will affect data flows and

[38] *Direct Marketing: Data Protection Act Privacy and Electronic Communications Regulations.* The Information Commissioner's Office (UK), 24 November 2013. Version 1.1

processes much deeper in the system with one option being shown in figure 18 where the flow back to the user is simple removed but the behaviour collection by marketing remains.

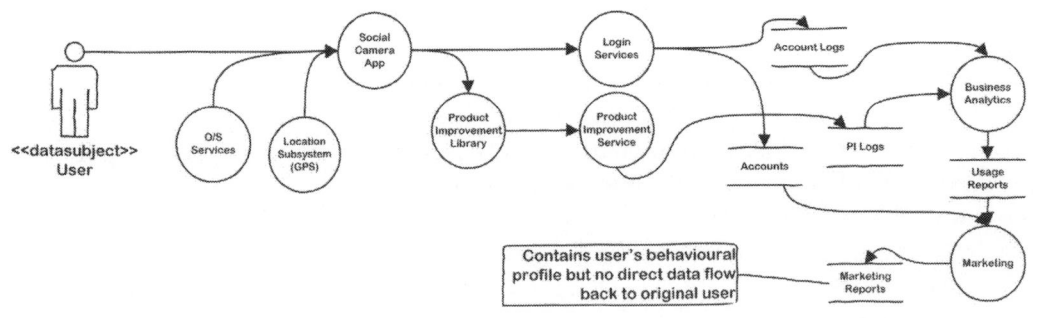

Figure 18: Data Flows with No Marketing Consent Given

This then generates the question about how much analysis the marketing process can make over a set of data: can we still perform marketing analysis and operations but just hold off on the return data flow, or do we need to sanitise data elsewhere across all the possible flows into this process? Furthermore, it is also probably clear that at the high level of abstraction we have in the model, we might not be able to capture all the necessary details for a properly informed engineering based decision at this time. This latter case is typical but one often missed from the point of view of just presenting a consent. For example, in figure 19 based upon both figures 18 and 16 we can perform a further refinement and may choose to use this particular model.

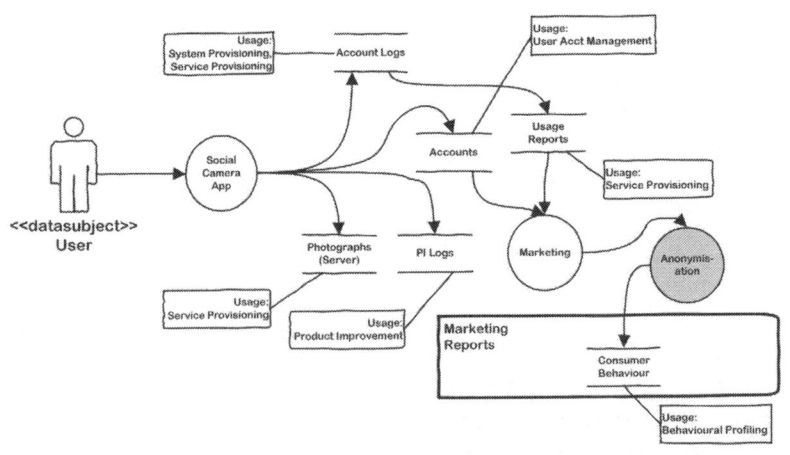

Figure 19: Refinement Data Flows with No Marketing Consent Given

Data Breaches

No system is ever perfectly secure nor private unless isolated completely from any network and any form of external monitoring. The bulk of data breaches are going to happen in situations not related to the technological design decisions; indeed most of these situations are human related[39] be it either malicious or accidental[40]. However, even here in comparison with the amount of malicious attacks, accidental breaches of data are by far the most common involving factors such as password and account mismanagement, data extraction to removable media, unencrypted media/laptops, printouts left on printers, etc. of this nature are relatively rare compared to the accidental breaches.

[39] Ponemon Institute. 2013 cost of data breach study: United kingdom, May 2013

[40] Glenn Greenwald, Ewen MacAskill, and Laura Poitras. Edward Snowden: the whistleblower behind the NSA surveillance revelations. *The Guardian*, 10 June 2013

There are a few heuristics that can be followed to understand where data breaches can occur:

- From the data subject themselves
- From any point outside of the control of the application, including file system storage, remote procedure calls of any nature
- Any data flow crossing an architectural boundary, implying some flow over a public (or even private!) network
- Any sink of data outside of the immediately control of the data subject

We can obviously continue with more refinements here. In the social camera *system* we have immediately the issue of the social media provider, the advertiser(s) and the 3rd party backup system as being of particular risk for a data breach. The nature of the breach must be both quantified and qualified in terms of its nature and effect upon the data subject. Most privacy breaches via a social media provider do not take the form of deliberate hacking or internal data release - it is not in the business interest to lose data in this manner. Accidental visibility settings by the original user or a misunderstanding on how social media's privacy system works are generally the cases here; along with too permissive or user-unfriendly privacy policies[41].

[41] Chang Liu and Kirk P. Arnett. An examination of privacy policies in fortune 500 web sites. *American Journal of Business*, 17(1):13–22, 2002

From the data subject's point of view, often the greatest danger is accidental or even deliberate over-sharing of information. We can obviously assist in this in the design of our application by making privacy friendly features available such as stripping of location and other meta-data from photographs, ensuring that interaction with social media providers is made on the most restrictive privacy settings by default and so on. Admittedly here there are limits as to what can be done and it can be a fine line between making applications 'idiot proof' and over-intrusive and complex privacy preserving features.

The interactions between the social media provider, advertisers and other 3rd parties which share information are likely to of significant concern to both the developer and the user. These can be mitigated by suitable agreements between the service provider and these 3rd parties if possible.

One of the major worries of any user is the trust and reliability of any service, especially when the geographical location of the data is unknown. Furthermore, given revelations about spying and other forms of subversion of data, unless explicitly known, all services should be considered to be potentially leaking data to parties unknown. For example in our model we have explicitly noted the breach of data to some 'three letter agency' from the backup provider.

While the above are often outside of our control, we need to consider the biggest attack vector as coming from the social camera service provider in our example. For the purposes of the data model we show six data stores, processes such as marketing and analytics and consumption of the data by internal users. Analysis of these has to take place during the development of the system and suitable security, data handling and data disposal practices put in place. Again we have a significant human factor once again which also needs serious consideration with the caveat that often such procedures, especially if too onerous[42] make day-to-day working awkward if not downright impossible.

[42] Kafka anyone?

Summary

WHILE THIS DISCUSSION HAS been long, it does present the place of a simple application in the wider information ecosystem. Engineering discipline requires that we construct models of our systems to fully understand and appreciate their functioning. It is only through the construction of said models that we can fully understand and control the flow of data through such a complex set of differentiated platforms, services and applications.

The other appreciation here should be the degree to which the concepts in privacy such as data, information, provenance, security, identity, identifiability, authority etc are all very tightly linked together. A change in any one of them results in seemingly chaotic effects upon all the others and finding the correct balance or equilibrium[43] between each of these aspects and the user and business environments almost unassailable.

[43] J.F. Nash. *Non-cooperative Games*. Princeton University, 1950

Throughout the rest of this book we will return to this case study to describe terminology, modelling and analysis. We use this case study as a basis for development and as such many of the models to be presented will take on various differing levels of detail, focus and architectural design. Indeed one of the most important reasons to model a a system and abstract away from many implementation issues is to have the ability to rearrange components, try out different designs and comprehend these changes.

Privacy Engineering Process Structure

ENGINEERING IMPLIES A FORMAL or rigorous method of working, with defined terminology, metrics and processes. All work under the banner of engineering whether agile or waterfall in process or whether dealing with privacy, security or some other aspect of software development needs to be placed in some kind of *process and terminological framework*[44] where particular actions and results are made accordingly. Indeed given the very nature of processes, especially in software engineering, it does seem quite a bit of a misnomer to talk about process in general.

[44] Thomas Finneran Michelle Finneran Dennedy, Jonathan Fox. *The Privacy Engineer's Manifesto: Getting from Policy to Code to QA to Value*. Apress, 2014

In this section we present the overall structure through which we can organise the inclusion of privacy aspects in the software engineering process, whatever that itself might be in any given organisation or project. We do not enforce a particular process other than that of a broad structure to follow that can be applied in differing situations accordingly[45].

[45] IBM Global Services. *Privacy Architecture Overview*. Government of Alberta, Canada, May 2003

Regardless of whether an agile process, or waterfall or any other kind of process[46] is used we are bound by requirements for the system being developed and the needs to communicate clearly what the system already does or is intended to do. The purpose of this section is to introduce the kinds of artefacts, processes and analyses that should, could or must be made in order to implement and audit privacy compliance.

[46] Ian Sommerville. *Software Engineering*. Addison-Wesley, 9 edition, 2010

In this chapter we outline a process, or rather a process framework, which we follow in the book and the structure into which we define our terminology about privacy and information.

'The' Process

REGARDLESS OF THE PROCESS chosen, we always progress from an overall, abstract understanding of a system towards fine-grained details and design. The kind of 'process' we are following here is depicted in figure 20 along with a list of concepts we must understand:

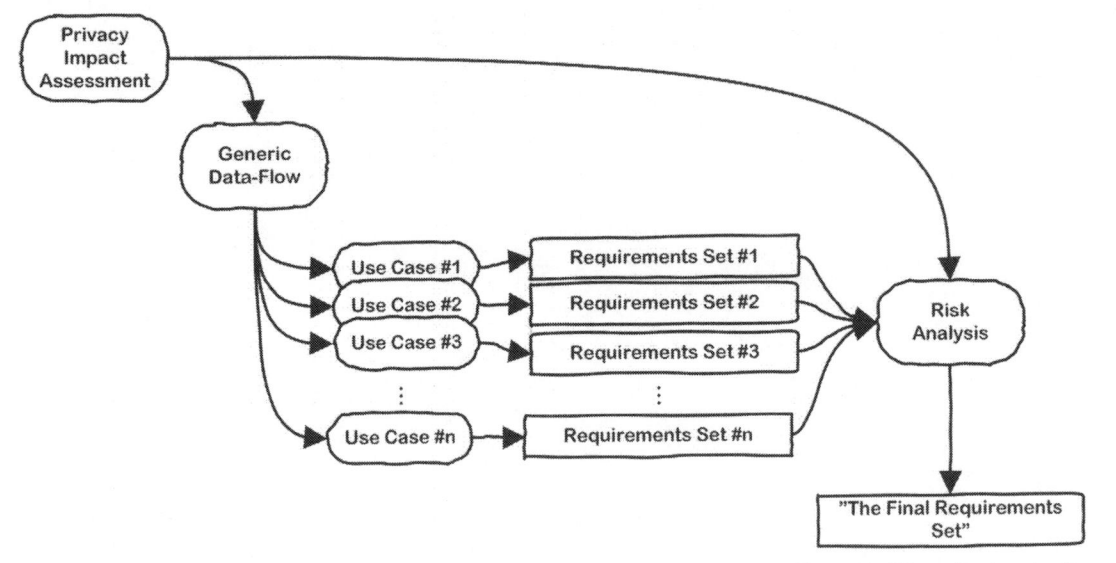

Figure 20: Privacy Engineering Process Flow

- the overall, or 'big'-picture of the system
- the specific use cases and their properties
- the requirements we generate from these use cases and analyses
- selection of relevant requirements that can be implemented
- the risks involved based upon the requirements selection

In supporting this modelling process which runs as an integrated part with whatever software development process is employed, we also need to understand how our role as privacy engineers[47] interacts with this in terms of requirements developing, auditing and testing:

[47] officers, lawyers, etc.

- one-off set of requirements and 'forget'

- continual interaction
- single, final audit

Generic Data Flow Model

WHEN WE CONSTRUCT A generic data flow model of any system, this assists us in the understanding holistically how information travels through the system and where the major components, that is sources and sinks of information, exist. The generic model does not take into consideration particular use cases but is largely a conglomeration of these. While this might make the model rather unwieldy in some circumstances is serves as a basis for the discussion of the overall requirements and the scope of the later detailed work. One point to be understood from the generic model is that it should show all the possible sources and sinks of information - this will assist in use case development later when we select specific areas to investigate in more detail.

To support documentation of the data flow we rely upon specific formalisations of various aspects[48], such as the types of information - whether the information contains location or identifiers, etc., and also aspects such as the provenance of information, the authority under which it was collected, i.e.: was the user logged in or not. These formalisations take the form of ontologies or taxonomies over pre-defined set of aspects to be introduced later in more detail.

[48] Ora Lassila, Mika Mannermaa, Marwan Sabbouh, and Ian Oliver. Aspect-oriented data. In *W3C Workshop on RDF Next Steps*, June 2012

Use Cases

DECOMPOSITION OF THE SYSTEM into the individual use cases means taking specific parts of the more generic model and adding detail that best describes the flow and kinds of information that are handled in that particular case. Constructing a set of use cases is usually driven by particular functional needs, though in privacy we can supplement these by further breaking these down to handling specific situations such as different processing under the situations of whether the user is logged in or not, or whether the data is being captured from a child or adult and so on. Use case based development is a well known technique in software engineering and we trust that the practitioner is familiar with this[49,50].

Model Layers

FOR EACH MODEL PRODUCED, be it a generic data flow or individual use case we are required to model a number of aspects. These aspects may be introduced separately for modelling convenience but must be understood as a whole as each interacts with the others within the context of the data flow. The aspects as their terminologies are described later but for now figure 21 shows how these layers and models relate in one possible structuring of models:

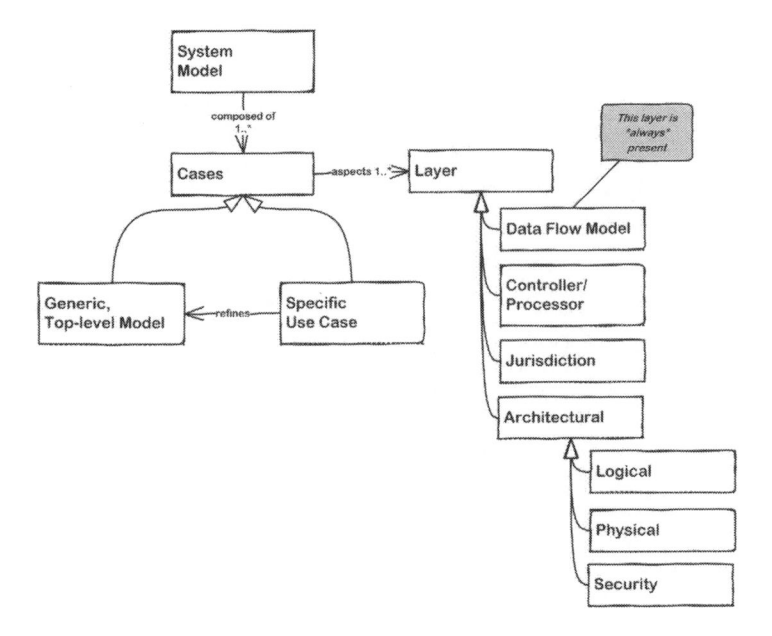

[49] Steve Adolph, Alistair Cockburn, and Paul Bramble. *Patterns for Effective Use Cases*. Addison-Wesley Longman Publishing Co., Inc., 2002. ISBN 0201721848

[50] Geri Schneider and Jason P. Winters. *Applying Use Cases: A Practical Guide*. Addison-Wesley Longman Publishing Co., Inc., 1998. ISBN 0-201-30981-5

Figure 21: Model Structure, Aspects and Layers

Note that regardless of the actual model and its usage, the data flow layer is always present. It is on top of this that we layer aspects such as the controller-processor distinctions, architectural aspects and so on.

The actual naming of models and relationships of the models of course varies by environment and context and so figure 21 should only represent a possible structuring. The meaning of relationships such as 'refines' while having some semantics would need to be defined more precisely in terms of local methods and requirements, for example, it could mean that one model refines another if all regression testing passes and so on.

Derivation of Requirements and Risk Analysis

FOR EACH USE CASE for each element in the associated data flow model we can generate a set of requirements that apply to that element. These requirements will be a mix of those directly generated by the properties of that element and those implied through the properties of the directly generated requirements.

This set of requirements may be further partitioned according to any logical or physical partitioning in the data flow model, or, over the generic model as necessary. Regardless of this we still end up with many sets of requirements.

If we take any one of these sets of requirements then we can analyse these to either accept or discard a particular requirement. If we choose to discard a requirement then obviously some justification is required and this justification should be accompanied by a risk analysis of some form, for example, using a technique such as failure mode and effects analysis.

After performing the filtering and risk analysis of requirements we should be left with a set of requirements that can be architected, designed and ultimately implemented.

There is always the danger that the selected requirements are not sufficient to construct a fully privacy compliant system. Indeed it is prerogative of the business to decide on the level of compliance and the amount of risk that business wants or even needs to take.

Auditing Processes

ASSESSMENT OF A SYSTEM through auditing is a requirement in its own right. Without the independent (as much as this is possible) check correct adherence to the requirements, risk analysis and their implementation cannot be fully guaranteed unless the system is *very* small, simple and isolated.

The integration of any auditing can vary widely between projects, but the three basic patterns area:

- Auditing at start
- Auditing at end
- Continuous auditing

To a point the use of the word 'auditing' is often a little onerous and this should be replaced with 'consultancy', 'mentoring' or something similar as required.

If we audit at the beginning of a project then this amounts to checking off the set of requirements and allowing the team to proceed unhindered. The danger here is that this only works if the requirements for the system are fully established and unchanging, along with a software development process that is sufficiently inflexible to admit change. Obviously this is not an ideal situation and one that now rarely occurs.

Auditing at the end of a project is reasonably common and usually results in a go/no-go decision with the latter being somewhat awkward for the development team. It does however have the advantage that all necessary documentation and implementation is available with the guarantee that very few changes will be made after the audit which might change its result. This kind of final audit works well with mature teams that already understand fully the necessity of implementing privacy requirements, or in already existing systems where only small changes have been made.

Continuous auditing probably suits best less experienced teams and also so-called agile environments where the functional requirements to a system may be rapidly changing. The disadvantage here is that it does require a great deal of interaction between the project team and auditor, but with the advantage that mistakes and problems can be dealt with quickly.

In reality, we typically work with a combination of all three and most certainly a combination of continuous auditing with a final sign-off tends to be the most typical. In all cases matching the timing of a privacy audit or mentoring with internal project milestones tends to be the most productive in that the idea of the audit is to help the development team rather than hinder its progress. Indeed it should always be remembered that the auditor's responsibilities include ensuring that the system being developed does actually make production and release rather than trying to mire a project in complicated, unattainable requirements.

A detailed description of how an audit is conducted is described in a later chapter.

Terminology and a Structure

WE HAVE BEEN QUITE lax with the use of terminology when talking about 'information systems' or 'services' etc and we must now place this into a more proper foundation. Conceptually all systems are a collection of components linked by data-flows and it is through this mechanism that we describe what the properties of these systems from a privacy perspective. At its most generic all systems follow the pattern of a source or sources of data; zero, one or more sink or sinks of data, and internal process and storage. We can see this visualised in figure 22 as a data-flow diagram.

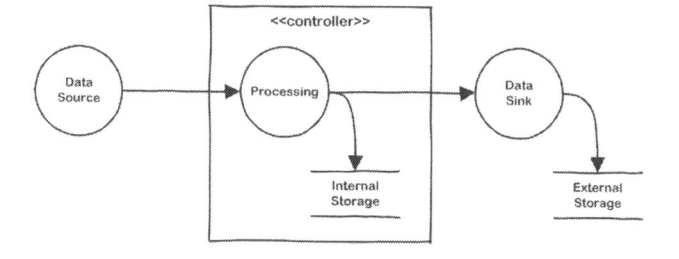

Figure 22: A Generic or Template Data Flow Diagram

Notice that the structure contains the following concepts:

- A data source (which will likely be the data subject)
- The application or service denoted by an element named 'processing'
- Some internal storage used by that application or service

- Some logical or physical boundary - typically a device, but could also be a jurisdiction, an access control boundary etc.

- Some external sink, such as an analytics provider, or advertising providers etc.

- Some external storage, not necessarily under the control of the application or service.

This model will be further refined in due course but for the moment is serves as a base for our models and scope the terminology.

Data flows between these components when instantiated and linked together by some means. Each of these links then denotes a communication channel of various kinds: interprocess communication, intraprocess communication, network links etc., all with various properties depending upon their construction, for example, REST style calls over HTTPS over TCP being a pertinent example.

One observation that we can immediately make is that data can only flow between two directly linked components - an obvious fact admittedly, but the repercussions of this are that if data is required to flow between two non-directly coupled components then it must flow via one or more proxies each with the possibility of extracting or modifying data in that data-flow. Thus the more components data has to flow through the less we can trust in the overall integrity of that data-flow and thus the greater chance that the privacy of information will be compromised. The alternative is to link more components directly with the disadvantage of overall system complexity which in turn provides more opportunities for the leakage of data from a component to many others. We are faced with a simple choice: no connections and thus sharing of data whatsoever or a compromise between privacy and security and the interconnectedness of a system.

Ontology and Classification

THE GREATEST DANGERS IN any discipline is that the terminology is ill-defined, used incorrectly and inconsistently; this leads to confusion between persons and teams and in the worst case is ultimately destructive to actually solving the engineering problems faced. In privacy this is common occurrence between those with a legal background and those with a (software) engineering background and as with any mix of areas those who understand both are a rarity.

Our goal is to ultimately generate requirements for our system and software engineers as well as ensure compliance with all necessary laws therefore we need to unify the terminology between lawyers and software engineers at least to allow some form of consistent and mutually understandable communication[51]. While terminology used by both groups appears to mutually understandable and may even have some form of common sense semantics, for example, the term 'database' has many subtle differences in meanings and especially implementations to a software engineer which would not be understood to a lawyer. Vice versa, legal terms when used by engineers sound similarly *weird*!

[51] Martin Kost, Johann Christoph Freytag, Frank Kargl, and Antonio Kung. Privacy verification using ontologies. In *ARES*, pages 627–632. IEEE, 2011. ISBN 978-1-4577-0979-1

We achieve this by developing a mechanism of classification through which we can abstract away from implementation technology issues to concentrate on and reason about the actual content and necessary privacy related aspects of our data[52]. The model that will serve as the basis for our models of information systems, information and privacy is shown in figure 23 and provides a structure which explains the relationship between data elements and the aspects over which we will reason and model. Note that this is just one way[53] of expressing the concepts and relationships between those concepts of information and as will be emphasised many times, such models are and must be open to modification and customisation as local processes and contexts require.

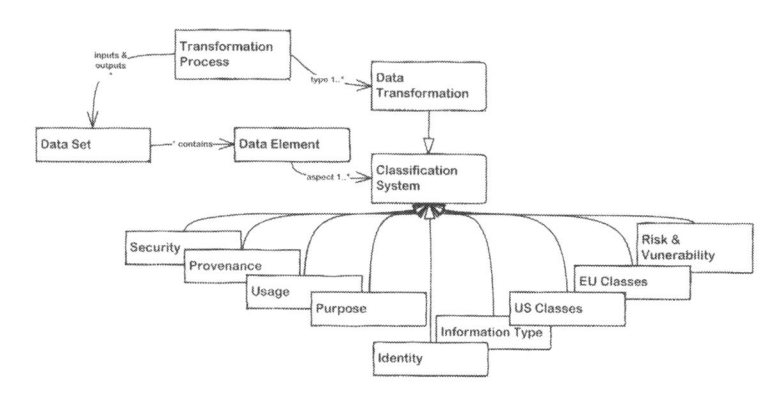

[52] Anya Kim. Position paper building privacy into the semantic web: An ontology needed now, 2002

[53] Philippe Kruchten. The frog and the octopus: a conceptual model of software development. *CoRR*, abs/1209.1327, 2012

From this we will define ontological or terminological structures

Figure 23: Relationships Between the Ontologies of Information

for the following aspects:

- Security
- Information Type
- Provenance
- Jurisdiction
- Identity
- Purpose
- Usage
- Controller, Processor and Data Subject
- Data Transformation

Each of these will be explained further in following chapters as we present the full ontology that we wish to use to classify data.

Our notions can be applied in many contexts and as may be seen in figure 23 we have deliberately stayed away from enforcing any particular notion of what a data element is. In figure 24 we can see how this might be applied to an object oriented system.

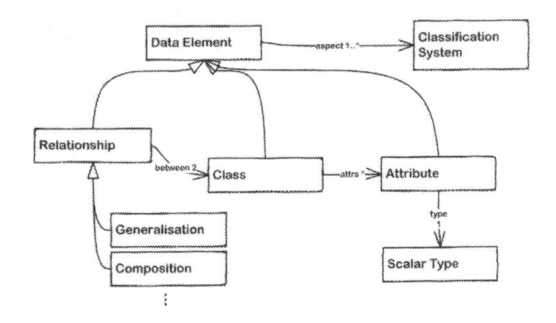

Figure 24: Aspect Structure in an Object Oriented System

The common usage of structured files such as log files in batch analytics processing can also be placed in such a structure as shown in figure 25.

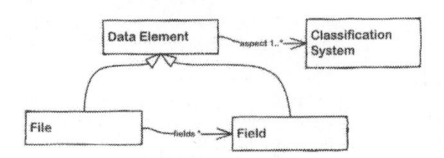

Figure 25: Aspect Structure in a File Oriented System

Finally we can show also how this might be applied in a 'traditional' relational database centric data centre as shown in figure 26.

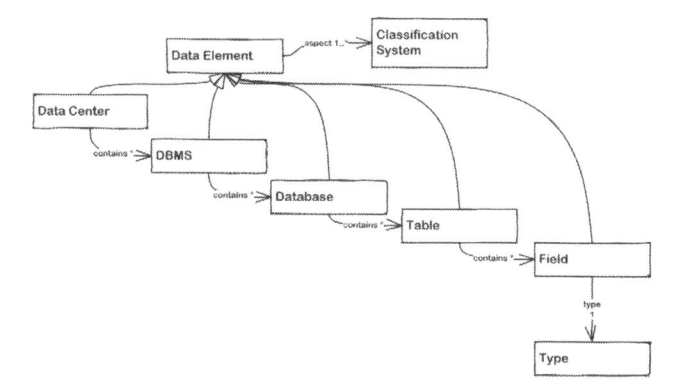

Figure 26: Aspect Structure in a Relational Database Structure

The models we create here are highly conceptual in nature and do cross various meta-level boundaries[54] and the models of the specific structure as seen in figures 24, 25 and 26 could be constructed differently depending upon local need. We could attach the meta-model of any language such as that of the UML or programming languages such as C or C++ into this scheme which would then give us precise control over how these aspects are integrated and used to implement privacy within these languages.

It must be noted that any attempt to define a taxonomy or ontology such as this and the ones to be presented later are always going to be incomplete[55]. There will be specific cases that require any classification to be extended and/or modified in various ways to accommodate this. Between environments (companies, divisions etc) there might exist further variation in the use and structure of these classification systems[56]. This is inevitable as subtleties become apparent and care must be taken to either ensure some degree of homogeneity of semantics even if the syntax and terminology are heterogeneous. Above all such taxonomies, ontologies and classifications are to promote communication.

[54] Cesar Gonzalez-Perez and Brian Henderson-Sellers. A powertype-based metamodelling framework. *Software and Systems Modeling*, 5(1): 72–90, 2006. ISSN 1619-1366. DOI: 10.1007/s10270-005-0099-9

[55] Ian Oliver and Ora Lassila. Integration in the large. In *W3C Workshop on Data and Services Integration*, October 2011

[56] Franz Baader, Diego Calvanese, Deborah L. McGuinness, Daniele Nardi, and Peter F. Patel-Schneider, editors. *The description logic handbook: theory, implementation, and applications*. Cambridge University Press, New York, NY, USA, 2003. ISBN 0-521-78176-0

Summary

WHATEVER PROCESS IS USED to develop software or an information system, from some highly regulated waterfall model to some incarnation of agile still requires that the system being built is understood, even if there exists just one developer with the model committed to mind rather than software tool or paper.

From any initial design are derived the various use cases and requirements, from those the code and tests at various levels of abstraction such as a formal behavioural specification, or some Java or Python code. Linking these together are tests which again might be a formal set of test cases or simply running the application with *printf*-style debugging. The structure of this always remains the same[57].

Understanding this structure and how various components fit together be they software components, process components or even high-level software engineering concepts such as how non-functional privacy requirements are engineered into functional code implemented is critical to any successful outcome[58].

[57] D L Parnas and P C Clements. A rational design process: How and why to fake it. *IEEE Transactions in Software Engineering*, 12(2):251–257, February 1986

[58] *ISO29100: Information technology - Security techniques - Privacy framework*. ISO/IEC, 29100:2011(e) edition, December 2011

Data Flow Modelling

WE WILL INTRODUCE A language and notation for modelling components, processes, structure and the flow of data within a system. Models can be annotated and partitioned to show further aspects including architectural, geographical and legal boundaries and so on. We then show mechanisms for the refinement, partitioning and analysis of these models.

For any given development project it will be necessary to construct a number of data flow models to fully capture the various use cases and scenarios of the particular system in question. Through this we can truly understand and reason about from and to where data is flowing, through which components, for what uses and where the control points over this data are.

Basic Notation

THE BASIC ELEMENTS OF a data flow language are those which show the source and target points of data and the data flows between these[59]. In our language we define five kinds of element, each with their own graphical notation depicted in figure 27.

- Processes
- Users
- Environments
- Stores

[59] Peter Gorm Larsen, Nico Plat, and Hans Toetenel. A formal semantics of data flow diagrams. *Formal Aspects of Computing*, 3, 1994

- Leaks

We make it compulsory to name all elements in the model, with the same name referring to the same element if used in a number of different diagrams or use cases.

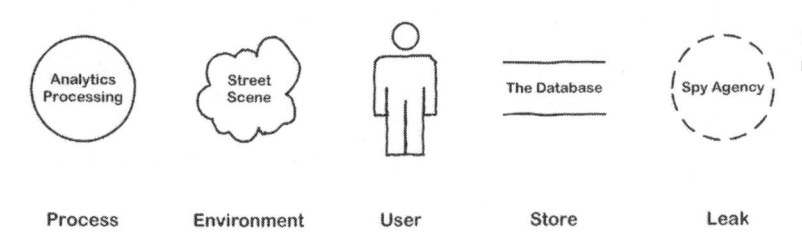

Figure 27: Processes, User, Environments, Stores and Leaks

Process | Environment | User | Store | Leak

Processes are places where data is processed by some computational entity, this could be anything from a small filtering function to a large analytics cluster environment or software component depending upon the specific modelling needs and the required level of granularity.

Users refer primarily to humans interacting with the system and **Environments** to things outside of the system that exist in the 'Real World' such a scenes for a photograph or other sources of data. **Leaks** are explicit notifications to the reader that some data flows in the model flow to unknown places or points where an unauthorised data flow would be especially problematical. Typically this would be used to bring into question any confidence about that particular component leaking that data.

Stores denote any place where data can be held for a period of time, for example: a database, a file (including temporary files), a log file or even a physical piece of media such as memory stick. Again the granularity depends upon how detailed a model is required and here we could even see internal partitioning even to table or some other structural level.

Data flows link elements of the above node types together and denote the general direction of communication - the precise meaning of this is explained later in this chapter. Data flows are named by default by referring to their start and end points. In cases where more than one flow exists between two nodes this uniqueness is not possible and a further distinguishing name should be given.

We make a syntactic distinction between 'normal' data flows and return data flows. This latter notation is used to emphasise where data might return back to a user. Data flows are always directional as we wish to emphasise the overall flow of data rather than any particulars of the underlying communications protocols. The basic form of a data flow between two processes (and this follows for other node types too) is shown in figure 28. Note that we have chosen to leave the flow unnamed, though we always have the option to do this for reference purposes.

Figure 28: Data Flow Between Two Processes

In figure 29 you will note that we have *two* flows from one process to another. As noted earlier, this shows two separate 'conversations' or channels of communication between these processes. The actual break down into separate channels is largely due to whatever granularity of modelling is required. Note that we explicitly name the data flows to distinguish between them in this case.

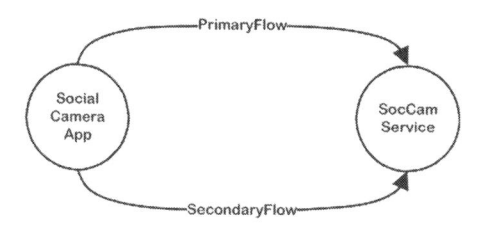

Figure 29: Multiple Data Flows Between Two Processes

If we need to emphasise a flow back to some originator of some data then we can utilise the return flow notation as shown in figure 30. This is purely syntactical and is meant just to place emphasis on this fact to the reader of the model. This reverse flow is not used to describe the ACK/NACK, error correction, key exchange or other two-way features of the underlying transport protocols. Note that neither data flow is named, though on the return flow we have provided information about the underlying protocol used for transporting information over this, i.e.: we do not model control flow data.

In the model shown in figure 31, we see four different elements together. This depicts the prototypical starting situation for many applications and systems. Here we show data is collected from both a human user and the street scene being

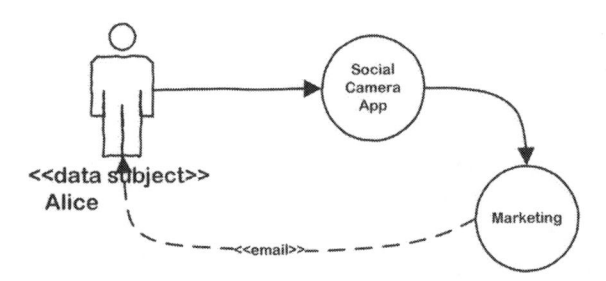

Figure 30: Return Flow Notation

photographed; data then flows via the application and its processing to some storage mechanism.

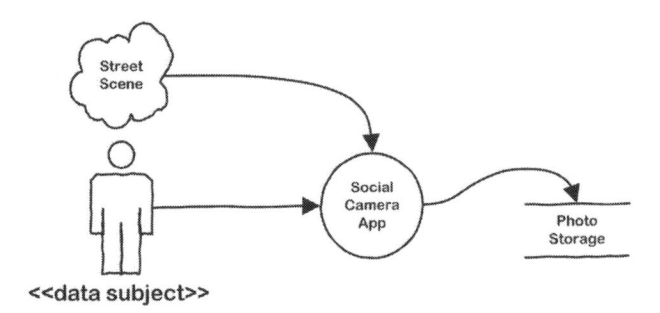

Figure 31: Example Prototypical Initial Data Flow

Note that the data from the street scene 'environment' flows, via the camera sensors and subsystem(s), to the camera application and not via the user of the application. Secondly the flow from the user to the camera application does not denote any control flow but that the user might be providing data such as personal details, picture meta-data, etc. Furthermore we are showing no partitioning of the model such that we can not infer whether the camera application and storage are on the same device, or whether there is even a device at all.

A further situation that we might wish to model are flows out to some 'unknown' entity - specifically to show some kind of potential leak of information that must be explicitly noted, reasoned about and maybe later protected from; this is shown in figure 32.

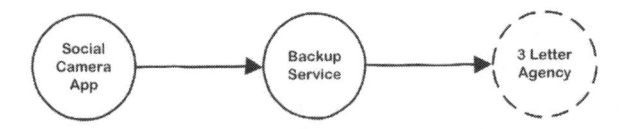

Figure 32: Example Leak to an Unknown Entity

Leaks are always modelled as sinks of information flowing away from a process, store or user via some data flow. Our syntax is defined such that showing a leak stemming from a data flow is not possible; data flows should always be considered liable to being breached and thus leak information. The purpose of the leak notation as has been explained is to alert the reader to possible sinks of data which might exist due to incomplete or poor specification of a system, or untrusted components and so on. Note that this is a separate concept from data being leaked due to user actions such as might occur due to incorrectly set privacy settings with a social media provider as might occur in the situation depicted in figure 33

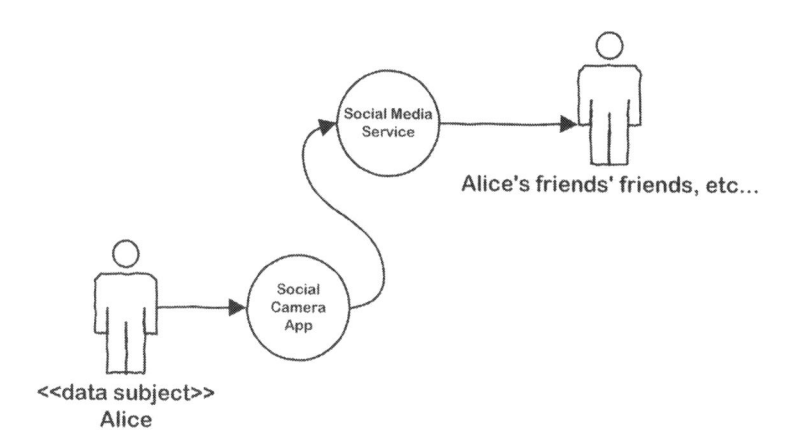

Figure 33: Example Leak to a Known Entity

The above examples, while simple, show the basic structure and concepts of a data flow model. It is important to remember to concentrate on the directionality of the flows and that we are not expressing how the underlying communication protocols work.

It is usual that a single data flow model does not show everything. Models should be constructed with consistent naming of elements and flows so that elements can be tracked across use cases and other models as required. If models become too complex or cluttered to read that it is good practice to split the models up into a number of individual diagrams. Models **must** also be backed up with textual descriptions and references to other documentation describing the system at hand.

Annotating Data Flow Models

EACH ELEMENT, FLOW AND even partition in a data flow model can be additionally annotated with information about its nature. The properties of these annotations should be formally defined in some ontological or taxonomical structure and a number of examples of these are given in the following sections.

Data Subject and Diagram Context

WHEN WORKING WITH DATA flow diagrams and privacy it is important that we annotate the initial source or sources of data and in particular the source about whom the diagram is constructed. The terminology used to describe this individual is 'data subject' and is derived from various pieces of privacy legislation. We will borrow this terminology and utilise the UML stereotype notation[60] as a convenient method of annotating this.

[60] UML Stereotype Notation - seems to fit well here, semiotically speaking

In the examples provided earlier we have seen this notation being used, for example in figure 33 it is unambiguous that we are explicitly referring to the data being collected from the marked data subject. The use of this annotation is not compulsory but its inclusion is strongly recommended and necessary when especially describing larger models or specific situations where there may exist ambiguity about the source or the context of the data.

Data Flow Transport Protocols

DOCUMENTING THE NATURE OF transport over a data flow provides much information about what kinds of data can be collected from the protocol layer and also give hints about what kinds of requirements need to be placed on that flow. The transport protocol is *generally* a combination of the layer 4 (HTTP, HTTPS, FTP etc.) protocol and any of the relevant higher level protocols[61,62] as necessary. Syntactically we denote these as a list of the protocol names and an example of this is

[61] Andrew Tanenbaum. *Computer Networks*. Prentice Hall Professional Technical Reference, 4th edition, 2002. ISBN 0130661023

[62] John Day. The (un)revised OSI reference model. *SIGCOMM Comput. Commun. Rev.*, 25(5):39–55, October 1995. ISSN 0146-4833

given in figure 34 which shows a number of data flows each utilising a variety of transport protocols.

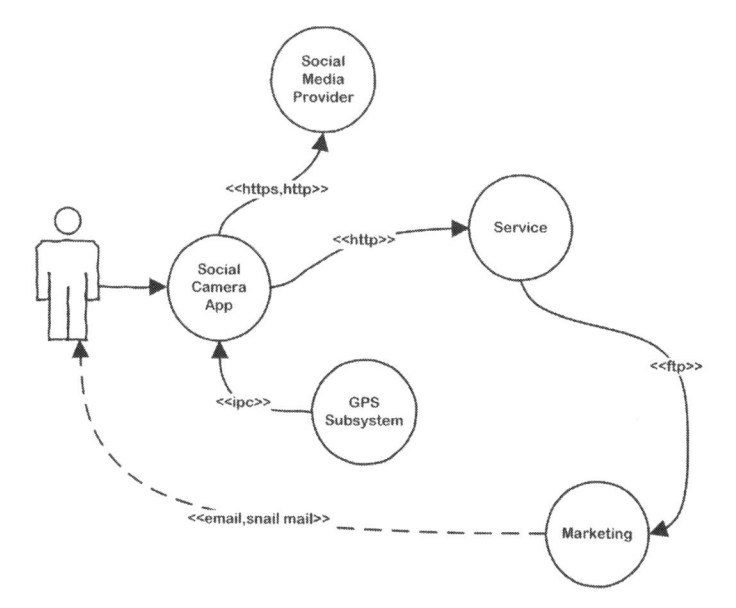

Figure 34: Annotating Data Flow Transport Protocols

If we write: <<*http*>> then we infer that we mean the HTTP protocol only. If we write multiple transport protocols such as <<*http,https*>> then this means that both are used for different parts of the data conversation over that particular data flow or that some choice of transport protocol might exist. In such circumstances it might be well worth decomposing the data flow to differentiate the parts of the conversation or performing more analysis of the system. If no protocol is provided then this means that either none is applicable or that this information is undecided or unknown.

The choice of protocol has implications regarding the data being carried and extractable over that channel. Typically most protocols provide source and end device addresses as IP addresses[63] and timestamps as a minimum. As described earlier this is what is termed 'traffic data' and this must be taken into consideration when calculating the whole information content of a channel.

[63] We rarely see non-IP based addressing these days and protocols such as DecNet and SNA

Data Flow Channel Content

THE SPECIFICATION OF WHAT content is transmitted over a data flow is the most critical piece of information in any data flow model. The transport protocols only state the mechanisms of how the conversation over a flow is mediated. Further annotation of a flow can show this information content as well as other aspects such as the security level and so on as necessary. We define later a classification system for expressing the contents of a flow, but here we provide a self-explanatory example of this as shown in figure 35.

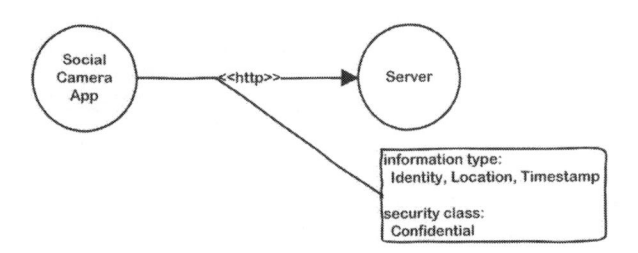

Figure 35: Annotating Data Flow Contents

In this example we state that we can expect identifiers of various kinds, location information and timestamps, and that this is *in addition* to anything provided by the HTTP protocol in this example.

The use of high-level 'types' or 'kinds' such as location or identifier is important in that it explains the content without getting confused with machine types or various representations of data. It is often seen that data flows are noted to carry 'JSON data' or are 'RESTful' - both of these **do not** describe the content but rather the syntactical representation of the content and an architectural style of calling an API.

Providing detailed information such as a schema or field names often leads to confusion - the naming of data structures does not necessarily provide unambiguous information about what the data contained therein really is. Providing a high-level type gives us the opportunity to focus discussion on the kind of information and not whether it is hashed, encrypted or contained in some machine type such as a VARCHAR or int. This is especially true when dealing with location data, especially when data such as geographical location typically is not typed using some geometrical type but as a structure of real numbers.

Calculating the Complete Information Content of a Channel

IN ORDER TO EVALUATE the complete set of information available via a channel it is simply a matter to add together the information types of the channel content and the information contained in the transport protocol together.

Each transport protocol can be mapped to a set of information types according to the parameters it uses for its own internal workings. For example, the HTTP protocol[64] over TCP/IP [65,66] provides a large number of headers as well as addressing and routing. For example, if we have a data flow that contains Device Identifiers over the HTTP protocol then the total content would be Device Identifier, Temporal, Machine Address and various kinds of Content which itself could be further refined to reflect significant parameters contained within the HTTP headers.

[64] R. Fielding, J. Gettys, J. Mogul, H. Frystyk, L. Masinter, P. Leach, and T. Berners-Lee. RFC 2616, Hypertext Transfer Protocol – HTTP/1.1, 1999

[65] J. Postel. Transmission Control Protocol, September 1981. Updated by RFCs 1122, 3168

[66] *RFC 791 Internet Protocol - DARPA Internet Programme, Protocol Specification.* Internet Engineering Task Force, September 1981

Annotating Processes

PROCESSES CAN BE ANNOTATED similarly to denote the kinds of processing taking place within that element in much the same way as we annotate the data subject. At high levels of abstraction obviously many tasks may be taking place and in these situations we can surmise that using no classification is an indication of such. However after decomposition of nodes or if we model at a suitably detailed level, then explicitly stating that a process does fall under certain data transformation classes is a useful indicator to the reader of a model about what might be happening.

Similarly analysing the incoming and outgoing data flows and their contents can be cross-checked against the process's data transformation classification. Any process with two or more incoming data flows is likely to be performing cross-referencing of the data; similarly any abstracting or filtering process can be checked by ensuring the output data flows contain less information than the incoming data flows. Furthermore in the latter situation, any process with two or more incoming data flows is relatively unlikely to be just abstracting or filtering. Such classification can also be applied to user elements as well as process elements, though this kind of usage would be rarely seen in practice. Applying this classification to stores, leaks and environments is not permitted. Examples of this notation can be seen in figure 36.

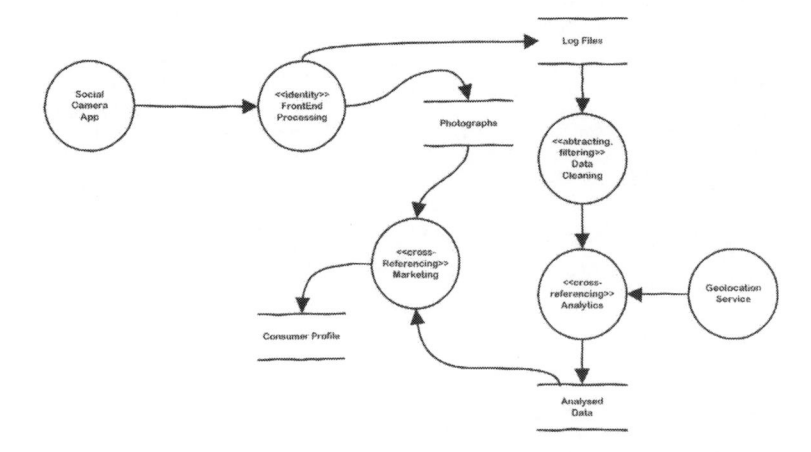

Figure 36: Example Annotation of Processes

In this example we see the flow of data from the application through the various stores via processes performing varying tasks upon whatever data is being consumed. As well as the three types presented above we also note that one process is marked << *identity* >> to denote that it does not perform any transformation of the data in any form. One process - Data Cleaning - is annotated with two kinds of processing, this means that both kinds of processing take place. It is possible that all four kinds mentioned here can be placed upon a process (see figure 37) which should act as an alert that much decomposition of that process is required to properly understand its internal workings.

The case where no annotation is provided is similar to the aforementioned case with annotating data flows and suggests that this description is not required, unknown or irrelevant in the current modelling context.

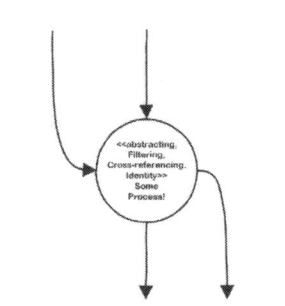

Figure 37: An 'Over Annotated' Process

Partitioning

JUST WORKING WITH THE flat data flow model as described earlier gives us information of the processes and other elements that make up a system as well as the various channels carrying the data between them. To go further we need to group those elements together in order to explore particular boundaries over which the data flows. When modelling a system we are required to group processes, stores and even users and environments together to express such as aspects as but not limited to:

- architectural boundaries, including both logical and physical distribution between devices, servers, cloud etc.
- operating system/application process boundaries
- security and trust boundaries
- controller and processor boundaries
- jurisdiction and geographical location

It is often necessary to show multiple aspects in a model. We can do this either by utilising multiple views to the model or by placing all the aspects on a single view and using a suitable naming or even colouring scheme to differentiate between the aspects. We now explain the partitioning notation.

Simple Partitioning

PARTITIONING IS TYPICALLY USED to show physical boundaries, for example in figure 38 we show the logical architecture between a user and an application which stores data locally and 'in the cloud'. Note particularly where data flows cross boundaries, especially in this case between the local device and the cloud which implies a flow outside the control of either. All processes, users, stores and any environments within a partition must be completely enclosed, only data flows can cross partition boundaries - other elements can not straddle the partition boundaries. If an individual model element is partitioned so then it must be decomposed to two elements and one or more partition crossing flows.

In the model in figure 38 we can clearly see the logical architectural partitioning, the interactions and various contained elements. It should be clear that the nature of the two data flows completely contained within their respective partitions

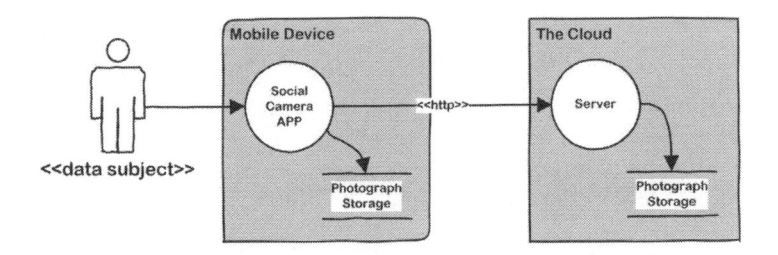

Figure 38: Example Simple Partitioning

will imply a different set of requirements and implementations to that which crosses the partition boundaries, specifically the flow between the social camera application and server.

Also note the naming of the two stores in this model, despite both having the same name they are easily distinguished by the partitions in which they inhabit. Care should be taken in such cases where the partitions are not shown that ambiguity or misunderstanding does not occur. This could be achieved by modifying the naming convention to take into account this fact.

Hierarchical Partitioning

THE PARTITIONING SCHEME ALREADY described is too simple for many cases and we have to introduce additional structure to capture the hierarchical nature of many properties such as process and execution boundaries or the controller-processor relationship. Within any hierarchy each subsequent partition is completely enclosed within a 'parent' partition. For example, in figure 39 we show a number of process and access boundaries.

In this example we show that processes (or any element) can occur at any level in a hierarchy as long as it is wholly contained or confined within that layer. As earlier elements which occur outside of given boundaries, for example the photograph store element implies that no partition has been assigned for this in the context of the current model. In this case we actually imply that there might be some access or other security or process related concern here with the flow to the leak element named 'snooper'.

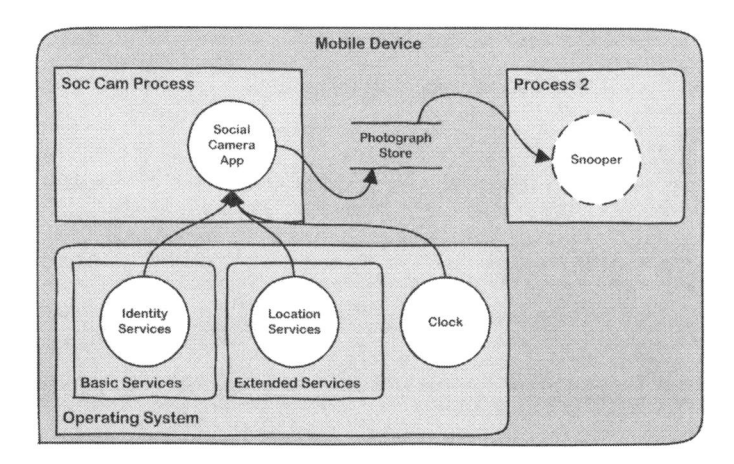

Figure 39: Example Hierarchical Partitioning

Overlapping Partitioning

WITHIN SOME ASPECTS THERE are situations where the strict hierarchical model does not capture the necessary properties we wish to model. A common scenario is when showing security domains where responsibilities and access may overlap as shown in figure 40.

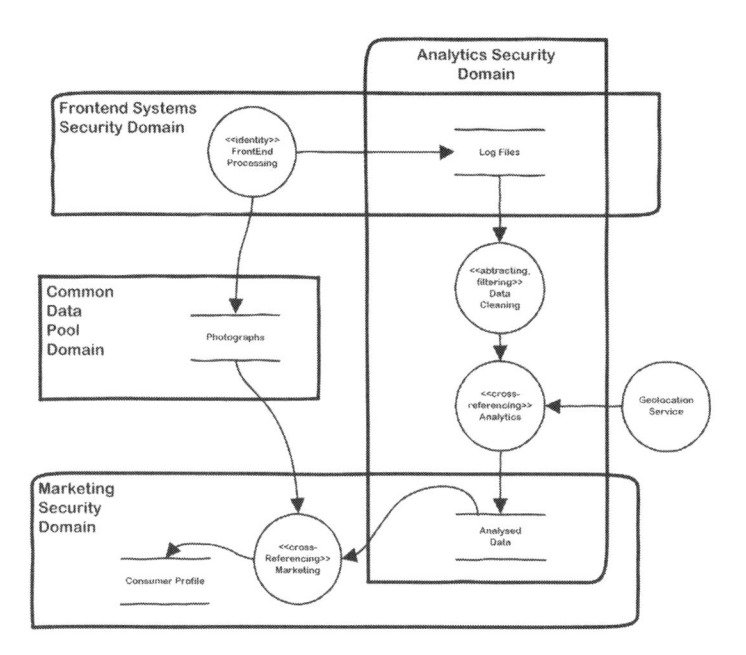

Figure 40: Example Overlapping Partitioning

In such cases we must note both the points where data flows cross boundaries but also elements that exist within one or more partitions.

Annotating Partitions

SIMILARLY TO DATA FLOWS and the various elements in a data flow diagram, partitions too may be annotated the syntax as we have already shown. This is necessary when presenting diagrams that are complex, having multiple aspects presented as partitions, or when there is any chance of ambiguity in the reading of the diagram from any externally provided context, for example, through a textual description of the diagram. This is especially necessary when showing multiple aspects simultaneously.

One particular case where this is particularly necessary and a good example of the use of this kind of annotation is when describing the controller and processor aspects of a system. For example in figure 41

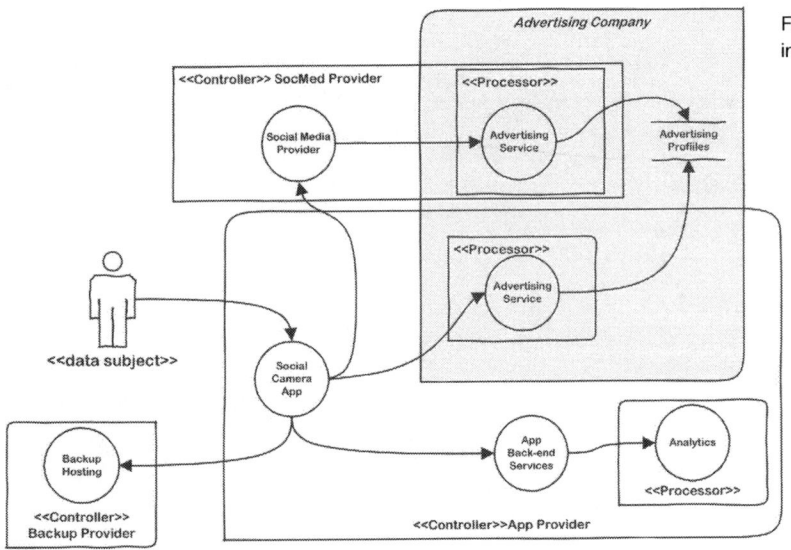

Figure 41: Example Annotated Partitioning

In this diagram we are showing multiple aspects - that of the controller/processor and the architectural or logical boundary of some advertising company. The first thing to note however is the hierarchical nature of the controller-processor partitioning and the way these are annotated. We have also annotated the user element with the data subject annotation and show the data flow from the user into a controller. This particular data flow is particularly important as it sets out the expectations for data processing and collection between the initial controller and the data subject.

From here data flows exit this initial controller to both other controllers and processors wholly contained within those. This is fairly straightforward until we examine the interaction between the controller-processor aspect and other aspects such as the logical architectural view which is shown additionally in this example.

Note how there would exist two contracts or agreements between the App Provider controller and the data processing services provided by the advertising company as a processor to the App Provider; and similarly between the social media provider and the advertising company. Finally take note of the positioning and data flows of the advertising company's data store[67].

[67] The stuff of legal headaches

This actually serves also as a good example of the complexities and discoveries that can be made during modelling and of the difficulties in confining[68] data to particular, neatly defined domains and aspects.

[68] Butler W. Lampson. A note on the confinement problem. *Communications of the ACM*, 16(10):613–615, October 1973

Decomposition

DECOMPOSING THE STRUCTURES IN a model is used to open up processes and channels to show more internal structure. Performing this in a systematic manner allows us to better reason and about how those particular elements are constructed without accidentally losing important data from the model. We will now describe decomposition over the nodes and data flows in our language. We do not consider decomposition of the partitioning as the specific semantics of this is generally out of scope of the data flow itself.

Decomposition of Data Flows

WE HAVE ALREADY STATED that a data flow is actually a conglomeration of a number of channels of communication. If we take a single data flow and split it into two then the following must hold:

- the start and end points of the new flows will be the same as the original flow

- the information carried over either of the new flows will be a subset of the original flow

- the union of the information carried over both the new flow will be the same as the original flow

- the transport protocol of either of the new flows will be a subset of the original flow

- the union of the transport protocols of both of the new flows will be the same as the original flow

We can demonstrate the above through an example. In figure 42 we have a simple system consisting of a single data flow between two processes. This data flow as the model shows carries data classed as Identity, Content, Location and Temporal by various means over the HTTP and HTTPS protocols.

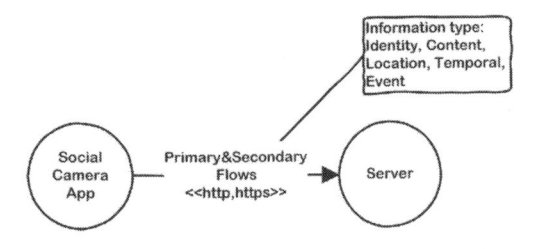

Figure 42: Data Flow Decomposition: Initial Model

Embedded within this data flow is a large amount of information at a high level of granularity. In order to extract the structures that exist inside here we decompose this as shown in figure 43.

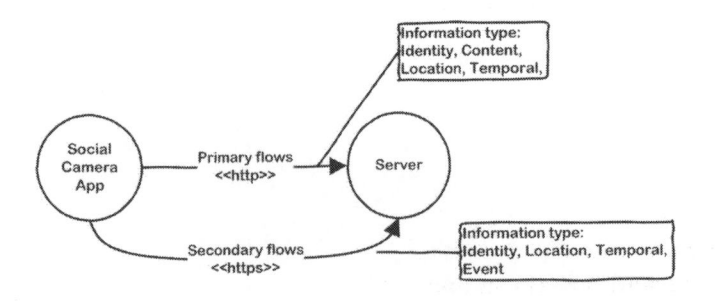

Figure 43: Data Flow Decomposition: Decomposed Model

The original data flow has been decomposed into two separate data flows between the original processes and we can distinguish which content and which protocols are in use over the two parts. To check that this is a correct decomposition from the modelling language perspective we add the information content and protocols of the two flows back together we should get the original undecomposed flow.

We can, if necessary continue with the decomposition of either of these flows as necessary in order to capture the relevant and salient points of our system in the model.

Decomposition of a Node

REFERRING TO PROCESSES, STORES, user and environments, when we decompose these the following remains true:

- Two new data flows are created between the new processes, each carrying the union of all incoming and outgoing data to the original process.
- The protocol of the new data flows is left undefined
- The original data flows are split between the two processes

In the example presented in figure 44 we have a two stage data flow between three processes. The information content and protocols of the flows are readable from the model as in earlier examples.

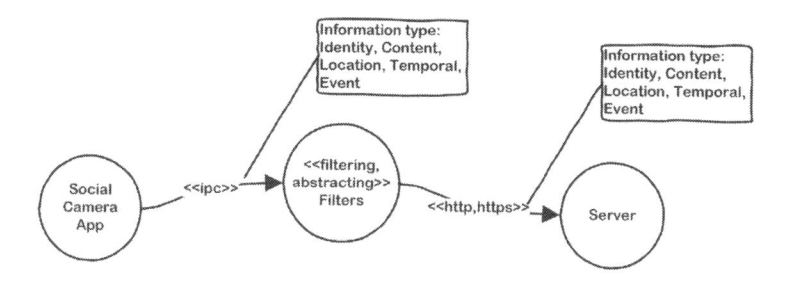

Figure 44: Node Decomposition: Initial Model

When a node is decomposed, then we effectively split the data flows over the two new nodes. The check here is again simple, if we recombine the two incoming data flows together then this should equal the original single incoming flow; similarly for the outgoing flows.

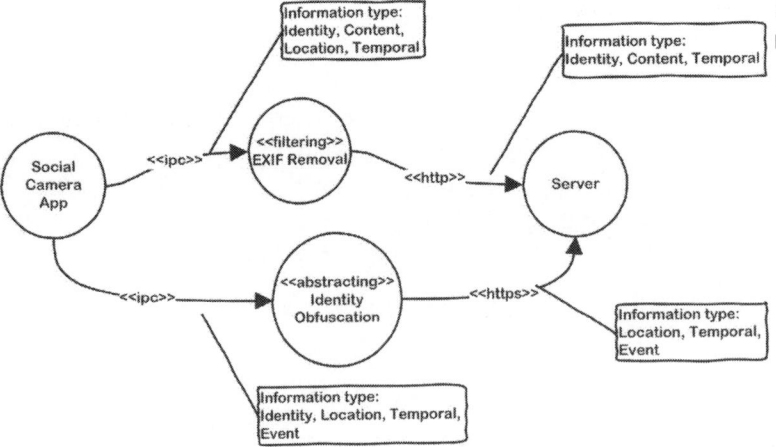

Figure 45: Node Decomposition: Decomposed Model

In figure 45 we have explicitly shown the logical partitioning of the model around the two new nodes and given a default naming to that partition. This is not necessary to explicitly show, but does provide information to the reader of the model that some kind of partitioning exists between those nodes. Of course, this partitioning might be purely for convenience or model granularity and it is really left to the modeller to decide whether to show this or not.

Refinement

REFINEMENT IS ANOTHER PROCESS used to develop the model but this time ensuring that the changes we make only restrict the model[69]. For example, developing a model such that the information in some store is no longer just an Identifier, but a particular kind of Identifier such as a Device Identifier is a refinement; that is we move from an abstract model to one that is more specific and detailed.

The places where refinement takes place are on the data flows and stores. In both case this is generally a simple matter of ensuring that the information types are more specific and any transport protocols similarly.

[69] Ralph J. Back and Joakim Wright. *Refinement Calculus: A Systematic Introduction (Texts in Computer Science)*. Springer, April 1998. ISBN 0387984178

In the example in figure 46 a data flow model with a single flow from a process to a store carrying information classified as Identity and Content over the HTTP protocol is shown. Furthermore we have a store which contains data of the same information type classification and also marked as being of the confidential security class.

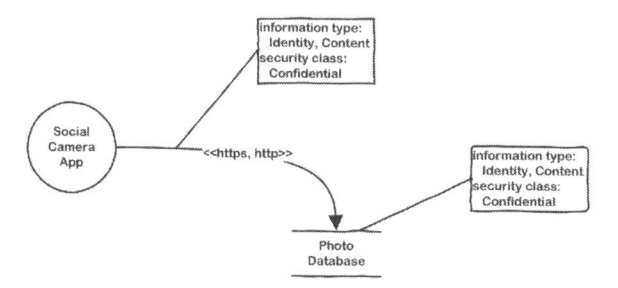

Figure 46: Refinement Example: Initial Model

When we perform the refinement here we will for convenience group four individual refinements together. These are refinement of the data flow content, refinement of the data flow protocol, refinement of the store's information content and refinement of the store's security classification. Figure 47 shows a possible result of this.

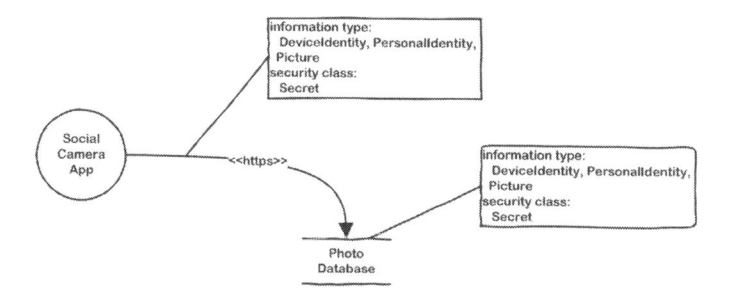

Figure 47: Refinement Example: Refined Model

In all cases the information types and other aspects become more strict; these are easily defined in terms of the ontologies through using deeper subclasses than the originals. Also note that the number of classifications might increase as we see with the information type in the refinement model: we have moved from just knowing that the flow carries Identity to knowing that there is data of Device Identity and Personal Identity classifications - both of which are subclasses of Identity and are thus more specific and detailed in nature.

Refinement of the protocols is more difficult and depends upon how the developer wishes to set up the relationships between the different protocols. We assume here that HTTPS is a better choice than HTTP from a privacy perspective and decide that this is therefore a refinement. We could not do the same between, say, HTTP and FTP for example, though there are arguments for the security and other properties of these that might help the decision over which is 'better' or more refining in any given situation.

The opposite of refinement is abstraction and in an ideal world we should only move forward to more refined models containing more accurate and detailed information. There is an additional technique which attempts to formalise changes that are not strictly refining known as retrenchment[70].

[70] Richard Banach, Michael Poppleton, Czeslaw Jeske, and Susan Stepney. Engineering and theoretical underpinnings of retrenchment. *Sci. Comput. Program.*, 67(2-3):301–329, 2007

If we do need to retrench a model, for example, if we notice that a Session identifier is really an Personal Identifier, then this needs to be traced back through previous models to ensure that our new, retrenched model is a refinement of the previous abstractions. This also implies further consistency checks made over the models and possibly some quite significant changes in the requirements to the system as a whole.

Channels and Data Flows

THE PRIMARY CONCEPT OF a data flow is based upon the notion of information channels[71] and understanding these is the key to not only understanding how a data flow is modelled and what it contains but also how to read a data flow diagram.

[71] J. Barwise and J. Seligman. *Information Flow: The Logic of Distributed Systems*. Cambridge Tracts in Theoretical Computer Science. Cambridge University Press, 1997. ISBN 9780521583862

The concept of a channel can be considered as a self-contained conversation between two participants. Over this channel flows items of information, or at least data which has meaning to the two participants. An additional property of a channel is (might be) that both participants *understand* the information being passed.

At any point in time there might be multiple, simultaneous channels between any two participants. The divisions are purely logical, though might have basis in some physical sense. For example, two entities, say, Alice and Bob might communicate both by voice *and* by Morse code sent by torch light. The most sensible way of modelling this would be to describe this system using two information channels. Of course both Alice and Bob in this example might be combining the information received.

The idea of a data flow corresponds to the overall flow of information from one participant to the other. From our case study earlier if we consider the data flow between the application and login service we see that this is modelled in one direction only. This is to capture the property that information is primarily flowing from the app to the login service. Obviously the login service would be responding at the application level protocol with tokens or failure messages and between the two participants with whatever the underlying protocol is using to acknowledge and manage the communication.

To decide on the primary direction of flow we need to consider the context in which we are modelling. In our case study we are primarily concerned with flow from the user to other services. If we had modelled the system in the context of the login service then our model would have been much simpler in that the only information it reveals about itself is the data of a login request (which isn't that particularly interesting here).

The above can be summarised as follows:

- a data flow model depicts a particular context, typically that of a user and the information that he or she is revealing to the World along with all the interesting cross-referencing and aggregation points.
- a data flow depicts the primary direction in which the information is flowing and does not take into consideration any application, transport or physical level protocols and their internal mechanisms for managing the information flow.
- a data flow may encompass many individual channels of communication.
- a channel is a logical, conversation between two participants.

Documenting APIs

WHILE THE DATA FLOW is probably the most important model required for privacy analysis, it is nearly always accompanied by other descriptions of a system. In particular architecture diagrams that describe the logical and physical organisations, class or ER diagrams showing relationships between data and/or objects, sequence diagrams, state diagrams, etc. Of concern however are the interfaces to the various components of a system which are expressed through application programming interfaces or APIs.

An API at its simplest describes the functions, parameters and return types, along with the calling mechanism and semantics to access the functionality of any given component. For example the API (or part of) to the user account service might be specified as follows:

Name	Parameters	Preconditions	Return
Login	u : String, p : String	The user identifier u already exists in the system. p is a non-empty string conforming to the SHA-256 structure	Returns a session identifier if the user exists and the password is accepted, else returns null.
Logout	u : String	The user identifier u already exists in the system	No return values. Always assumed to work

We describe the function name, parameters and machine types, return cases with data and types for scenarios such as success, failure and other cases such as network failure[72] during the call, etc. Furthermore it is always good practice to present the pre and post-conditions: the contracts that must hold for the function to operate and those conditions that hold after the function has completed[73]. Providing such contracts also helps significantly with many security issues relating to poor data validation such as SQL injection.

Continuing further we notice that the above only presents the specification and nothing about the implementation. At the next level of detail we present more information about how the calls are actually made. Many systems now provide a number of implementations to any given API: RESTful via some web interface, via a JavaScript library and so on. For each of these it is necessary to provide a description of the implementation so that the traffic data collection can be properly analysed. Table 2 gives an example; note the field labelled 'call' includes the function name, HTTP verb, protocol(s) and call semantics.

An all too common error is to just specify the data representation - XML, JSON etc. - or the calling semantics such as REST (Representational State Transfer)[74,75]. An API specification that

Table 1: High Level API Specification

[72] Gregor Kiczales. Towards a new model of abstraction in the engineering of software. *IMSA'92 Proceedings (Workshop on Reflection and Meta-level Architectures)*, 1992

[73] Richard Mitchell, Jim McKim, and Bertrand Meyer. *Design by Contract, by Example.* Addison Wesley Longman Publishing Co., Inc., Redwood City, CA, USA, 2002. ISBN 0-201-63460-0

[74] Roy T. Fielding and Richard N. Taylor. Principled design of the modern web architecture. *ACM Trans. Internet Technol.*, 2(2):115–150, May 2002

[75] Roy T Fielding. *Architectural Styles and the Design of Network-based Software Architectures.* PhD thesis, University of California, 2002

Name	Call	Preconditions	Return
Login	GET /acct/login HTTP, REST	In HTTP body as JSON {u:<username>,p:<password>} User must exist and the password must not be empty *and* password must be correct	OK 200 along with the authentication token in the message body JSON {$token :< UUID >$}. BAD REQUEST 400 if not successful
Logout	GET /acct/logout HTTP or HTTPS, RESTful	In body as JSON {u:<username>} User must exist.	OK 200 always returned regardless of the internal result

Table 2: API Specification with Protocol Details

does not list each of the calls, parameters, return types, etc. as described above is not by definition a description of an API. REST or RESTful is not a description of an API, nor a component of the system, but a style of of interacting with a system. Typically REST is used to describe a stateless method of communication on top of the HTTP family of protocols using the HTTP verbs GET, PUT, and so on. Stating 'REST API' as a description is incorrect at best and does not offer any information to the developers, users and auditors of a system. Stating that 'an API is RESTful' is correct, but must be accompanied by a description of what functionality, preconditions, parameters, return values and types the API provides.

As described in an earlier section, each API might describe one or more 'conversations' between a client and component over some channel of communication. These might be grouped together for modelling purposes and an overall direction of flow of information described giving us a data-flow between client and component.

Analysing and Checking the Model

A MODEL IS CHECKED or analysed in three ways:

- Syntactic Check

- Semantic Checking

- Requirements Analysis

The first two aspects apply to the internal consistency of the model. The first is the basic syntactic consistency of the model which has been explained in the previous sections as we have introduced the notation, that is data flows connect together elements, elements are not divided by partitions, etc.

The second aspect is ensuring that the model is correct from the various aspects of security class, information type, etc. This is an exercise analogous to that of type checking a computer program[76,77,78]. Finding inconsistencies here denotes that either the model is incomplete or that the model is wrong. The former requiring more information, the latter requiring more analysis and correction.

[76] Simon Thompson. *Type Theory and Functional Programming*. Addison-Wesley, 1991

[77] Jean Yang, Kuat Yessenov, and Armando Solar-Lezama. A language for automatically enforcing privacy policies. pages 85–96, 2012

[78] Thomas H. Austin, Jean Yang, Cormac Flanagan, and Armando Solar-Lezama. Faceted execution of policy-agnostic programs. pages 15–26, 2013

The inputs to a process or store must match any output form that element. For example, if a process takes financial data as an input and outputs health data then there is likely to be a misspecification. Similarly we need to check for cases where the information types and other classifications change in unexpected ways. If a process is marked as abstracting and the information types become more specific then this is cause for concern. Particular elements and their annotations may provide important information on what to expect. If a process cross-references many inputs then the outputs can be surprising in their information content and new information derived.

One aspect to be considered always is the amount of information being presented in a model. It is often the case that a model describes a specific situation and that many details may be suppressed for simplicity or readability reasons. Such suppression of information must be explicitly noted when presenting a model for analysis.

Requirements Analysis

WHEN PREPARING A MODEL for requirements analysis either for the purposes of checking or deriving/generating requirements we have a number of lines of 'attack':

- Individual Elements - nodes and data flows
- Partition Relationships

- Element-Partitioning

- Cross-Partition Flows

The first is that we check each element in the model as a distinct entity: that is we generate or check requirements for each node, each individual data flow - taking into consideration the source and target ends of the flow and each partition of the model.

The second requires that we check the relationships between the layers of the model. As has been explained earlier we can consider the model to be constructed from any number of interacting layers each representing a different aspect of the system (viz. figure21). The relationships between each of these layers must be investigated, for example when partitions in one layer conflict with another as might happen with architectural or geographical jurisdiction and the controller-processor partitioning. Also included here of course is the semantics of any particular layer with checks on items such as whether all processors are wholly contained inside controllers and so on.

Each element in a model exists wholly within a set of partitions layered over it. While and element such as a process might have its own set of requirements, further requirements are imparted by each of the layers in which that element exists. Each of these must be ascertained and calculated appropriately.

Finally any data flow which crosses a partition in any one of the partitioning layers needs to be investigated as particular crossing suggest certain requirements. For example, a data flow crossing from the EU geographical jurisdiction to the US may imply the Safe Harbour requirement. A data flow crossing from one device or process to another requires checking of the security of the transport protocols be they some IPC mechanism or some call over the public Internet and so on.

Summary

THIS CHAPTER HAS INTRODUCED the data flow notation, an overview of its semantics and shown how it is used within the context of privacy modelling to express how information flows not just between processes but between partitions of various aspects. The data flow model is central to understanding the application and generation of requirements and mitigations[79] as well as the effects of architectural decisions.

A system however can not be modelled by data flow models alone and care must be taken to ensure that any data flow model and its partitioning are consistent with other models of the system including the code and deployment - which themselves are models albeit at a very low-level of abstraction.

As development of systems continues patterns emerge in the models, their partitioning and annotation and amongst the requirements and architectural development paths. Documenting the patterns[80,81,82] that develop over time and their analyses greatly enhances the overall speed (or velocity!) of the privacy engineering processes. Indeed even the simple models presented earlier in figures 6 and 7 are themselves patterns of the initial models that can be constructed for almost any information system.

[79] privacypatterns.org

[80] Erich Gamma, Richard Helm, Ralph Johnson, and John Vlissides. *Design Patterns*. Addison-Wesley, 1995. ISBN 0201633612

[81] Munawar Hafiz. A collection of privacy design patterns. In *Proceedings of the 2006 Conference on Pattern Languages of Programs*, PLoP '06, pages 7:1–7:13, New York, NY, USA, 2006. ACM. ISBN 978-1-60558-372-3. DOI: 10.1145/1415472.1415481

[82] Sasha Romanosky, Alessandro Acquisti, Jason Hong, Lorrie Faith Cranor, and Batya Friedman. Privacy patterns for online interactions. In *Proceedings of the 2006 conference on Pattern languages of programs*, pages 1–9, Portland, Oregon, 2006. ACM. ISBN 978-1-60558-372-3

Security and Information Type Classifications

THERE ARE MANY CLASSIFICATION structures for denoting the security level of a given set of data: that data being a report, file, database or any other structure containing data. From the simple 'secret', 'classified', 'public' to the seemingly James Bond inspired 'Top Secret' and 'For your eyes only'. Such markings need to state clearly what the responsibilities of the readers and authors of those data sets are. Such security classifications form the backbone of data set and document management.

When working with sets of data it is equally important to understand exactly what data exists therein and not just its sensitivity; what that data is and the purposes for which that data is being used. Precisely or rigorously understanding the contents, provenance and other aspects of a data set gives meaning and justification to the assigned security classifications. When working with personal data it is critical to understand how each of these aspects, and especially that of the content of a data set, come together.

Just relying on lists of data fields is not sufficient for truly understanding the content and semantics of a data set. One of the problems when working with field names and their programming language types is that the names are largely arbitrary and the types are to do with machine representation rather than the actual semantic content of the field. Abstracting away from field names and machines types to concentrate on what the information content *really* is rather than its naming is critical to properly understanding the very nature of the data and information we are dealing with.

In this section we shall explore both security and information type classification systems, their application to various elements in a data flow model, the implied requirements arising from applying these classifications and finally the relationships and semantics of these classification levels to other aspects of data modelling. In further sections we will introduce additional classification structures and aspects for the description of data.

Security Classification

WE MAY INVENT AND apply any number and complexity of levels of security, from a trivial two state public and private system to a massively more complex system as might be applied in some military environments with many concurrent levels each denoting a set of particular requirements to be followed. The structure of a simple, linear security classification structure is shown in figure 48 with the implication that the relationship between security levels being transitive in nature.

The United Kingdom's security classification system described in [83] describes a 6 level system: Top Secret, Secret, Confidential, Restricted, Protect and Unclassified. Additional descriptors are used to inform the reader of particular content of note, for example, budgetary, commercial, medical or other kinds of information. These additional descriptors are used to further restrict information to particular persons or countries. For example, a document marked: Top Secret - CANUKUS EYES ONLY - MEDICAL - NATSEN would indicate a document of the highest security classification, restricted to UK, US and Canadian personnel only, that the information contained is of national sensitivity and contains medical information. Associated with these, particularly the basic security classifications are a large set of procedures and requirements describing the storage, handling and vetting necessary to see the contents of that document.

The US classification system [84] and its implementation [85] is similar to that of the UK's in many respects. Indeed within the G8 community there is a mechanism called the Traffic Light Protocol[86] for denoting the security classification of documents that need to be shared amongst nations, this system is an abstraction of the various national classification systems.

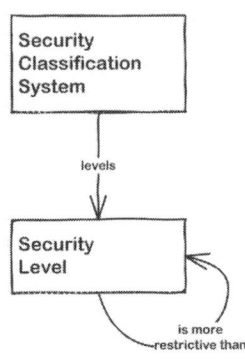

Figure 48: A Security Classification Meta-Model

[83] The UK Cabinet Office. Security policy framework, April 2013

[84] US Administration. Executive order 13526 - classified national security information. Technical Report Section 1.4, US Government, 2009

[85] US Dept of Defence. *National Industrial Security Program Operating Manual*, inc, change 1, march 28 2013 edition, February 2006

[86] OECD. Development of policies for protection of critical information infrastructures, 2007

We can choose as many levels and be as complex as we like, however erring of the side of simplicity is generally the best approach. For example a three class system and the ordering in terms of sensitivity as shown in figure 49. Secret is more restricting than confidential, confidential more restricting than public; with the relationship being transitive so that it follows that secret is more restricting than public by implication.

$$Secret > Confidential > Public$$

For each level we are required to define what handling, transmission and storage procedures apply amongst others. For example:

Public May be distributed freely, for examples by placing on public websites, social media etc. Documents and data-sets can be stored unencrypted.

Confidential Only for distribution within the company. May not be stored on non-company machines or places on any removable media (memory sticks, CD etc.). Documents and data-sets can be stored unencrypted unless they contain personal data.

Secret Only for distribution by a specific denoted set of persons. May not be stored on non-company machines or places on any removable media (memory sticks, CD etc). Documents and data-sets must be stored encrypted and disposed of according to secure deletion standards.

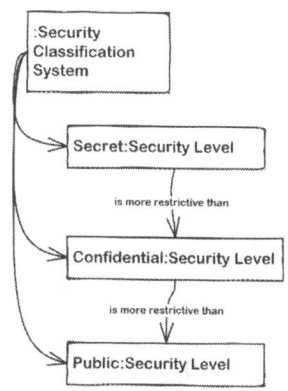

Figure 49: Security Hierarchy

Another variation often seen in business environments is the four class system which includes the notion of data sets and documents being 'internally public' to the business environment:

$$Secret > Confidential > Internal > Public$$

We can of course have additional levels, further descriptors and even 'partial orders'[87], but this just adds to the complexity and is often not required upon detailed analysis and in practice in most business environments. We have actually seen this kind of security classification with the earlier example, but rather dealing with this inside the security classification structure itself we split this kind of specific information typing into a separate classification structure. Similar splitting is also done

[87] A partial order is a binary relation that is reflexive, antisymmetric, and transitive.

across other attributes and aspects such as provenance, usage etc. and is explained in following sections in more detail. The linking of these together is made then explicitly through the requirements rather than trying to bind everything together in one homogeneous classification structure. Ultimately simplicity in this system a major key to its usage and acceptance

The Classification of 'Unclassified'

WHILE SOUNDING COUNTER-INTUITIVE, a classification of 'unclassified' simply means that no decision has been made. And if no decision on the actual classification has been made then it is possible that in the future that classification might be decided to be 'secret'. Which implies that if 'unclassified' needs to be at least as strong as the highest explicit classification.

It could be argued that data sets without classification be 'public' in nature; however it is more likely that either classification has been forgotten or that the classification to any of the given categories has not happened yet and so no decision can be made regarding how 'public' that data set might be. Consider a data set without classification that is found to contain personal identifiers and medical information; should this be default public or secret?

The procedure of Controlled Unclassified Information[88] used by the US Government is a mechanism for marking unclassified information along with a set of requirements on their handling[89]. While this serves as a good example of how to work with material classified in this way, we shall describe here a somewhat more restrictive starting point from where notions of how to handle unclassified information in all senses might be developed. There are two choices:

[88] US Administration. Executive order 13556 controlled unclassified information. Technical report, US Government, April 2010

[89] *What is CUI?* Controlled Unclassified Information Office, National Archives and Records Administration

- Either an explicit classification is given, for example, secret, confidential and public
- Or, no classification is given and the author remains the authority for instructions on how to handle that document

In the latter case the author's instructions may be more restrictive than the highest, explicit classification, which implies that unclassified is more restricting than, say, secret.

If the unclassified data set is communicated by some means[90] then we have a data breach. The document implicitly becomes public through this means and over time the document might become explicitly public knowledge but still remain officially secret. For example, if an employee of a company leaks future product specifications to the public media, even though they are now effectively public, the employee (and others) who handled the data would still fall under whatever repercussions leaking secret or confidential data would imply.

Still this is awkward to reconcile, so we need more structure here to understand what unclassified and the other classifications mean. We must therefore apply to a notion of authority: all data sets and document *must have an owner* and that owner:

[90] say, to the whole company by a reply-all accident

- Either assigns an explicit security classification, and all handlers of that document refer to the standard handling procedures for that security classification: referring to the security classifications standard as the authority

- Or, keeps the document as being unclassified and makes themselves the authority for rules on how to handle that document - with the added implication that prevention of any data breach is then their responsibility

The latter comes with the implication that the owner of the document here is also responsible for ensuring that whatever handling rules are implied are consistent with the contents of the document. For example, if the document contains sensitive data then the author will themselves be responsible for ensuring that the rules that come from his or her authority are as at least as strict as the highest implied security classification.

In summary, if a document or data-set is unclassified then the owner of that document is the authority deciding on what the handling rules are and that by default the rules must be *at least* as strict has the highest explicit security category:

$$Unclassified \geq Secret > Confidential > Public$$

Information Type

TO DESCRIBE INFORMATION CONTENT we can not rely upon arbitrary field names and machine types; neither of these describe the *meaning* of the data contained therein. We present here a classification system that concentrates on what the information is without reference to its syntax, structure, naming, representation and machine typing.

We define a seven high-level information types, which can be subtyped (and these are presented later) as necessary. Data contained within a data set may be classified according to a number of information types at any point time; including the possibility that some data may remain unclassified. If information is classified according to one of the higher levels in the classification structure, then this means that its specifics have not been defined and we treat that as if it might also be in any of the more specific levels; this usually means that more investigation into the information content of the data is required.

These categories are not exhaustive and have further subdivisions refining and specialising those more general classifications[91,92]. Certain categories also imply additional constraints on the data, for example the Medical subcategory of Heath implies HIIPA compliance, financial data can be further refined into that data which requires PCI compliance.

We have already seen examples of these classification structures being used in data flow models presented earlier, for example, in figure 35 which shows a data flow containing identifiers, timestamps and location data. The format and structure of this data is not specified, nor are aspects such as whether the identifiers were hashed, or the location data encrypted or abstracted in some way. This forces the discussion onto the content rather than arbitrary representation, and decisions such as whether there is sufficient anonymity to drop the, say, identifier type can be addressed in a more rigorous manner.

The seven top level information type classes are shown in figure 50 along with an abstract 'generic' top class which provides some structuring within the ontology only.

[91] Barbara Liskov. Keynote address - data abstraction and hierarchy. *SIGPLAN Not.*, 23(5):17–34, January 1987b. ISSN 0362-1340

[92] Barbara Liskov. Keynote address - data abstraction and hierarchy. In *Addendum to the Proceedings on Object-oriented Programming Systems, Languages and Applications (Addendum)*, OOPSLA '87, pages 17–34. ACM, 1987a. ISBN 0-89791-266-7

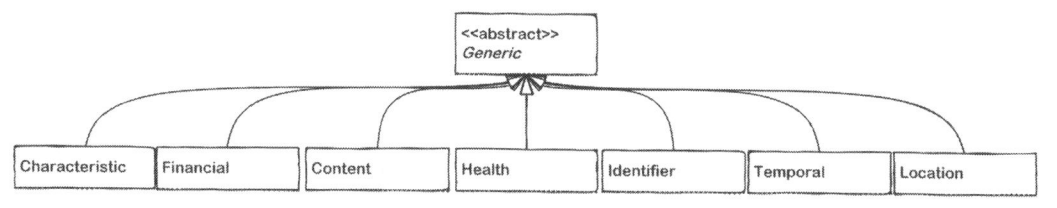

Figure 50: Top Level Information Type Classes

- **Characteristic** pertains to any data that can be used to identify a person. Typically this means names, contact information, email addresses, gender, age, dates of birth and other demographic data.

- **Location** refers to items that depict location.

- **Temporal** refers to time stamps rather than specific dates and times such as dates of birth. However, depending upon the context, it may be that a given time is classified in both the Temporal and one of the Characteristic categories.

- **Health** includes both medical and personal health details such as exercise information such as heart rates.

- **Financial** includes information that pertains to monetary data including credit/debit cards, monetary amounts, account information, purchase transactions, receipts etc.

- **Identifier** includes user IDs, device IDs, sessions IDs etc. This category also includes certain kinds of addresses, specifically machine addresses such as IP.

- **Content** relates to user generated content generally of a free-form nature such as the body of an email, social network postings and various kinds of media, for example, photographs. This also takes into consideration structures such as events, log entries, passwords etc. This classification implies that the data has further structure.

These classifications can refer to both individual fields and structures, for example, the fields *lat, long, accuracy* would be classed together as being of the location type.

If fields have been encrypted or hashed, then these will be classified accordingly. For example, if a user identity is hashed then it *still acts as an identity* of some kind. This is critical to understand as transforming the representation of a field does not necessarily change the information type - this is a common mistake when hashing or encrypting identifiers and other data in a mistaken belief that this somehow makes things anonymous. In most cases hashing and encryption usually change the information type to something more generic, for example, from a 'user identifier' to just a generic 'identifier' as we lose information from the syntax of the original data.

In many cases a field might be classified according to two or more types simultaneously, for example, an email address might be both a characteristic and an identifier (or suitable subtype of these). There are also similar cases with data such as IP address which itself can be classed as both a machine identifier *and* a location. When a subtype is used, then the field is implicitly also of one of the parent types[93] by default so we only need to express the most specific subtype and none of the parent types.

[93] cf: inheritance in OO programming languages

Personal Characteristics

ANY SET OF INFORMATION that can be used to uniquely identify a person. Typically this means user IDs, names, dates of birth, certain locations; but can also include multiple location instances, various demographics, certain kinds of addresses and identifiers.

Firstly we define two broad categories: Contact and Demographic with further subdivisions as necessary. This is depicted in figure 51 and this particular model must be considered incomplete as we can add further subclasses as required.

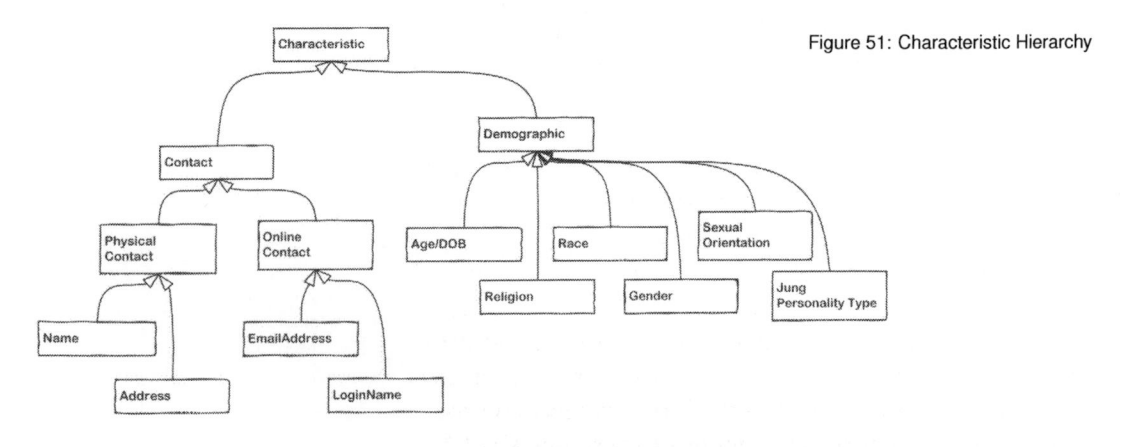

Figure 51: Characteristic Hierarchy

Information is placed in the Physical Contact class if it relates to 'real-world" data and that relating to one's physical nature such as names, addresses etc, whereas the Online Contact class refers to that data which describes data points such as email or social networking identities etc. Note that there is some overlap when dealing with data classified as Physical Contact when dealing with addresses that can be simultaneously classified as the Location class. This kind of classification, especially in this case, required further understanding of the role and usage of those data points within the data set.

Demographic is an easier category and the subcategories here are fairly self-explanatory and specific in nature. Due to the nature of this particular category, the classification here is necessarily not complete as explained earlier. In the case of a missing category this can be added as a sub-category of demographics or just the higher-level Demographic category can be used.

Location

LOCATION PERTAINS TO MORE specific notions of place such as coordinates, geographical entities and 'point of interest' (POI). The reference which can be used to define location is 2002/58/EC[94] - this would be authoritative in at least EU jurisdictions but can be applied more widely as necessary and states:

[94] EU. Directive 2002/58/EC of the European Parliament and of the Council Concerning the Processing of Personal Data and the Protection of Privacy in the Electronic Communications Sector, 2002

> "any data processed in an electronic communications network, indicating the geographic position of the terminal equipment of a user of a publicly available electronic communications service"

The structure of this classification is shown in figure 52 with a number of additional, non-exhaustive, subclasses.

As we have previously mentioned, in some case data may be classified simultaneously as Location and one of the subclasses of Characteristics and/or Identifier (eg: device address) as necessary. This latter case is particularly true when processes such as geolocation are being employed to derive location data from data such as IP addresses or mobile base-station CellIDs.

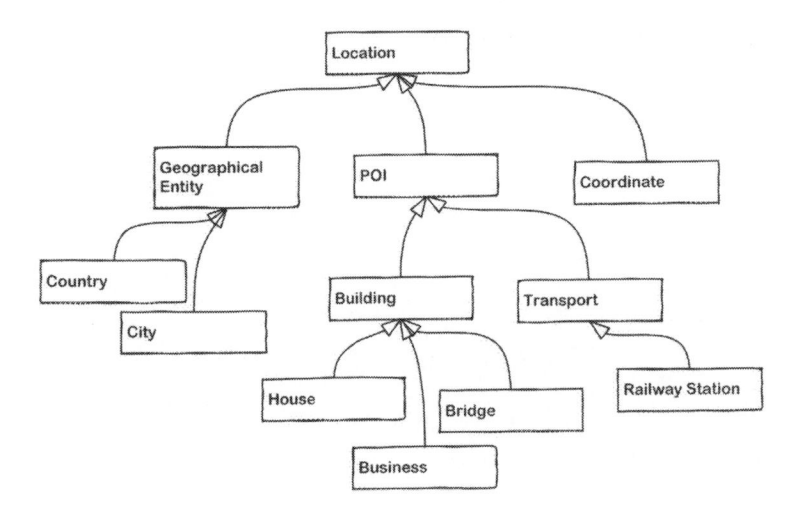

Figure 52: Location Hierarchy

The classification we have shown here goes fairly deep into specific subclasses, for example, those under the POI class. Additional subclasses and even the use of these subclasses will very much depend upon the amount of detail required in the system being developed and the analyses being made. Deep subclassing such as this is very context dependent and often just use of fairly high level classes such as POI to describe data is sufficient.

One interesting case that can occur is where data sets contain what appears to be location information but is really a different form of existing data. Consider a data set which contains fields such as country, lat and log. Does this data set contain both geographical entities (countries) *and* coordinates? Investigation must always be made to ascertain this as it might just be that the inclusion of lat and long here might be for convenience for drawing some user-interface and have been derived from the country field - in which case the data set would be deemed to contain just geographical entities. The opposite can also be true in that we might have very specific coordinate data being supplied and a country being derived from this; in which case either the data set can be classed as containing coordinates or both coordinates and geographical entities.

This also suggests that there are relationships existing in this classification regarding the sensitivity of data. Typically coordinates and types of POI are more sensitive than Geographical Entities. This must be considered during the analysis of the data set and during the formulation of requirements pertaining to location data.

Financial

GENERALLY PERTAINING TO ALL things related with money, this classification denoting that the data set contains fields and structures describing various financial mechanisms information and probably implies that the data set and processing must be treated under specific stronger regulations such as those set out in the PCI[95] requirements. The structure of this classification is shown in figure 53 and again the specific subtypes can be extended as required.

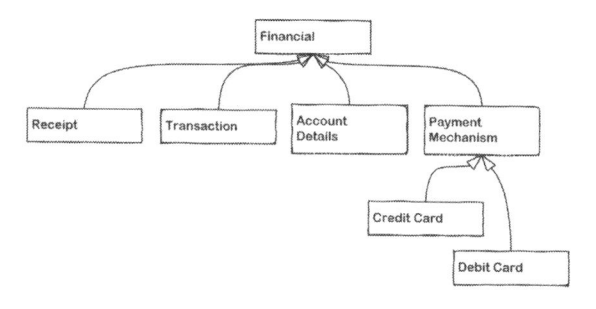

[95] T.M. Virtue. *Payment Card Industry Data Security Standard Handbook*. Wiley, 2008. ISBN 9780470260463

Figure 53: Financial Class Hierarchy

Receipts relate to specific details of payment, while transaction relate to particular details about processes such as money transfer and so on. If transaction data is present then it is often likely that receipt information will also be present and vice versa.

Another case is where a data set is marked as containing Account Details - that data set will also invariably contain information such as identifiers and characteristics. However the presence of account information will likely imply a different security classification and certainly different handling, storage and transmission requirements.

Health

THE HEALTH CLASSIFICATION is applied any data that contains information about the human condition. At its simplest

– presented here – the Health data classification contains two subclasses that specifically denotes data of a recreational or medical nature and is shown in figure 54.

Recreational data is regularly seen in exercise or lifestyle applications, for example, weight, height and heart-rate are fairly common. Generally such data does not fall under the more strict requirements for storage and usage of medical data such as the HIPAA regulations[96].

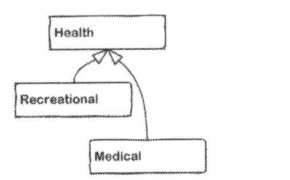

Figure 54: Health Class Hierarchy

[96] Centers for Medicare and Medicaid Services. The Health Insurance Portability and Accountability Act of 1996 (HIPAA), 1996

To decide whether data is recreational or medical it is necessary to consider whether this data has been supplied by a medical authority. However data that pertains to a medical condition, which may include conditions such as pregnancy does not by itself imply the medical classification. For example, if a user decides to record details of their pregnancy then this is recreational data; if a doctor specifies this then this will most likely be made in a health care information system and therefore fall under the medical category. Specific rules on this can be found in the HIPAA regulations and should be checked and confirmed in all cases.

Identifier

IDENTIFIERS ARE MANY, VARIED and complex and have obvious overlaps with other classifications especially those in the Physical and Online subclasses of the Characteristic classification structure. This category is specifically used to denote artificial identifiers of various natures. The structure of this classification is given in figure 55.

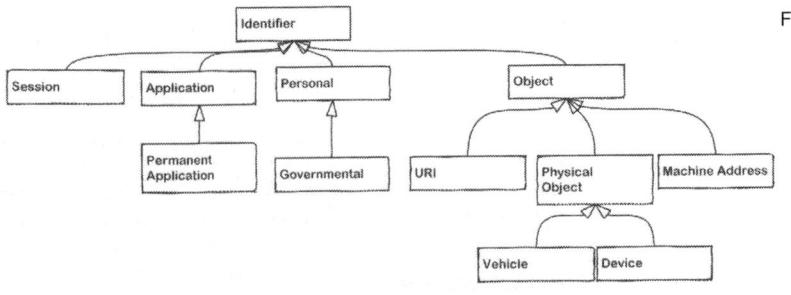

Figure 55: Identity Hierarchy

While session are temporarily assign identifiers for usually the purposes of a set of closely related interactions within a relatively short period of time. Such identifiers are often found in relation with structures such as cookies and so on.

Applications are often uniquely identified either through an identifier assigned at compile time, or in rarer cases at installation time. We make a specific distinction between these two cases in whether an application is identified by a permanently assigned identifier or whether this is something more temporal in nature.

Personal identifiers are those which are artificially assigned to identify a unique individual but being distinct from a Characteristic. However in many cases there is a very close relationship between data classified as Online Contact such as email addresses and this should be taken into account when using this classification. If an email address is used for contact information then despite it probably being unique to that person it is not being used as an identifier; whereas if one uses an email address as an account name then its primary use is as an identifier in which case it should be classified so.

We also note the specific cases where identifiers have been provided by government such as social security numbers, passport numbers, etc. These typically require specific handling and the requirements from data of this kind should reflect this.

Finally we have the Object Identifier classification to denote the identification of both physical and virtual objects, for example, car registration numbers, serial numbers, URIs, URLs and other schemes for identifying 'objects' in the internet[97] such as web pages, API locations, etc., or the physical world. Given the wide variety of identifiers and some confusions about terminology[98,99]

The subject of device identifier is used for those identifier uniquely referencing a single device and include data such as IMEI codes on mobile devices or MAC addresses used in networking equipment. A further subtype of this - Machine Address - takes into consideration those device identifiers that can be used as addresses, specifically data such as IP addresses.

Care must be made to be clear about the semantic differences with certain kinds of object: for example a street address can

[97] Michael Mealling and Ray Denenberg. Uniform Resource Identifiers (URIs), URLs, and Uniform Resource Names (URNs): Clarifications and Recommendations. Internet RFC 3305, August 2002

[98] D. Stuttard and M. Pinto. *The Web Application Hacker's Handbook: Finding and Exploiting Security Flaws*. Wiley, 2011

[99] URL vs URI vs URN: *"The correct technical term for a URL is actually URI (or uniform resource identifier), but this term is really only used in formal specifications and by those who wish to exhibit their pedantry"*. (See above citation)

function as a characteristic, location and a physical object depending upon how it is used.

As we have seen with the Location classification one can form an ordering between the different kinds of identifier in terms of their uniqueness with reference to a human being. Session and application identifiers are very hard to trace to a person whereas a governmental identifier is a reference. Identifiers falling into the Device class could be considered as personally identifying or at least personal data in many cases.

Note that certain classes such as Machine Address or Personal here can be transformed into or have a close correspondence with other classifications as we have noted. In particular it is always worth noting that Machine Addresses have the possibility of being transformed into Location data.

Quasi-Identifier

A QUASI-IDENTIFIER IS ONE where a set of fields when combined together[100] can be used as an identifier in their own right. For many data sets, even when anonymised, it is possible to construct an identifier from various permutations and combinations of fields, such as those classified in the characteristic, location, identifier classes and so on. This very generic relationship can be visualised in figure 56.

[100] Rajeev Motwani and Ying Xu. Efficient algorithms for masking and finding quasi-identifiers. In *Proceedings of the Conference on Very Large Data Bases (VLDB)*, 2007

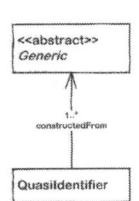

When modelling data flows after some anonymisation or filtering process it may be necessary to explicitly denote which fields when combined together could or do act as quasi-identifiers. Figure 57 shows a simple example of this.

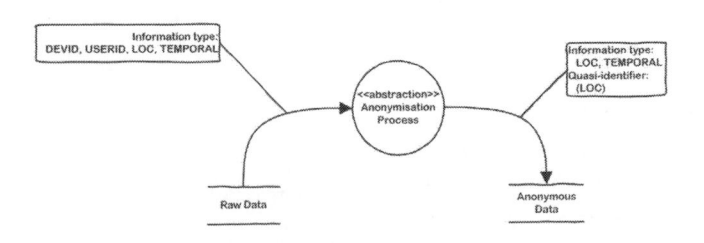

Figure 56: Quasi-Identifier Construction

Figure 57: Denoting Quasi-Identifier Fields in a Data Flow Model

Furthermore, even if steps are taken to remove quasi-identifiers, given a large enough data set then various kinds of fingerprinting can be used, even in cases where the denoted identifiers are constructed out of comparatively fuzzy data[101].

[101] Benjamin Coifman and Michael Cassidy. Vehicle reidentification and travel time measurement on congested freeways. *Transportation Research Part A: Policy and Practice*, 36(10):899 – 917, 2002. ISSN 0965-8564

Temporal

THE TEMPORAL CLASSIFICATION REFERS to most expressions of instantaneous recording of times - in particular time stamps as opposed to dates such as birth dates which typically come under the Demographic classification. Inclusion of data that can be classed as Temporal is always cause for concern as this can lead to tracking of behaviour over time. The Temporal classification will occur is almost all data sets, especially in log files, transaction logs, receipts, and so on.

Typically no subtypes of this exist in any meaningful form and so the structure presented already in figure 50 suffices to describe graphically this ontology.

Content

CONTENT IS A BROAD category and relates to data points of a generally of a free-form or opaque nature such as the body of an email, social network postings and various kinds of media, for example, pictures or photographs. Numerous subclasses of Content exist each of which may infer additional classification in the other aspects. For example, pictures or photographs may contain identifiers of various kinds, characteristics and location. The certainly non-exhaustive set of subclasses of Content is shown in figure 58

There are three main subclasses, the media subclass and its further subclasses are self-explanatory. The event classification refers to data collected as part of some logging activity and may actually refer to a whole data set rather than a specific field depending upon how that data set is constructed. It has subclass that specifically refers to data such as that found in memory dumps and is so named.

108 PRIVACY ENGINEERING

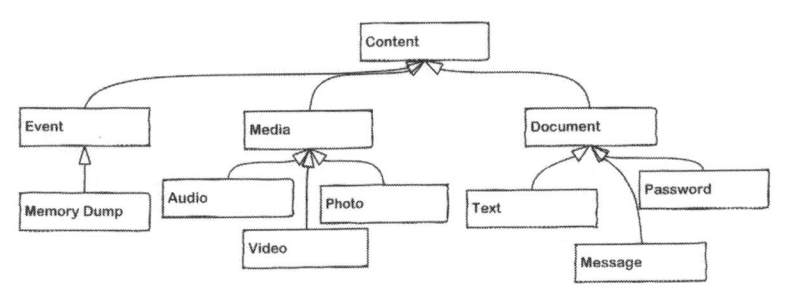

Figure 58: Content Hierarchy

The document subclass refers to again opaque data such as that found in free form text fields. The subclass of Text is used to describe such fields, especially those that are human readable. We also include a specific classification for Messaging referring specifically to email, SMS and social media posting message bodies. Finally the Password class is used for password and other passkey related fields.

Nearly all data in this category can be transformed through filtering and abstraction processes into its constituent data. An example of this is shown in figure 59

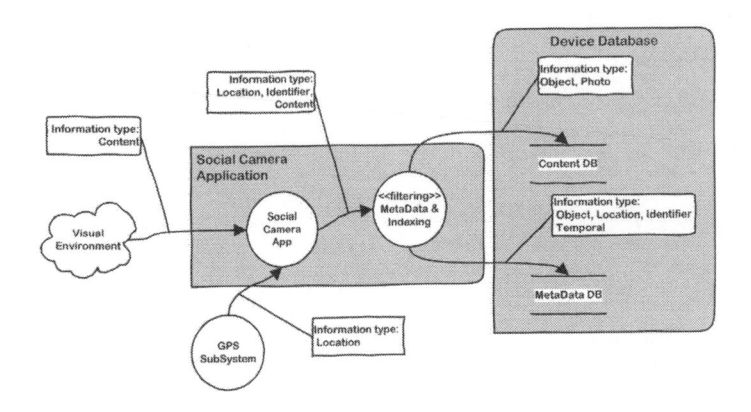

Figure 59: Content Transformation Example

In this example we expose the path of data from a visual environment through the application that processes. Within this application the collected visual image - Content - is combined with Location from the GPS and various other kinds of data such as an Identifier which probably has been randomly assigned, such as a default file naming convention. This data which contains Location, Identifier and Content data is passed to a process which splits this into two flows. The first flow contains data classified as Photo and Object; these are subclasses of Content and Identifier respectively. The second flow shows the extraction of meta-data form the incoming data.

Summary

THE SECURITY AND INFORMATION type classification systems are the core of understanding privacy in an engineering context. It is by these classifications that we understand *what* information is being carried without all the baggage of *how* in terms of machine types, field names and structures and therefore derive the requirements for the storage, handling and transmission of that data.

We have **not** defined some familiar terms, such as *personal data* and *personally identifiable information (PII)* at this point, nor provided mechanisms for ascertaining whether a given set of data does contain personal or personally identifiable data as defined in many privacy legal texts. The terms personal data and PII do have particular meaning but are often extremely broad in nature, it is for this reason that we have explicitly avoided any attempt to define these without first introducing a mechanism for the classification of information content.

Additional Classification Structures

IN THE FOLLOWING SECTIONS we describe a number of additional classification structures that can be used to further describe data sets and elements of the data flow models such as the processes and partitions, some of which have already been introduced. We also include a number of important *externally* defined classifications such as those for privacy risk and definitions of terms such as 'Personal Data' and 'Personally Identifiable Information'.

These additional classifications are much smaller and more contextually dependent than the security or information type ontologies. This means that their use and content is typically more customised and sparingly used and that they are used to denote more specific properties of a system. These classifications are often introduced later in the development and modelling processes after the model of the information system has been developed sufficiently and refined to such a degree where these aspects are better known and understood. As in all cases, we reiterate here that these classification structures, as those earlier, are open to modification as local practice and context demands.

Data Transformation

CLASSIFYING THE KINDS OF data transformation that occurs in the information system being modelled is necessary to better reason about the properties of those processes[102]. The fact that data can be extracted or cross-referenced is a major concern of privacy, for example, a log that collects the IP address and

[102] Benjamin C. Pierce. Differential privacy in the programming languages community, October 2012. Invited tutorial at *DIMACS Workshop on Recent Work on Differential Privacy across Computer Science*

timestamps of a user is a much richer entity in information content terms when IP addresses can be mapped to locations of reasonable accuracy. Similar concerns exist when collecting, for example, CellIDs of mobile network base-stations and many other cases are easily envisaged.

The processes by which data can be transformed from one type into another can be similarly classified to express their processing properties[103]. Firstly any process over data is capable of transforming it into some other form and to express the types of transformation we define four classifications: Abstracting, CrossReferencing, Filtering and Identity to describe that process as shown in figure 60 and described further below:

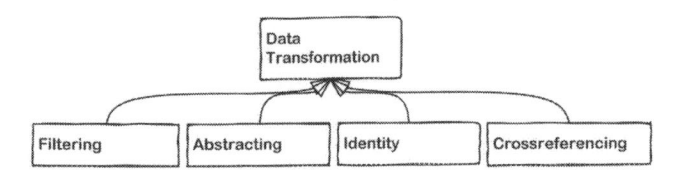

[103] Jason Reed and Benjamin C. Pierce. Distance makes the types grow stronger: A calculus for differential privacy. In *ACM SIGPLAN International Conference on Functional Programming (ICFP), Baltimore, Maryland*, September 2010

Figure 60: Data Transformation Hierarchy

A **filtering** data transformation is any which extracts data from a structure through the suppression of certain fields or certain items of data. This is commonly seen with data that is classified as Content and then more specifically one of the media types. Pictures contain not just the data from the image but much meta-data about the image, the conditions under which it was taken, copyright data, location etc. The EXIF standards [104,105] define the file format and a large number of standardised fields though it must be noted that camera manufacturers are free to and do add additional propriety fields.

[104] Technical Standardization Committee on AV & IT Storage Systems and Equipment. Exchangeable image file format for digital still cameras: EXIF Version 2.2. Technical Report JEITA CP-3451, JEITA, April 2002

[105] Japan Electronics and Information Technology Industries Association. JEITA CP-3451 exchangeable image file format for digital still cameras: EXIF version 2.2, 2002

An **abstracting** transformation is any which reduces the information content as opposed to extracting or suppressing specific content as seen when filtering, though commonly applied together. Processes such as the tokenisation of data and the generalisation of data are good examples of abstraction transforms. An example of this is when processing location where we might map GPS coordinates to countries or cities. Another example is seen when processing identifiers over a dataset to reduce their longevity, or to remove the most-significant bit from IP addresses.

Cross-referencing is the only transformation which potentially adds information and so requires more than one source of data. The crossreferencing transformation is almost ubiquitous when performing tasks such as data analytics over multiple data sets, user reidentification etc. The canonical example for this would be geolocation[106] where IP addresses are mapped to locations [107]. Other commonly seen examples are where inputs from two data stores are combined and an output with cross-referenced data is produced with all the privacy repercussions that might entail.

An **Identity** transformation is one where no change to the data is made. While seemingly at odds with the whole notion of transformation, this is used in cases where the process more represents some control mechanism than processing. Its use should however always act as a warning to ensure that data is not being changed during its passage through such a process.

When a category is assigned to a process then this should be used as alert to potential privacy issues; especially in cases of cross-referencing and identity classifications. At one level this can be checked from the number of incoming and outgoing data flows and the sum of their contents.

Ideally an individual process should only be classified in one of the above but it is more likely that multiple classifications will be used in order to keep models readable and at a higher level of abstraction for simplicity. In the case where more than one classification is present it is implied that the process can be can be decomposed into individual steps and each step further examined regarding its properties.

Provenance

PROVENANCE DEALS WITH THE nature of the source of any data - in particular the data subject. In this chapter we present the classification system for expressing properties about the nature of the source of any data. This is particularly important when working with systems that are collecting data from outside parties such as companies or library sources, or, when from humans, especially when information is sourced from children.

The W3C has a standardised ontology for the structure of provenance[108] which we can take advantage of[109]. The core of the

[106] Andrei Popescu. Geolocation API Specification. World Wide Web Consortium, Working Draft WD-geolocation-API-20081222, December 2008

[107] Yuval Shavitt and Noa Zilberman. A study of geolocation databases. *CoRR*, abs/1005.5674, 2010

[108] Khalid Belhajjame, Helena Deus, Daniel Garijo, Graham Klyne, Paolo Missier, Stian Soiland-Reyes, and Stephen Zednik. Prov model primer. Technical report, W3C, 2012b

[109] Li Ding, Jie Bao, JamesR. Michaelis, Jun Zhao, and DeborahL. McGuinness. Reflections on provenance ontology encodings. In DeborahL. McGuinness, JamesR. Michaelis, and Luc Moreau, editors, *Provenance and Annotation of Data and Processes*, volume 6378 of *Lecture Notes in Computer Science*, pages 198–205. Springer Berlin Heidelberg, 2010. ISBN 978-3-642-17818-4

W3C's PROV-O ontology[110] is shown in figure 61.

[110] Khalid Belhajjame, James Cheney, David Corsar, Daniel Garijo, Stian Soiland-Reyes, Stephan Zednik, and Jun Zhao. PROV-O: The PROV Ontology. Technical report, W3C, 2012a

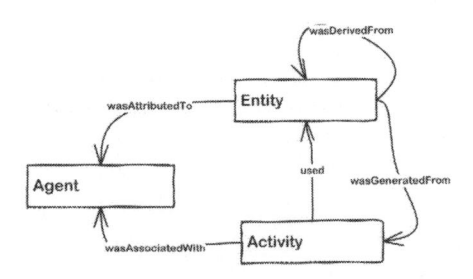

Figure 61: W3C PROV-O Provenance Ontology Core

We concentrate on the agent which in our usage is the source or owner of the data and in most models is both a user element and a data subject. This need not just be the data subject of the system in question, but includes 3rd parties, library calls etc. The concepts and relationship with PROV-O can be seen in figure 62 with the provenance classifications we will use described below:

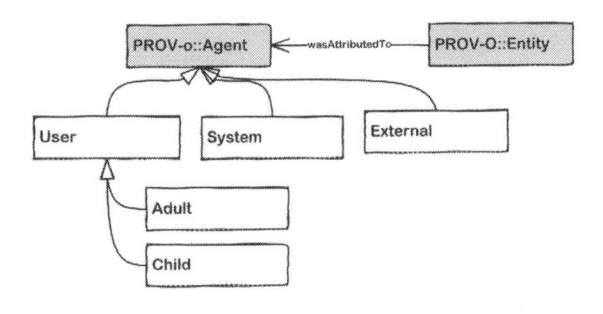

Figure 62: The Provenance Classification

User Typically referring to a human owner of data, i.e.: the user which input or owned that data

System Referring to data generated by the operating system of a device, for example, the location provided by the GPS hardware in a mobile device. The ownership of course must be reconciled against that of the User based on local policy, but this allows us to make the distinction

External Referring to any data generated outside of the system, for example OAUTH tokens or data provided by some service, e.g.: geolocation services. This class would likely need to be subclassed to describe particular licensing situations and usages but that is best left again to local policy[111]

[111] As already stated, these ontologies are designed to be flexible and customised as context dictates

We further subclass the User with the overlapping types of Adult and Child to give us information in the cases where information is specifically collected from just adults or those over the age of consent, or whether we are specifically collecting data from children or other minors[112].

An aspect of provenance is that it refers to the **sources** of information and this is carried forward over all the data flows from that point across the model as a whole. If two data flows meet at a process, then the output data flow will take the sum of all in the incoming provenance classifications. In this respect provenance acts as a kind of 'dual' to the usage classification in its application to the data flows expressed in the model.

Provenance is often found at the source elements combined with various identity classifications to form the basis of various use cases related to whether users are logged in and to the degree of validation of their identity; combined with their 'status' of various kinds such as whether they are acting as themselves, as an adult, on the behalf of an adult or as child, etc. In this respect provenance normally appears as an identifier to a use case rather than being explicitly noted on a data flow diagram - both cases are shown in figure 63

[112] United States. Congress. House. Committee on Commerce. *Child Online Protection Act: report (to accompany H.R. 3783) (including cost estimate of the Congressional Budget Office)*. Report. U.S. G.P.O., 1998

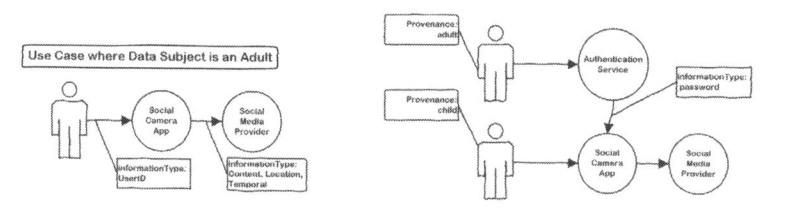

Figure 63: Annotating Provenance in Data Flow Diagrams and Use Cases

Data flow models and privacy analyses are constructed in the context of a given data subject - which will be defined later - which provides the starting point for understanding the context in which a model is constructed as well as the legal owner or source of any data.

Jurisdiction

IT IS CRITICALLY IMPORTANT to understand from where the information is geographically sourced and where it resides and therefore from this under what jurisdictions that data will be held. For example, in the transfer of personal data from the EU to US we have legislation such as Safe Harbour[113] to provide requirements on data handling, storage and processing, knowing which data falls under this legislation is necessary for the functioning of the service and related business in a compliant manner.

Cases where data flows between differing legal jurisdictions becomes critical important when there are significant differences in the treatment of personal data (or any data). Furthermore when working with geographically distributed systems where there controller and processor aspects vary between countries[114] then specific legislation will need to be ascertained. For example, as has been stated between the EU and the US exists already Safe Harbour legislation, while between the US and China exist a completely different set of rules including trade restrictions etc.

The ontology for jurisdiction can be simply defined in terms of countries of the World and the various legal groupings of these. However this must be taken with some caution as even within well established legal entities such as the EU or the US there can be significant differences in interpretation of laws between individual countries or states. Indeed it might be the case that data can not be transferred between certain jurisdictions[115] as is the case when dealing with data flowing into and out of China or other sensitive areas; for example, the US Patriot Act[116] may provide numerous and onerous restrictions.

We provide no specific classification or ontology for jurisdiction other than that of providing the already known set of countries of the World and their various groupings. Jurisdiction is best presented as a partition within a data flow model and an example of this is seen in figure 64

In this particular model we show not only the data flows but two aspects: jurisdiction and architectural. Note how these two aspects overlap and partition the model and their interactions. For example, we have a backup provider which provides its front-end services in the EU but its storage in the US and/or Ireland. Similarly an advertiser providing services in both EU and the USA.

[113] EU. 2000/520/EC: Commission Decision of 26 July 2000 pursuant to Directive 95/46/EC of the European Parliament and of the Council on the adequacy of the protection provided by the safe harbour privacy principles and related frequently asked questions issued by the US Department of Commerce (notified under document number C(2000) 2441) (Text with EEA relevance.), 2000

[114] Rebecca Iglesias, Rob Nicholls, Anisha Travis, and Webb Henderson. Private clouds with no silver lining : Legal risk in private cloud services. *Communications and Strategies*, 84(1), 2012

[115] Abhishek Vaish, Abhishek Kushwaha, Rahul Das, and Chandan Sharma. Data location verification in cloud computing. *International Journal of Computer Applications*, 68(12):23–27, April 2013. Published by Foundation of Computer Science, New York, USA

[116] USA Congress. Public Law 107 - 56 - Uniting and strengthening America by providing appropriate tools required to intercept and obstruct terrorism (USA PATRIOT ACT) act of 2001, 2001

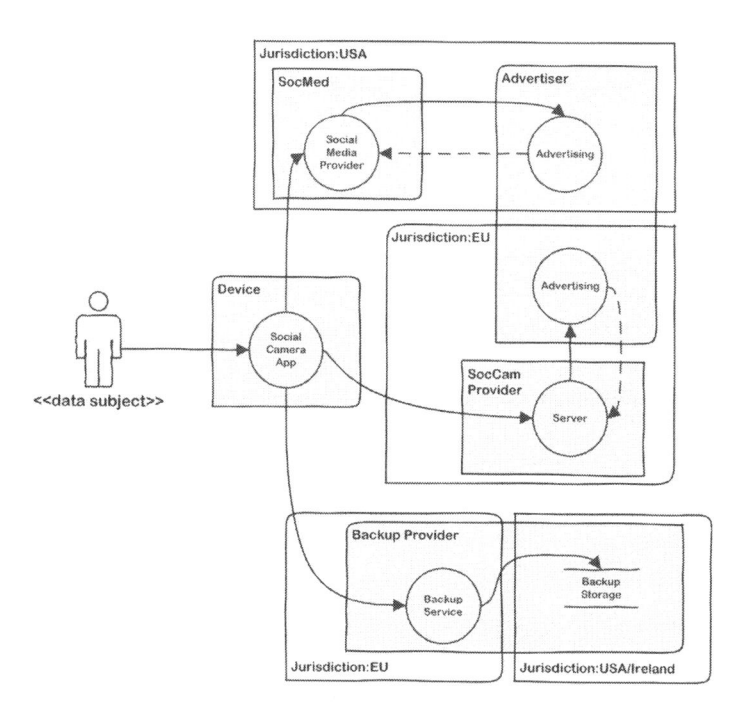

Figure 64: Example Annotating a DFD with Jurisdiction Information

Purpose

PURPOSE DESCRIBES THE REASONING behind why data is being collected and provides a context for this. Data is generally collected to allow the application and associated purposes to function, which is the primary purpose of the data. If we collect data that outside of this then we term this secondary data, that is, data about the functioning of an application. From this we can simply define these two basic categories of purpose as shown in figure 65 and described below. Note that not all jurisdictions this distinction between primary and secondary usages.

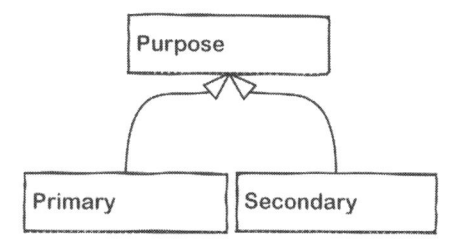

Figure 65: Purpose Ontology

- Primary data is the data that is gathered for the purpose of providing a service, or, data about the user gathered directly

- Secondary data is the data that is gathered from the provision of that service, i.e.: not by the user of that service, or, data about application gathered directly

When modelling we can either note whether the data being collected is primary or secondary using annotations or by decomposing the data flow into two separate data flows to explicitly note this as depicted in figure 66. Much of this will however be decided by architectural concerns such as the use of instrumentation libraries for application analytics.

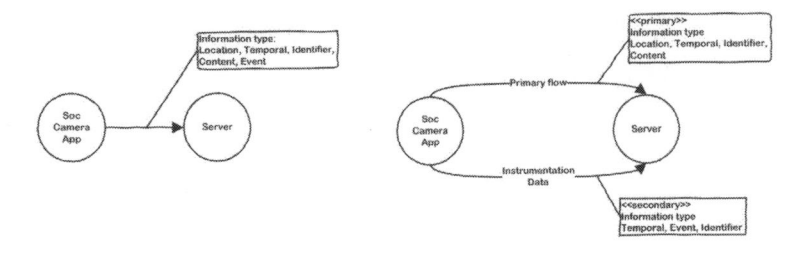

Figure 66: Annotating Purpose in a DFD

While it can be argued that the primary-secondary distinction is often complex to decide upon, the use of the terms is used in data collection and so means for annotating and expressing this are provided.

Usage

USAGE PERTAINS TO WHAT is intended and allowed to do with the information we have obtained and is one of the major considerations for privacy. For any application or system we *have* to collect data to provide the various services that the application or system provides. For example, it is necessary to collect GPS coordinates if one is trying to augment a photograph with a location for example; similarly it is exceptionally difficult it at all possible not to collect location data when working with location aware services, regardless of the amount of data minimisation and despite attempts to the contrary.

As data flows into and around any information system it is split, combined, cross-referenced and processed and eventually ends up in various 'silos' for specific purposes. Generally we can split this into two categories: system provisioning and service provisioning. The former relating to that data which is collected, kept and used for monitoring the behaviour and health of the system providing the service. The second category relates to the necessity of data collected, kept and used for the actual service itself.

However data is used for further purposes such as marketing, product improvement, consumer profiling and so on. We can therefore construct a set of further classifications covering each of these usage cases. A suggested ontology is shown in figure 67 with the following meanings below:

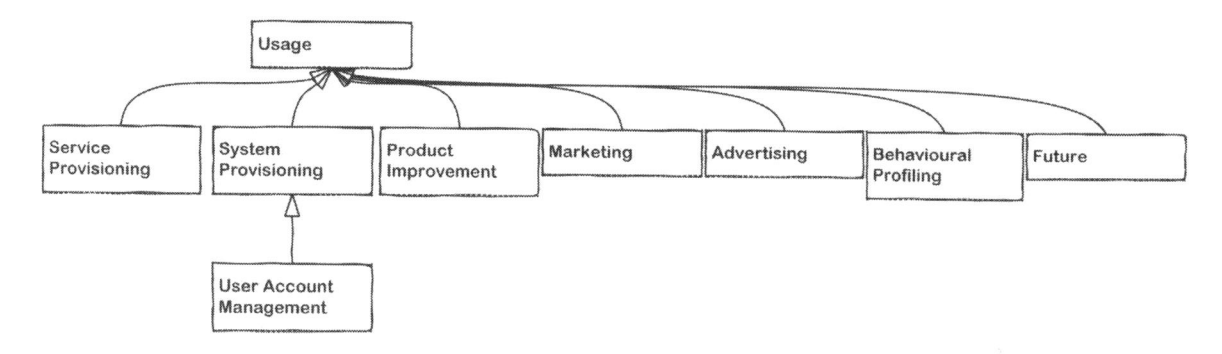

Figure 67: Usage Ontology

Service Provisioning the data is required for the application or service to provides the stated functionality

System Provisioning the data is required for the (operating) system to provide its functionality

User Account Management the data is required to provide for user accounts (subtype of system provisioning)

Advertising the data is required for advertising mechanisms

Marketing the data is required for advertising mechanisms

Behavioural profiling the data is required to generate a profile the user's behaviour for their application or service usage

Product Improvement the data is required by research and development teams for understanding product usage and for debugging purposes

Future the data has no explicit usage, but is planned for

The usage classifications, while they can be applied across a model, have particular importance at the **target** elements of the data flows. It is at these points that the usages are sufficiently granular, partitioned and specific for this particular classification to start having specific meaning. Therefore when modelling usages are ascribed at the target elements, which typically tend to be stores. In figure 68 we show an example of a number of target data sets being annotated with the usage classification - the explanation on the flows from the data subject is explained below.

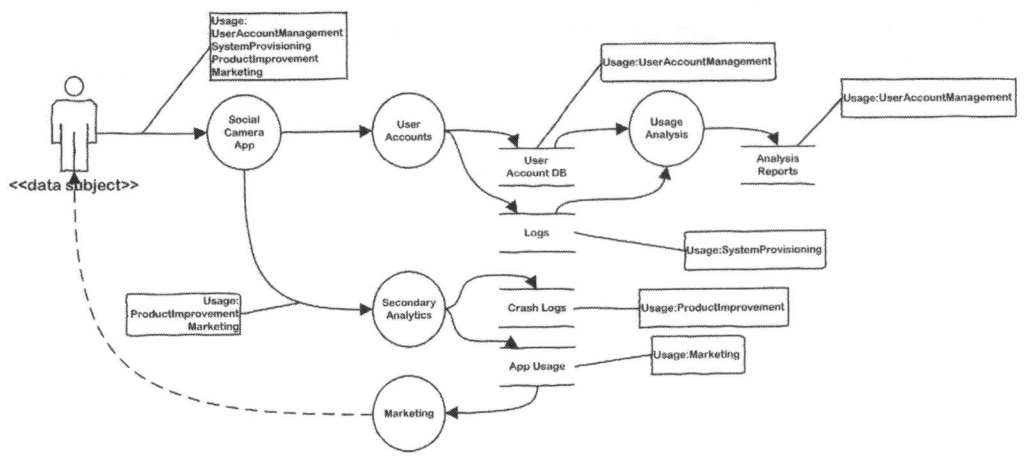

Figure 68: Example Usage Annotation in a DFD

In a well-constructed and detailed model all data sets and therefore points will have a usage ascribed. One of the clear principles of privacy is that data is not collected without a usage being known and defined for that data. We include a 'future' category to capture cases where the usage has not been decided upon rather than a case where no usage is given. If no usage is given then then investigation must be made on the necessity of that data.

While usage is typically annotated on target elements, we can calculate that all the data feeds into that point must also contain data of that usage category. This should result in the usages ascribed to the totality of all data flows from a data subject being the sum of all usages over the targets reachable via data flows from that data subject. Note that in figure 68 we show the usages ascribed to the initial data flow from the data subject as the sum of all target usages and similarly the data flow between the social camera app process and the secondary analytics process as being the sum of the individual usages thereafter.

This calculation of the sum of usages applied to the data flows from a data subject is important in the construction of the rules for the agreements between the data subject and the controller-processor structures as we shall see later on.

Data Subject, Controller and Processor

THE TERMS DATA CONTROLLER and data processor are defined by the EU Article 29 Working Party[117] to clarify the roles that an individual or organisation plays in the processing of personal data. While these terms are EU specific, their inclusion here is both for completeness and that this distinction often plays a significant role in understanding the roles and responsibilities between differing organisations.

[117] http://ec.europa.eu/justice/data-protection/article-29/

The classification is shown in figure 69 and is as would be expected with only three terms rather simple but also shows the relationship between these; in particular the hierarchy between these through the agreements between these parties.

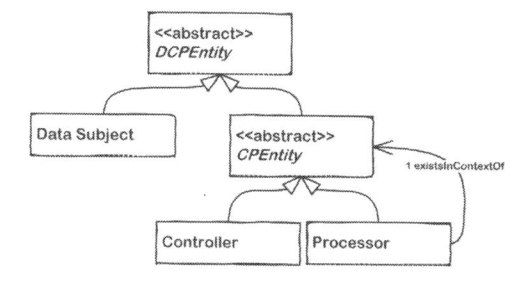

Figure 69: Data Subject, Controller and Processor Classification

The formal definitions are, starting with data controller:

> the natural or legal person, public authority, agency or any other body which alone or jointly with others determines the purposes and means of the processing of personal data...

and for data processor:

> a natural or legal person, public authority, agency or any other body which processes personal data *on behalf* of the controller

and finally for the data subject:

an individual who is the subject of the (explicit or implicitly derived) personal data.

In more simple terms if an individual, an organisation or even you decides what personal information is going to be collected, kept and the purposes to which that information is to be put, then you, that individual or organisation is a data controller.

If an individual, an organisation etc. however holds and uses personal data but the bounds on this are provided from elsewhere then that individual or organisation is a data processor. Examples of data processors include cloud service providers that are not directly providing an applications services, payroll processing companies and generally anyone being provided or subcontracted with data. Data processors may only process personal data on behalf of a data controller.

It is possible that an individual or organisation be both a data processor and a data controller simultaneously but in different contexts with regards to the data. There are a number of other specific aspects related to the above, particular relating to the *necessary* processing of information as part of, for example, legal compliance. In those situations the individual or organisation utilising the data may be considered a data controller. In all cases above and as this is not a discussion on the vagaries of law in this areas specifics would need to be confirmed given the local context.

When modelling with these classifications, as we have already seen earlier in figure 41 when defining annotations of partitions in the data flow language definition we can explicitly mark logic partitions or a user element in a data flow with these classifications. Note that the classification here has some additional rules which must conformed be to. While a data subject may have data flows to both controllers and processors, due to the hierarchy between controllers and processors the processors will be diagrammatically inside the controllers. Additionally if a processor further subcontracts processing then this too will be diagrammatically inside a processor. Any flow from a data subject will be implicitly 'via' a controller.

It is permissible to *draw* a data flow diagram that does not adhere to these rules - this might be done for simplicity of expression in that the diagram might become too complex to read.

However the relationship between the data subject, controller and processor must be fully clarified and the structure correctly in place when analysis of the models (and not necessarily the diagrams) be made.

When constructing agreements between these parties, the flow between the data subject and the controller should express the maximal amount of purpose, usage, information content and other related data. This maximal amount of information on the flow is calculated in a similar manner to that expressed when calculating the usages ascribed to a flow as described earlier.

Identification and Authority

A DATA SUBJECT OR other entity that communicates and interacts with any information system will provide some kind of identification and will also likely to rely upon some kind of authority to prove their identification. We can classify the various levels of detail of identification to express the continuum of degrees of identification. This is closely related to the Identifier classifications present in the Information Type classification system as when identification is made then identifiers will be present; however the presence of any identifier, even something such as a user identifier is not proof of identity. In order to gain trust in that the identifier is identifying the correct human or entity we must appeal to some form of authority to validate this.

To make things simpler we can work with a number of discrete categories to express this level of identification and authority. For example, when dealing with a bank account it is necessary to show proof of identity by multiple means through a process known as Know Your Customer (KYC) which includes manual inspection of specific approved identification documentation such as a passport. Other mechanisms however are more familiar such as the ubiquitous user name and password, which may be backed up with authentication tokens and other two-factor mechanisms for some systems.

Often systems allow access without explicit identification and appeal to authority - any passing access to a web site is typically made pseudo-anonymously and login is not required. Identity might be provided through cookie mechanisms, collection of IP addresses and session identifiers, but none of these are authenticated as being indicative of an identified unique human being.

We construct a simple classification system that allows us to capture the level of authentication made on the source of the data. Furthermore we can also divide this classification into two higher categories - weak and strong - that convey the difference between actively versus passively providing authentication information.

Strength	Classification	Description
Weak	Unauthenticated	no authenticated identity was made or unknown for this data
Weak	Observed	user's identity was established by reference to identifier, eg: email address, device identifiers
Strong	Authenticated1	user was established through normal login
Strong	Authenticated2	user was established through two-factor or better means
Strong	Proven	user's identity was established through KYC procedures

Table 3: Identity Classification Levels

Similarly to the previous security classifications these form an ordering of identification:

$Proven > Authenticated_2 > Authenticated_1 > Observed > Unauthenticated$

A further property of the **strong** identity classes is whether the identity was authenticated locally or through federated means. We include the classification of **Federated** in any annotation of identification to express this.

Knowing this is be critical to knowing what is and is not allowed regarding the processing of that data. For example, if we have authenticated the user then we might be allowed to process that data without any anonymisation, which might not be the case if we have just observed the user's details. For example, every access to a web server is logged and will contain device addresses such as IP address, and IP address can be linked with a person, this means we have just observed a user's identity but not established it through any authoritative means. This then might imply that any processing such as analytics over this log file could not be used for specific targeting of the user whom we have observed.

While identity can be authenticated, there still lies the problem of whether the person using the system is the one who provided the identity credentials. A typical case here is where an adult provides an account for a child to use as does happen with services that are ostensibly blocked for children, such as many social media services. From a privacy compliance view we can only assume that any data comes from the one who has provided the identity credentials.

In figure 70 we show a data flow diagram with identity annotated and discuss some of the implications of this.

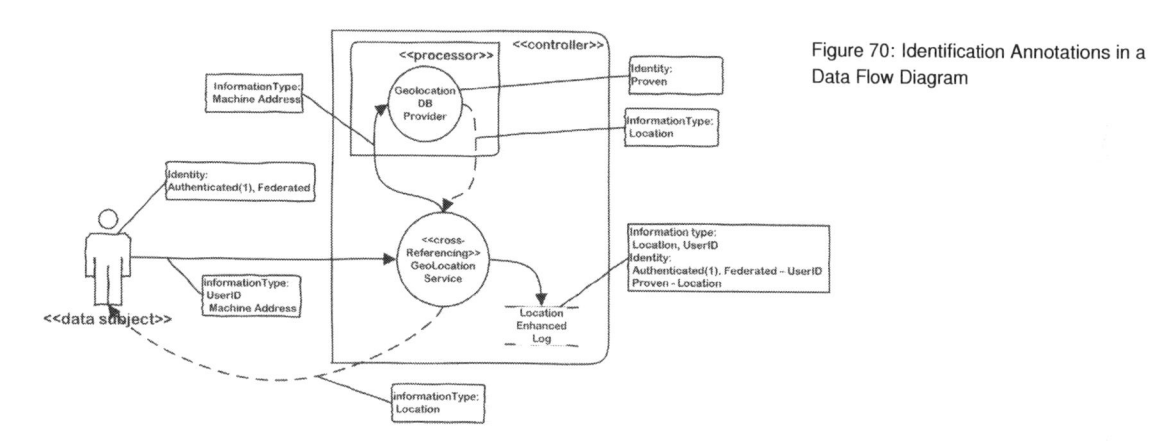

Figure 70: Identification Annotations in a Data Flow Diagram

Starting with the data subject, we immediately notice that in this use case (and maybe to use the service in first place) the user here has provided authentication details and had these authorised by a 3rd party through federation. This potentially means that the user identity data in the flow from the data subject to the controller will contain details about this federation which might then have to be mapped to a local user identifier if such things exist. This also requires trust in whatever federation mechanism has been used. It does however give us some confidence in that the data subject in this case is who they state they actually are.

Geolocation DB Provider's identity is proven and in this case the authority is likely to be defined in the controller-processor relationship through contractual means and also through some API key means shared between the two parties.

The identification data set that we eventually construct in the log files and also report back to the user is also marked with these identification properties, though in the storage element this is now mixed and in the return flow traceable back to its proven source. When data is mixed as we see in the storage element this may be repercussions regarding processing and the trust of the data later, especially if data has been or is due to be cross-referenced when, for example, reconstructing the identity of the original owner. If we consider the case where data from a data subject whose identity has been observed is cross-referenced against known person then the level of identification class does not necessarily improve. Expressing this in a data flow model means that we can trace the level of trust in the identification of the source and any data and therefore quantify the risk of poorly sourced and identified data.

Personal Information and Personally Identifiable Information

IN THIS SECTION WE present the terms **personal data, personally identifiable data** and the refinements thereof. In our information classification system earlier we did not define explicitly what is *personal data* nor the equally ubiquitous term *personally identifiable information* (PII) - often seen as synonyms of each other. These terms and their subclasses shown in figure 71 come from external sources and specifically EU[118,119] and US directives and legislations. In order to use these terms consistently we can define these in terms of our information type classification.

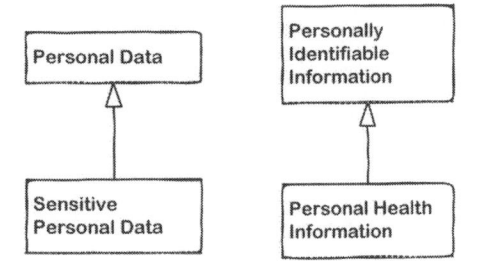

[118] EU. Opinion 4/2007 on the concept of personal data. article 29 data protection working party, June 2007

[119] E. U. Directive. 95/46/EC of the European Parliament and of the Council of 24 October 1995 on the Protection of Individuals with Regard to the Processing of Personal Data and on the Free Movement of such Data. *Official Journal of the EC*, 23, 1995

Figure 71: Personal Data, PII and Subclasses

We show here not only the definitions of these terms as given but also demonstrate how they can be derived from more detailed information classes. It often assumed that personal data means that the identity or thereof is directly given by the contents of a dataset. In most cases this is of course true, but by forcing justification of these terms we not only place the terminology on a more sound basis but also encompass datasets which appear not be person data or personally identifying data. Figure 72 shows how these terms map together and also shows links to further more detailed metrics, classifications and theories which can be employed in the justification of the personal data classification or not.

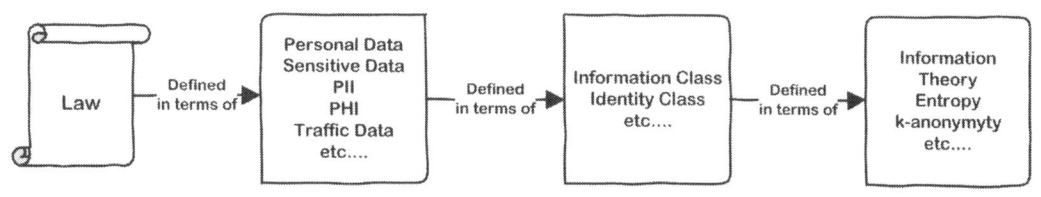

Figure 72: Derivation of the Personal Data Terminology

Furthermore we avoid a common scenario where some development teams avoid admitting that they hold personal data to avoid the additional privacy requirements this would entail. By concentrating on the *content* of the data we can infer the classification of personal data with, as written above, more justification. This is especially useful when working with location data, obfuscated data such as when identifiers have been hashed, tokenised data and time-series data.

Firstly we present these terms as defined: within the European Union the term Personal Data is defined[120]:

> ...any information relating to an identified or identifiable natural person ('data subject'); an identifiable person is one who can be identified, directly or indirectly, in particular by reference to an identification number or to one or more factors specific to his physical,

[120] Dag Elgesem. The Structure of Rights in Directive 95/46/EC On the Protection of Individuals with Regard to The processing of Personal Data and the Free Movement Of Such Data. *Ethics and Inf. Technol.*, 1 (4):283–293, February 1999. ISSN 1388-1957

Also from the above directive we have the following statement:

> Whereas the principles of protection must apply to any information concerning an identified or identifiable person; whereas, to determine whether a person is identifiable, account should be taken of all the means likely reasonably to be used either by the controller or by any other person to identify the said person; whereas the principles of protection shall not apply to data rendered anonymous in such a way that the data subject is no longer identifiable; whereas codes of conduct within the meaning of Article 27 may be a useful instrument for providing guidance as to the ways in which data may be rendered anonymous and retained in a form in which identification of the data subject is no longer possible

In the definition of Personal Data, "relating to" is considered to mean "data which relates to an individual if it refers to the identity, characteristics or behaviour of an individual or if such information is used to determine or influence the way in which that person is treated or evaluated"

A further refinement to the above is the use of the adjective 'sensitive'[121], ie: 'sensitive personal data' which refers to data such as:

- Racial or ethnic origin
- Political opinions
- Religious or similar beliefs
- Physical and/or mental condition
- Sexual life, sexuality etc.
- Data relating to any offences committed or alleged; including proceedings of any legal trial
- Political affiliations, Organisation membership (some jurisdictions only)

It is likely that the scope of the term personal data will increase within EU Law with the publication of the General Data Protection Regulation (GDPR)[122], which includes the following statement:

> "personal data is any information relating to an individual, whether it relates to his or her private, professional or public life. It can be anything from a name, a photo, an email address, bank details, posts on social networking websites, medical information, or a computer's IP address"

The term personally identifiable information or PII as defined in US law which broadly coincides with the definitions of personal data and traffic data given above. The definition of PII is mentioned in a memorandum from the Executive Office of the President, Office of Management and Budget [123] and also in the NIST standard Guide to Protecting the Confidentiality of Personally Identifiable Information [124]. The definition given is as follows:

[121] *Handbook on European Data Protection Law.* European Union Agency for Fundamental Rights, April 2014

[122] European Commission. European Commission's press release announcing the proposed comprehensive reform of data protection rules, 25 January 2012

[123] Executive Office of the President. Safeguarding against and responding to the breach of personally identifiable information. Memorandum M-07-16, 22 May 2007

[124] Erika McCallister, Timothy Grance, and Karen A. Scarfone. SP 800-122. Guide to Protecting the Confidentiality of Personally Identifiable Information (PII). Technical report, NIST, Gaithersburg, MD, United States, 2010

Information which can be used to distinguish or trace an individual's identity, such as their name, social security number, biometric records, etc. alone, or when combined with other personal or identifying information which is linked or linkable to a specific individual, such as date and place of birth, mother's maiden name, etc.

This means that any data classified as a Characteristic and especially within the Demographics subclass would imply that the data can be *additionally* given the Personal Data classification. Any data set from which behaviour of an individual can be ascertained, for example, a data set containing Location, Identifier (of some kind) and Temporal data would also denote Personal Data.

Placing the above in the context of the already presented information classification systems and the measurement of identity as presented earlier means that we can not take any individual piece of data alone as being indicative of being personal data or PII. We must examine the whole record and in many cases where aspects such as time are involve, the set of records and their evolution over time to determine this. Consider the case where a data set contains just a list of religious and political affiliations.

ID	Religion	Political Affiliation
1	Christian	Labour
2	Muslim	Conservative
3	Christian	Liberal
4	No-Religion	Pirate Party
5	Jedi (Alderan Sect)	Free Occupied Shetland Party
6	Christian	Conservative
7	Christian	Nationalist

Table 4: Example Anonymised Data set

For the most part, the above list even though it contains religious and political information, these categories even when taken together form a too large sample to identify a person and as such would not be personal data. This of course *assumes* that the sample the above refers to is *suitably large* such as the population of a country. However even here one must be careful that even here we can have records which can be easily associated with a unique person even in large populations - such a record can be easily detected in the above[125]!

[125] Hint: The Jedi from certain northerly, Scottish islands

- The context in which the data is gathered could improve its identifiability dramatically. For example, if we stated that the above data set was collected from people living on a remote, very sparsely inhabited island with a population of 10.

- Even when the context is very large in terms of sample population, some specific elements might be extremely specific and thus revealing. For example, pro-Shetland independence supporters of a specific sect of the Jedi faith are likely to be very few

Similar cases exist when we deal with health data [126,127], especially those relating to particular rare diseases. Even in cases where the context is extremely broad such as the infamous AOL data breach [128], which was less of a breach but poor anonymisation practices, identification can take place rather easily.

These are in no way the only definitions and many jurisdictions have further refinements to these, for example the UK's Data Protection Act[129] introduces a further category refining personal data to *sensitive personal data* which would take into consideration many of the demographics fields presented above.

In the US, PII can be further refined in the context of health information which introduces the term Protected Health Information (PHI). This term is often referred to and covers any information that is ostensibly medical in nature and related with a person. The set of data which falls under PHI is extensive and the context defined by the HIPAA legislation, in the classification system provided here any information related with the Medical class would be considered PHI as well as any Characteristic information in any context under which HIPAA applies.

Information Theory and Entropy

IN 1948 CLAUDE SHANNON published a theory[130] of properly unifying the notions of the nature of information, communication, error correction and entropy. Shannon's work serves as the basis not only at a theoretical level but at an everyday, practical level. Simply put, Shannon effectively formalised the criteria by which all communicating systems behave: from today's mobile

[126] Khaled Emam, Fida Dankar, R+'egis Vaillancourt, Tyson Roffey, and Mark Lysyk. Evaluating the risk of re-identification of patients from hospital prescription records. *The Canadian Journal of Hospital Pharmacy*, 62(4), 2009

[127] Fida Dankar, Khaled E. Emam, Angelica Neisa, and Tyson Roffey. Estimating the re-identification risk of clinical data sets. *BMC Medical Informatics and Decision Making*, 66, 9 July 2012

[128] Michael Barbaro and Tom Zeller Jr. A face is exposed for AOL searcher no. 4417749. *The New York Times*, Aug 9, 2006

[129] Information Commissioner. *Data Protection Act 1998 Legal Guidance: a reference document for organisations and their advisers that provides a broad guide to the Act as a whole*. Information Commissioner's office, September 2009

[130] Claude E. Shannon. A mathematical theory of communication. *The Bell System Technical Journal*, 27:379–423, 623–656, July, October 1948

telephone networks to human-human communication. The key concept is that of **entropy**.

Entropy is the measure of randomness of a system and in information systems this relates to the amount of *expected* information content of a message[131]. Informally the greater the entropy the more random the system and thus more difficult to predict the outcome of any given scenario. For example, in the case of a coin toss, the outcome will either be heads or tails and predicting correctly the result of a particular coin toss is in the fair case will happen on average 50% of the time. The possible states of a coin toss can be expressed using a single binary digit, 0 for heads, 1 for tails (or vice versa). This we can use as a measure of the amount of information a system contains, in the coin toss case, just 1 bit[132] of information[133].

More relevant for privacy is the possibility of identifying an unique person in some context. At the time of writing there are approximately 7.2 billion individual human beings living on planet Earth at this moment. To assign a unique identifier to each of those people we require a binary digit containing 32.74 bits, or 33 complete bits[134,135].

Every piece of information we have provides us some additional bits of information. For example, similarly to our coin toss, gender is either male or female, or expressible in a single bit of information, 1 for female, 0 for male (or vice versa). If we know the gender then we have identified approximately one half of the population. If we can identify the country, for example, Finland we require approximately $\lceil log_2(6 \times 10^6) \rceil$ or 23 bits of information. The state space size for any item of information can be expressed in a number of bits of information.

The above measurement in bits is additive, so if we know the country (Finland) and gender then we have 24 bits of information which in this case works out to identifying around 2.5 to 3 million people; out of 7.2 billion in the context of all living human beings. Still a large figure, but if you consider the IP address of a network endpoint or router identifies a particular physical address and the number of people at that address is anything from a single occupant to an average family to a large multinational company then at best we've uniquely identified a person or a family and at worst a major, multinational corporation with a few million employees; the average number of employees in a company worldwide is in the 100s.

[131] M.V. Volkenstein, A. Shenitzer, and R.G. Burns. *Entropy and Information*. Progress in Mathematical Physics. Birkhäuser Basel, 2009. ISBN 9783034600774

[132] Bits meaning 'binary digits'. There are other measures: nats, bans or Harleys but the concept is the same regardless of measurement system

[133] I. J. Good. Studies in the History of Probability and Statistics. XXXVII A. M. Turing's statistical work in World War II. *Biometrika*, 66(2):393–396, 1979

[134] $\lceil log_2(7.2 \times 10^9) \rceil$

[135] 33 Bits of Entropy: The End of Anonymous Data and what to do about it, retrieved from http://33bits.org

More pressing for privacy and identification is when fingerprinting of data where the values contained within a data set act as identifiers[136]. Consider the browser identification string automatically supplied by web browsers over nearly all HTTP protocol calls which contains information such as the operating system, the browser, its version, installed features etc., then a person's overall profile becomes unique [137] even if many personal data fields aren't present. This actually is one of the major risks with data minimisation and particularly that the traffic data component is not considered in the minimisation.

[136] Ian Oliver. An advertiser's paradise: An adventure in a dystopian post-'do not track world?'. In *W3C Workshop: Do Not Track and Beyond*, November 2012

[137] Peter Eckersley. How unique is your web browser? Technical report, Electronic Frontier Foundation, 2009

Measuring Identifiability

GIVEN A SUFFICIENTLY LARGE number of people then being anonymous within that group is relatively easy as has been shown in the previous section. As the group size decreases then the chances of being identified by a particular piece of information becomes easier - the amount of bits required to assign a unique identifier to any member of that group decreases.

The cases where people have been identified from IP addresses of home routers bears witness to the above. If music has been pirated and traced to an IP address which identifies a house then we might identify a small group of people, say two adults and two point four children. Using knowledge about who might like a particular type of music we can further reduce this down to the probably likely suspect. Indeed this is the mechanism used to convict persons of music piracy[138].

[138] The actual legal complexities of going to trial notwithstanding

Similarly if we report the location of a person to within fifty metres then to actually identify that person we need to examine the actual surroundings. Within fifty meters in a city or a shopping centre might provide some degree of anonymity as the density of people would be quite high - high entropy. In a countryside location then the density of people will be much less, that is low entropy. We can take this to extremes when dealing with very sparsely populated areas where even a 50 kilometre radius might only reveal one or two people. This is seen in situations where location is inferred from GSM cell tower identifiers or even Wifi and Bluetooth tracking technologies employed to track customer movements in shopping centres and malls. Taking data points the above over time and even with large group sizes and imprecise locations we can track and identify unique persons given enough data[139].

When presented with a data set we can infer the amount of information pertaining to identifiability through simple examination of the various information types present. For any given information type we can map the particular kinds and granularity of data present to a scale ranging from non-identifying to identifying (though in both cases we should quality this with the word 'potentially') as shown in figure 73. Note that this diagram should not be read as an absolute scale of identifiability but rather as a guide to understanding this concept.

[139] Gayathri Chandrasekaran, Tam Vu, Alexander Varshavsky, Marco Gruteser, Richard P. Martin, Jie Yang 0003, and Yingying Chen. Tracking vehicular speed variations by warping mobile phone signal strengths. In *PerCom*, pages 213–221. IEEE, 2011

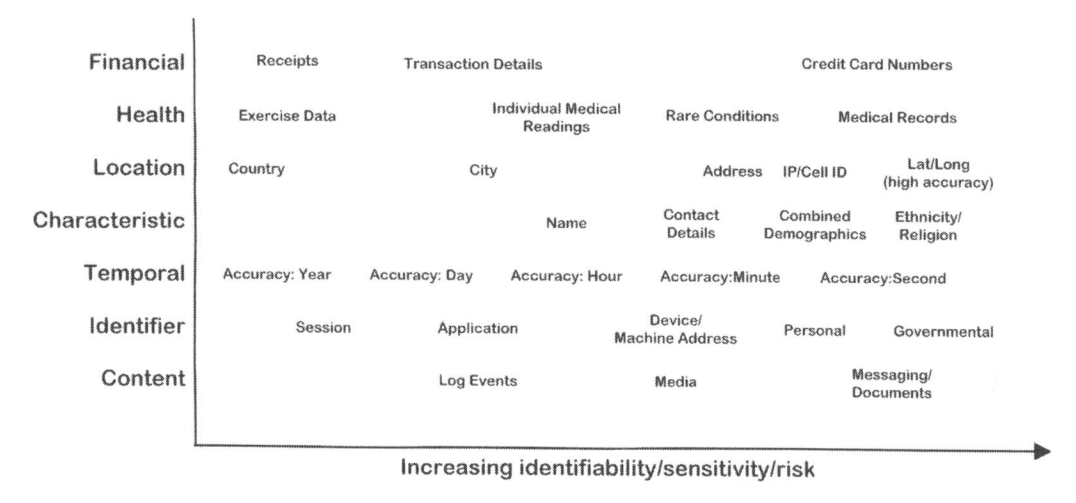

Financial	Receipts	Transaction Details		Credit Card Numbers		
Health	Exercise Data	Individual Medical Readings	Rare Conditions	Medical Records		
Location	Country	City		Address	IP/Cell ID	Lat/Long (high accuracy)
Characteristic			Name	Contact Details	Combined Demographics	Ethnicity/ Religion
Temporal	Accuracy: Year	Accuracy: Day	Accuracy: Hour	Accuracy: Minute	Accuracy: Second	
Identifier		Session	Application	Device/ Machine Address	Personal	Governmental
Content			Log Events	Media	Messaging/ Documents	

→ Increasing identifiability/sensitivity/risk

Figure 73: Measuring the information content of different information types

Once we have identified the degree of identifiability for each individual information type we still need to combine these together to obtain a fuller picture of how identifiable or fingerprintable the data is. Techniques for further analysis such as κ-anonymity, ℓ-diversity and others are presented later. If we have details of the sample size of the data and the population to which it pertains then we can make very accurate entropy calculations over this.

Assessing identifiability, or the concept of *nymity*[140] in some approaches, for most of the cases is relatively simple, if we have credit or debit card information in the case of the financial aspect then we most certainly have all the information we need not just to identify a unique person but to gain his or her actual identity too. Similarly for the health aspect: as soon as we get information that is medical in nature then typically this identifies a person. In cases where medical data is stripped

[140] Ian Avrum Goldberg. *A pseudonymous communications infrastructure for the internet*. PhD thesis, University of California, 2000

of much of its content, for example, if we just state that some anonymous person has a particularly rare disease then the identifiability is particularly high. This latter case is a classic example of entropy and information content and is of special concern for health data where a rare disease identified in a data set relating to a small population (such as health district or city) provides enough information to unambiguously identify a person even if all other personally identifying information is removed.

Content is normally broken down into its constituent structures which makes it difficult to evaluate in isolation. Similarly temporal information in the form of time-stamps by themselves do not reveal any identifying information, though it is critical to note that collection of data *over time* can be used to identify patterns of behaviour and therefore be used in fingerprinting.

The three aspects actually of particular concern are identifier, characteristic and location. In each of these cases in particular we must take into consideration the context in which the information is being used. As we discussed with the location case above, even if we have relative accurate information about someone's location, in some situations we might still have a large amount of uncertainty about whom this information pertains.

If a data set contained location data to the nearest 5 degree lat/long then at any point in time then the amount of people would effectively been in the many millions for populated areas and many hundreds in the sparsely populated areas. However given *enough* time individuals could be tracked, though how long enough time could be a considerable and impractical duration. Even at finer resolutions such as 50 square meters could be enough to admit anonymity such as might be found in a crowded shopping centre. This assuming no other information was available such as device identifiers being matched over a number of network end-points.

Location provides a good example[141] of the difficulty in determining *when* a dataset or, more likely, an extract of a set of records from a dataset becomes anonymous or non-identifying. It is the growth of information content that is extractable and derivable from a single record or set of records that must be taken into consideration when deciding whether that element is personal data or not.

[141] Yves-Alexandre de Montjoye, César A. Hidalgo, Michel Verleysen, and Vincent D. Blondel. Unique in the crowd: The privacy bounds of human mobility. *Scientific Reports*, 2013a

Traffic Data

THE TERM TRAFFIC DATA is defined in EU directive 95/45/EU and makes the distinction between the data carried in the data flow or communication channel from the data used to support the communication protocols:

> ...any data processed for the purpose of the conveyance of a communication on an electronic communications network or for the billing thereof

Typically referring to the data used in the whole supporting protocol stack, this data contains various kinds of Identifiers and Temporal data at a minimum. This must be taken into consideration when evaluating the whole content of a data flow. This has been presented earlier when we described how to calculate the whole content of a data flow channel.

Risk and Vulnerability Taxonomies

WITHIN PRIVACY THERE ARE a number well known taxonomies[142] for describing risk and in this section we develop a taxonomy based upon the Solove classification[143] based on the earlier work in this area[144] to set out a general framework for privacy, and the Antón-Earp Taxonomy[145] which was developed to capture concepts of privacy in web application design focussed upon vulnerabilities and the protection goals.

The Solove taxonomy conceptualises privacy into four major sections: information collection, dissemination, processing and invasion; and then within each of these a number of subcategories as necessary. This taxonomy is shown in figure 74.

The taxonomy attempts to conceptualise privacy according to a number of social and legal aspects rather than any technical aspect. This said, it does actually provide a number of areas which are particularly relevant to risk.

A different point of view to the conceptualisation of privacy

[142] *Risk Taxonomy.* The Open Group, 2009

[143] Daniel J. Solove. A taxonomy of privacy. *University of Pennsylvania Law Review*, 154(3):477 pp., January 2006. GWU Law School Public Law Research Paper No. 129

[144] Daniel J. Solove. Conceptualizing Privacy. *California Law Review*, 90(4):1087–1155, 2002

[145] Annie I. Antón and Julia Brande Earp. A requirements taxonomy for reducing web site privacy vulnerabilities. *Requirements Engineering*, 9(3):169–185, 2004

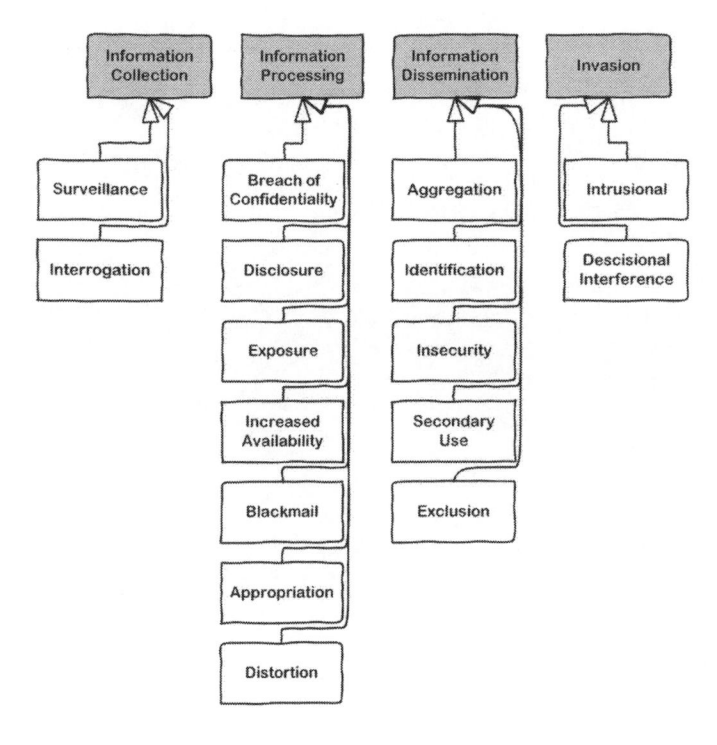

Figure 74: Solove's Taxonomy for the Conceptualisation of Privacy

is made in the Antón-Earp Taxonomy which was developed from analysis of e-commerce privacy policies. This taxonomy shown in figure 75 uses two major classes: protection goals and vulnerabilities.

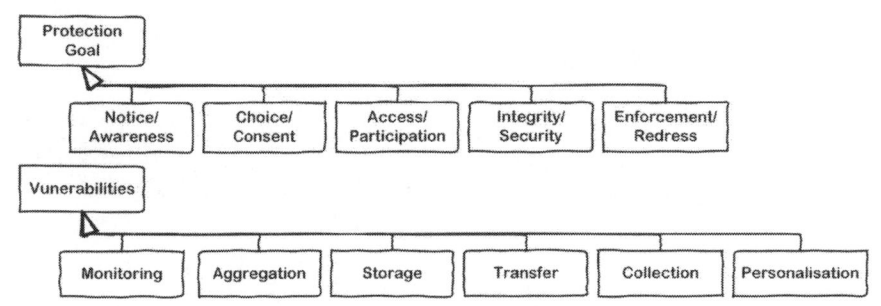

Figure 75: The Antón-Earp Taxonomy of Privacy Vulnerabilities and Protection Goals

A further risk classification system worth drawing attention to is The Human Factors Analysis and Classification System (HFACS) which was developed from the aviation and medical areas for the analysis of accidents caused by humans. The system shown in figure 76 has four major categories that classify human factors in accidents and risks. We present this particular classification system for completeness but at this time do not develop it further in any formal manner here, though its existence should be utilised especially in privacy accident investigation.

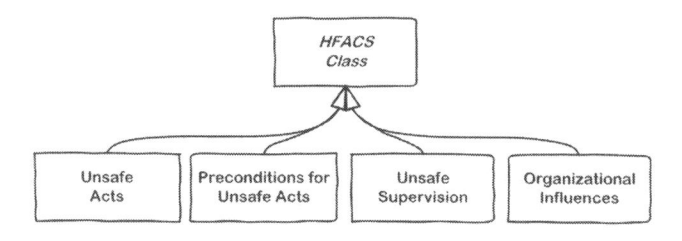

Figure 76: Human Factors Analysis and Classification System Taxonomy

Unsafe acts is further divided into errors and violations; and then further again to specific categories of unsafe act. Of the four categories it is this category that is most relevant when dealing with classification of privacy accidents. During an analysis of an accident we can use the subclasses from the Preconditions class to better describe the events and processes leading up to the accident, these include environmental and personnel factors. The latter two categories of unsafe supervision and organizational issues more related to the whole environment in which the system exists and often the factors from management leading to the accident.

Threat Taxonomies

WITHIN THIS AREA ALSO exist many other classification systems for risk and threats, primarily coming from the security domain rather than privacy, though there is much overlap and relevant material here. These include MITRE's Common Weakness Enumeration (CWE)[146,147] and Common Attack Pattern Enumeration and Classification (CAPEC)[148]. We do not continue discussion of these here but encourage reference to such classification standards as part of understanding risks and vulnerabilities across both the security and privacy domains.

Of particular interest is the STRIDE taxonomy of security threats used as part of the Microsoft Security Development Lifecycle[149] which itself integrates with the software development process in its many forms. STRIDE stands for the six elements in the security threat taxonomy:

- Spoofing identity
- Tampering with data
- Reputability

[146] Robert A. Martin and Sean Barnum. Common weakness enumeration (CWE) status update. *Ada Lett.*, XXVIII(1):88–91, April 2008. ISSN 1094-3641

[147] cwe.mitre.org

[148] capec.mitre.org

[149] M. Howard and S. Lipner. *The security development lifecycle: SDL, a process for developing demonstrably more secure software*. Microsoft Press Series. Microsoft Press, 2006

- Information Disclosure
- Denial of Service
- Elevation of Privilege

It is applied by checking and cross-referencing threats in each category against the various elements in a model - typically a data flow model. While not all categories are applicable in all cases it does provide a framework for classifying and organising the threat analysis process. Of particular interest for privacy are repudiation[150] and information disclosure. The latter case covering all aspects of cross-referencing of data, usage of identity, re-identification etc.

[150] Panagiotis Louridas. Some guidelines for non-repudiation protocols. *SIGCOMM Comput. Commun. Rev.*, 30(5):29–38, October 2000

As an alternative or privacy complimentary classification to STRIDE there also exists the LUNDDUN classification[151] of privacy threats which can also be used:

[151] Mina Deng. *Privacy preserving content protection.* PhD thesis, Katholieke Universality, Belgium, 2010

- Linkability
- Identifiability
- Non-Repudiation
- Detectability
- Disclosure of Information
- Content Unawareness
- Policy and Consent Noncompliance

The semantics of which are well established in much of the privacy literature.

General Privacy Risk Classification

THE PROTECTION GOALS IN the Antón-Earp Taxonomy can be used within requirements generation and in system design in general to outline what needs to be achieved in order to build a system with inherent privacy. However in the above cases it is the commonality between these taxonomies in how they relate and classify privacy risks that is of interest. We simply and combine[152] the above to classify a number of areas of risk and vulnerability in a system - this combination is shown in figure 77.

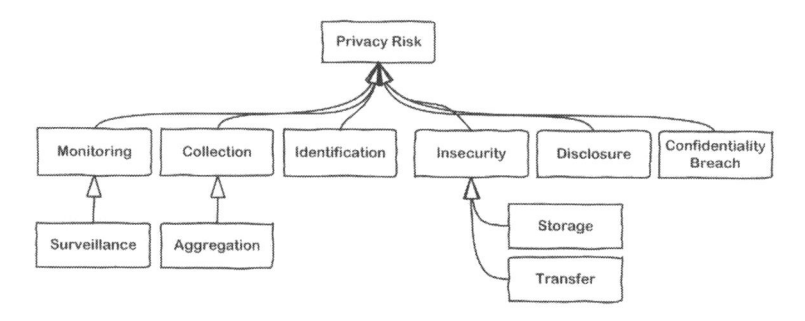

[152] Aaron K. Massey and Annie I. Antón. A requirements-based comparison of privacy taxonomies. In *Proceedings of the 2008 Requirements Engineering and Law*, RELAW '08, pages 1–5, Washington, DC, USA, 2008. IEEE Computer Society. ISBN 978-0-7695-3630-9

Figure 77: Risk Area Classification

These risk classifications are described below and reference other classification systems such as usage and identity as part of their descriptions.

Monitoring and Surveillance

THESE DESCRIBE THE RISKS that actually stem from necessary operations but in one case are typically required for the functioning of a system and in the second the overreach of that functionality.

All systems are required to be monitored, this might be achieved through regular monitoring of log files for system maintenance procedures and so on. The risk here is that the data being collected here is either too much or often neglected as in many cases the traffic data that collects in web server logs and temporary files[153] is never considered in the whole data collection of a system.

[153] Check to see what gathers in /tmp and /var for example

Going further the analysis of this information can then tell the system administrators and other about the functioning of the system over time and is again an essential component for system administration. When this data which is normally collected for the usage of 'system provisioning' gets used for purposes outside of this then we have a surveillance risk.

Surveillance also takes into consideration external activities such as espionage. While preventing this kind of access is often outside the scope of a system, protection from this via technical means needs to be taken into consideration. Legal means already exist through lawful intercept and authority request procedures - at least to a point.

Collection and Aggregation

ALL SYSTEMS NECESSARILY COLLECT data so it might come as a surprise that we include this as a risk but contained within this is the notion of too much collection of data. This is mitigated by the very basic principle of data minimisation, that is, collect what is necessary for the functioning or 'service provisioning' of a system.

As collection increases then we need to consider the risk of aggregation which relates to the combination and build-up of data within a system.

Identification

WE HAVE INTRODUCED THE ideas and degrees of identification earlier through the information type and identity classification systems. This particular risk tends to pertain not to the fact that we are collecting data that can be tied to a particular individual but more to the risks of reidentification of anonymous data and the necessity of requiring identification.

Consider two use cases where a user can access the system both in a weak or strong manner. In the latter case it should be obvious that all data collection can be tied to an individual whereas in the former case the data collected should not be mappable back or reidentifiable.

Insecurity, Storage and Transfer

THESE RISKS PERTAIN TO the general security aspect of a system from both architectural and operational perspectives, for example operating system hardening, physical security of equipment, whether a system is cloud based or hosted locally and so on. We can additionally take into consideration here any number of human issues relating to overall system security.

Particularly important when discussing security are the basic protection mechanisms when data is stored, i.e.: at rest, or in transit. Choices relating to risks here might include whether a system employed file system encryption versus field level encryption in the database, or whether data is sent over an insecure protocol and so on.

Disclosure

THIS RISK PERTAINS TO points where control over the information is lost and in particular refers to situations such as when information passes from a controller to a processor, processor to processor or even controller to another controller.

While suitable agreements should be in place, this risk not only covers areas such as whether that agreement is favourable to the data subject but also whether the receiving parties themselves can fulfil the clauses of that agreement.

Furthermore we can also envisage situations where data appears quite legitimately via a processor or controller but occurs to the surprise of the data subject.

Breach of Confidentiality

THIS CLASSIFIES A WHOLE set of risks pertaining to the loss of information from some given data subject[154]. This includes specific references to the legal aspects such as the economic effects as well as personal effects of such a data breach.

[154] Neil M. Richards and Daniel J. Solove. Privacy's Other Path: Recovering the Law of Confidentiality. *The Georgetown Law Journal*, 96:123–182, 2007

Summary

WE HAVE INTRODUCED A number of additional classification systems in this chapter beyond those of just security and information type. We have also introduced various externally defined classification structures of particular importance to privacy, particularly the definitions of personal data and PII, and shown how these relate and can be defined in terms of the structures we have presented.

While the number of classification systems appears large, each exists - to a point - independently of these others and focusses on a particular aspect of information. The reader should expect that any data set, be it large or small, can be classified from field level through to the organisational structures that data set inhabits in all of these systems simultaneously leading to some complexity. The use of any particular system or combination of systems is therefore made on an as needed basis as the modelling and analysis needs of the system require.

Requirements

THE REQUIREMENTS THAT ARE presented to the developers constructing any information system must be detailed enough that decisions on their implementation can be properly made: statements such as 'sufficient security' are not acceptable. A development team can not work from high-level legal texts but need detailed, specific engineering requirements that can be applied to the myriad of different aspects of system design[155]. Similar criteria apply to those that work in system operations and even the general personnel who handle any data.

In this chapter we will show how requirements[156] are derived and structured from the various classification systems presented earlier, the areas to which these apply and the level of detail required. We examine how these fit together to build the 'final' set of requirements and later show how requirements can be analysed in cases of *weakening* to actually admit a system to be constructed.

Requirements are derived from a combination of societal norms, business ethics and law; these are brought together as a set of high-level, formal statements that define a/the policy for handling data[157]. This policy is then consequently refined over the various aspects of data handing and eventually becomes the individual engineering requirements. This process may be visualised as shown in figure 78 which depicts derivation structure for the requirements. Note the level of cross-referencing between the various classifications systems.

The purpose of the requirements is to give a clear and concise set of rules for the applications developers to follow in order to construct systems and software with privacy as an inher-

[155] Merlin Dorfman. System and software requirements engineering. In *IEEE Computer Society Press Tutorial*, pages 7–22. IEEE Computer Society Press, 1990

[156] Gerald Kotonya and I. Sommerville. *Requirements engineering: processes and techniques.* Worldwide series in computer science. J. Wiley, 1998. ISBN 9780471972082

[157] Annie I. Anton, Julia B. Earp, Colin Potts, and Thomas A. Alspaugh. The role of policy and stakeholder privacy values in requirements engineering. In *Proceedings of the Fifth IEEE International Symposium on Requirements Engineering*, pages 138–145, 2001

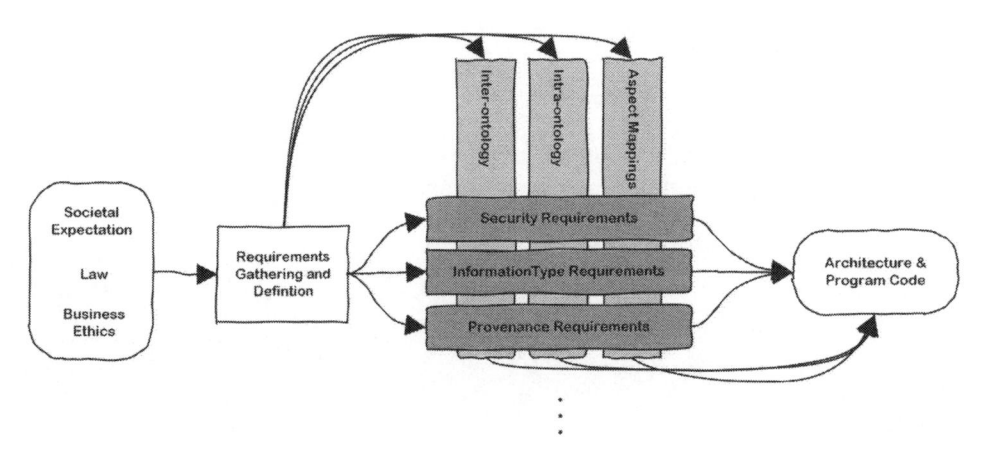

Figure 78: The Derivation of Requirements

[158] *NIST Special Publication 800-53: Security and Privacy Controls for Federal Information Systems and Organizations.* National Institute of Standards and Technology, April 2013

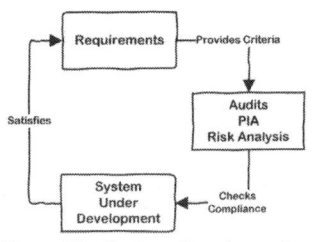

ent property of the system[158]. The following and selection of requirements also gives metrics from which we can estimate compliance and risk in the system or business as a whole. As we shall see later, this aspect will be checked through privacy impact assessments and audits. This symbiotic relationship is depicted in figure 79.

Obviously in the following sections we will not be able to give a precise and detailed set of generally applicable requirements - this would require a world-wide standard which is out of scope (and question) here. However we show how this structuring mechanism works through examples where we will mainly stay at the policy and high-level architecture levels. We will provide some more worked examples of requirements for the security classifications and selected information types. The requirements presented here are deliberately kept short for presentation purposes but should suffice to explain what is *required* of the requirements.

Figure 79: System, Requirements and Audits

Types of Requirements

To PRECISELY DEFINE REQUIREMENTS will require the audience and thus the abstraction level being taken into account. It is all too easy to remain at the policy level rather than define the 'how' of implementation[159], whereas what is required is a continuum of requirements from policy, this architectural level, design, coding and even testing. Each level of abstraction effectively

[159] Jeroen van Rest, Daniel Boonstra, Maarten Everts, Martin van Rijn, and Ron van Paassen. Designing privacy-by-design. In Bart Preneel and Demosthenes Ikonomou, editors, *Privacy Technologies and Policy*, volume 8319 of *Lecture Notes in Computer Science*, pages 55–72. Springer Berlin Heidelberg, 2014

refining the previous layer, for example:

Policy ⊑ Architecture ⊑ Design ⊑ Coding

We can further subdivide each requirement into a particular focus area such as storage, transmission, handling etc. This structure can be visualised in figure 80. Many and varied methods exist for requirements development in software engineering, and even some specialised for privacy requirements[160]; we try here to be agnostic to these as much as possible.

Each point in this structure represents one or more requirements relating to the abstraction level, classification element and aspect. The requirements at any point can both make and explicit statement and provide reference to any other point in the requirements structure. In the cases where no requirement exists at that point then we either take the requirements for a more general class, aspect or abstraction level. If the requirements for handling information of the 'userID' class at the design level of abstraction do not exist, then we refer to the requirements for the more generic 'identifier' type, or higher abstraction level or even a more general aspect if it exists. There is no restriction on how many individual requirements may be present at any point, nor any on at how many points in the structure any individual requirement might exist.

We have already introduced a number of classification systems for information and above a list of abstraction level. We have not yet however introduced the various aspects of requirements and this we do in the next section in more detail.

[160] Christos Kalloniatis, Evangelia Kavakli, and Stefanos Gritzalis. Addressing privacy requirements in system design: the PriS method. *Requirements Engineering*, 13(3):241–255, 2008

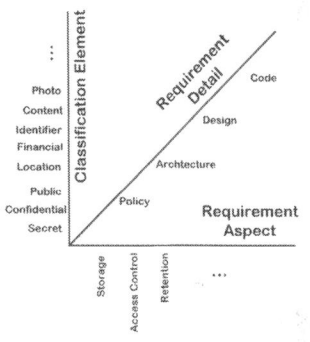

Figure 80: Three Dimensions of Requirements

Requirement Aspects

REQUIREMENT ASPECTS SUBDIVIDE THE requirements so that each may focus on a particular task, such as storage, transmission. etc. We make these aspects fairly broad and actually extend them out from privacy specifically to include other aspects of information handling. It is therefore likely that these *will* overlap with other areas, especially that of security - there is no issue here, overlaps *are* necessary and desirable; they act as interface points between different disciplines and a better overall, more holistic understanding of the interplay between requirements.

We divide our the aspects into a number of discrete areas as listed below. We of course can expand and specialise (or shrink) this list as local context dictates, for example it is useful in many environments to split storage into specific areas such as device storage, company data centre storage and cloud based storage - indeed we do this in later examples and show this in figure 81 for completeness of example.

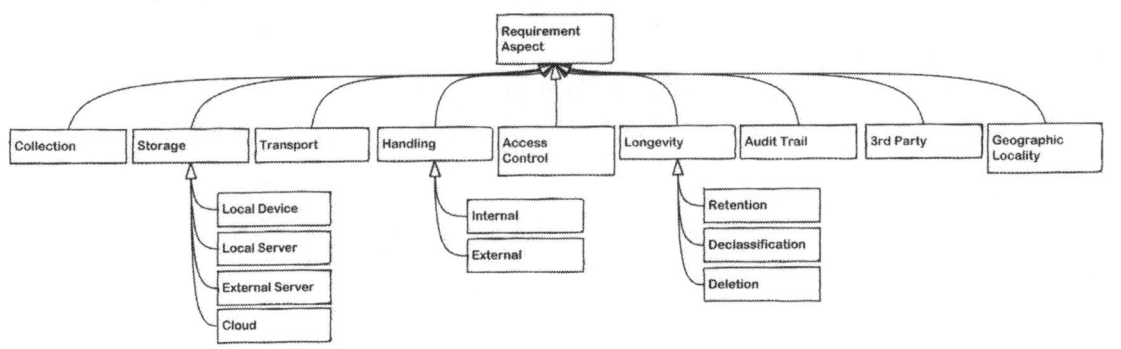

Figure 81: Classification of Requirement Aspects

The main point of any application is to collect data and the collection requirement sets out what is required for collect to take place. These requirements expressed under this classification are often very expressive in their content and therefore can sometimes overwhelm other requirements. This however becomes particular useful when checking individual information types and other classifications against higher-level requirements such as those for personal data. In terms of analysing privacy it is also extremely useful to cross-reference this particular requirements aspect against the risk classifications (viz.figure 77) and their subsequent analyses later.

Data is going to be stored at some point, whether on some long-term storage device or even temporarily in memory; furthermore, data may be retained in those areas for varying period of time depending on whether the user wants permanent storage or some kind of temporary storage as we see with a cache. We are particular concerned here with the specific protection mechanisms of storage such as encryption or access control and even possibly considering aspects such as database partitioning, key management, field level protections etc. Storage is further complicated by the locality of the data, for example it is common now to use cloud based storage where the actual physical location is unknown beyond possibly being at country level at best.

Transport of data is concerned with a similar set of concern as storage: whether it is itself secure or whether the contents are required to be secured, the degree of security and what transport protocols are acceptable. In a reverse sense it is also necessary to choose the transport protocols based upon what data can be collected at the protocol level (traffic data) for purposes such as system administration and take into consideration what this data might be utilised for.

Handling specifically refers to the human handling of data such as when computers, devices, USB drives and even paper copies are be transported or stored. We can also make the distinction between the environments; typically within a company, we would consider that environment to be "safe" where personnel are bound by company contracts and within corporate IT security systems such as VPN etc. However it is normal that data leaves this environment either through necessary means such as communication with users or other companies, or, but less explicit means such as when an employee takes home a laptop computer.

Access control is almost omnipresent in that every system has some degree of access control, either through user accounts or physical means. In fact we can expand access control into a number of areas to include physical security of systems additionally.

Closely related with access control is the ability to create an audit trail of access and thus handling or viewing of the data. Some standards require such audit trails to be kept, for example, PCI-DSS and SOX have audit trail requirements. Similar to access control, the ability to create an audit trail is omnipresent amongst all requirements, for example, recording when data was deleted or declassified. Most of the time audit trail tends to refer to the creation and management of log files as may be generated by web servers or other transaction mechanisms such as those found in e-Commerce system for purchase and payment.

The Longevity classification pertains to the rules on the length of time that data can be kept. We divide this classification into the retention of the data, declassification procedures and deletion.

Retention rules in this area can vary significantly by jurisdiction and even by business area. For example, a 2 year limit on personal data becomes 6 or 7 years when applied to financial data and even longer working with employee data in many cases. For raw intake data as might be processed by analytics system then these times might change dramatically depending upon the sensitivity of the data and kinds of processing and end data set. All of these considerations must be made under this requirement aspect.

Once data is no longer required then it must be deleted and this may be achieved by physical means (such as burning or drilling through disk platters) or logically by using specialist deletion software which targets the content[161]. Operating system file deletion often works by altering the index of files and not the actual content itself[162], though this might not apply to all filesystem structures. Associated with this aspect are the procedures for accurately auditing (see the audit trail requirement aspect) the deletion. Deletion can also pertain to how memory is handled, for example, flushing of cache memory upon application termination is just as necessary as deleting files and indeed has many of the same issues regarding content. For example a process may dynamically allocate memory, write to that area and then deallocate. The next process might then make a similar memory allocation request and find that content is still present from the previous process.

One area of concern relating to the above is the predominance of cloud storage and the fact that the virtualisation means that data can be replicated over many physical disks and sites in a transparent manner. Destruction of the data through secure means such as disk wiping may have little or no meaning. Similarly storage technologies such as flash memory has a very different deletion semantics than physically wiping a traditional hard disk[163].

Data sets rather than being deleted might be declassified for more general or even public release. We need also to consider the opposite where a data set becomes more secret thought this is rarely a privacy problem. We would specify here the procedures including technical procedures[164] such as what level of anonymisation is to be applied.

The requirement aspect for 3rd parties refers to specific requirements pertaining to external entities which might consume data

[161] Khaled El Emam, Emilio Neri, and Elizabeth Jonker. An evaluation of personal health information remnants in second-hand personal computer disk drives. *Journal of medical Internet research*, 9(3), 2007

[162] Microsoft DOS FAT filesystem being a good example

[163] Michael Wei, Laura M. Grupp, Frederick E. Spada, and Steven Swanson. Reliably erasing data from flash-based solid state drives. In *Proceedings of the 9th USENIX Conference on File and Storage Technologies*, FAST'11. USENIX Association, 2011

[164] Daniel Abril, Guillermo Navarro-Arribas, and Vicenç Torra. On the declassification of confidential documents. In *Modeling Decision for Artificial Intelligence*, pages 235–246. Springer, 2011

either explicitly or implicitly due to our or the user's interactions. In particular we refer to the use of other controllers, processors and considerations to voluntary user sharing such as is often made to social media providers.

Finally we must always consider the impact of geographical locality to any data. This especially so where specific agreements such as Safe Harbour are not in place or where there is the necessity for forms of censorship as exist with a number of countries.

Example Security Requirements

STRUCTURING THE REQUIREMENTS FOR the security classes is relatively simple, in that we only need to take into consideration the ordered nature of the classifications themselves and ensuring that higher classifications are more restrictive overall than the lower classifications. In the security classification example provided earlier in figure 49 there are three security classifications: Secret, Confidential and Public. Using this as a basis the following table shows an example of these requirements across these various aspects from earlier defined at some **policy** level:

Taking an entry from the table:

> **Handling (Internal) Secret, Policy** : *Designated personnel only*

For such a requirement we are required to define, in this case as an example, *who* are the designated personnel, how does one contact these and what are the procedures around becoming on of the designated personnel. for further clarifications. Similarly we have the case:

> **Storage (Cloud), Public, Policy** : *Unencrypted, approval required before public release*

Which states clearly that there is some kind of process associated with handling public data in such scenarios. Obviously such processes must be documented *and* most importantly *communicated*. Furthermore as good policy and process good practice,

	Unclassified	Secret	Confidential	Public
Collection	Not be made until security classification has been ascertained	Only under special, approved circumstances	Allowed upon presentation of necessary notices and consent received	as Confidential
Local Device Storage	encrypted file on owner's machine only	encrypted file on designated machines	unencrypted filesystem on internal machine only	unencrypted, approval required before public release
Local Server Storage	not allowed	encrypted file on designated machines	unencrypted filesystem on internal servers only	unencrypted, approval required before public release
Cloud Storage	not allowed	not allowed	unencrypted filesystem on designated servers only	unencrypted, approval required before public release
Internal Handling	owner's discretion	designated personnel only	all company	public
External Handling	not allowed	not allowed	company approved machines, encrypted on removable media	no restrictions
Access Control	owner's discretion	named persons only	company employees only	public
Retention	owner's discretion	2 years in secured storage	2 years in secured storage	unlimited
Disposal	DoD wipe	DoD wipe	standard wiping procedures	n/a
Transport	encrypted transport only. approval required	encrypted transport only. approval required	encrypted transport if containing personal data.	unencrypted allowed
Declassification	upon owner's discretion, then to secure class only	pending approval to confidential or public as required	pending approval to public as required	n/a
Audit Trail	Documents must be classified and approved before release	All accesses and changes to the data must be logged and approved	as secret	Public release date and approval must be logged

Table 5: Example Security Classification Requirements

these also need to be easy to use and transparent to those who have to go through such processes. Obscuring said procedures will lead to efforts being made to circumvent these with all the attendant privacy risks amongst others.

Another kind of requirement seen is of a more technical nature, for example:

> **Storage (Local Server), Secret, Policy** : *Encrypted file on designated machines*

Which refers to a need for encryption to protect the data. It does not state what kind of encryption nor the mechanisms around things such as key management and its implementation etc. While this might be fine for at the level of abstraction of a policy it does set the basis for the next level of abstraction which will be required to define the set of approved encryption mechanisms and algorithms.

A further example from the above is the requirement for transport of data:

> **Transport, Confidential, Policy** : *Encrypted transport if containing personal data.*

There are two aspects here: the first is deciding whether the information being transported contains personal data and also a second requirement for a suitable encryption mechanism to be chosen - similarly to the storage example above. In this case further refinement is complicated by a choice of mechanisms from encrypting the contents, removing information content so that the content no longer contains personal data and implementing the protection through the transport layer, say, using HTTPS. Furthermore it is likely in such a case they we will both have to refer to the whole information content due to the presence of traffic data, key management, etc., and, refer to other non-functional aspects such as performance.

An example of how refinement of these might work is given in the example below starting with the policy for the storage of confidential data:

> **Confidential, Storage, Policy** : *This data must be secured, e.g.: encryption*

which becomes more detailed as we move to the next level of abstraction:

> **Confidential, Storage, Architecture** : *Protected storage, either internally sandboxed or through the O/S or DBMS encryption mechanisms, i.e.: file system or DB level encryption. Key management should be utilised*

Note how the description becomes more specific or refined from the previous requirement - this follows the rule that each level of detail for any given classification and requirement aspect is more refined than the previous: $Req(C, A, policy) \sqsubseteq Req(C, A, architecture)$ where C and A are any classifications or requirement aspects. As we move to the next level of detail, that of design, the necessary refinement of the requirements follows ($architecture \sqsubseteq design$):

> **Confidential, Storage, Design** : *AES-256 bit keys in custom cases or known encryption technology, e.g.: bitlocker etc. If encryption not possible at this level, then field-level encryption can be employed instead. Particular field types, e.g.: password, certain contents, demographics will require field-level encryption with 1024-bit keys and asymmetric mechanisms being employed.*

It must be checked that each level is more refined than the previous, not only in description but in the contents of the description. For example we would not want to see at the architectural level a requirement for 2048 bit keys for some encryption algorithm and then just 1024 at the design level.

As already stated, deriving such requirements is a complex process and so when developing these some structured mechanism should be in place to ensure that said requirements are kept relevant to the business and specific to the particular aspects being discussed. Choosing a suitable requirements elicitation framework is a necessary aspect of good software engineering.[165]

[165] Qingfeng He, Annie I Antón, et al. A framework for modeling privacy requirements in role engineering. In *Proceedings of REFSQ*, volume 3, pages 137–146, 2003

Example Information Type Requirements

SIMILARLY TO THE SECURITY classifications we can construct a similar set of requirements for each of our information types.

There are a few things however to be aware of when working with a hierarchical classification structures as we have with the information type system. The first is that the lower levels are going to *relax* the requirements specified at the upper levels. This might appear counter intuitive at first but this is explained by that if we are using the more generic concepts then we are obliged to make further investigation to correctly identify the true nature of the information being conveyed. Working with this assumption consider the following example requirements in the table below:

	Generic	Credit Card	PersonalID	SessionID
Collection	as per security classification requirements	Under PCI-DSS rules	as per confidential security classification requirements	Allowed
Storage	not allowed	encrypted AES-256 or better	encrypted storage, encrypted or hashed. EU data in US see Safe Harbour. Data set partitioning must take place	as data set
Handling	not allowed	designated personnel only	per application basis, restrictions under analytics	as data set
Access Control	not allowed	named persons only	as required with approval	as data set
Retention	not allowed	7 years in secured storage	2 years in secured storage	unlimited
Disposal	DoD wipe	DoD wipe	standard wiping procedures, or anonymisation through aggregation	aggregation or removal
Transport	not allowed	encrypted. PCI certified channels	secured	as data set
Declassification	never	finance approval required	not allowed	n/a
Audit Trail	Every action	As per PCI-DSS	access, modify, delete	as data set

Table 6: Example Information Type Classification Requirements

As we might expect, for information that is 'generic' - that is, we have not performed any classification or investigation over that data - we need to assume the effective worst and ensure that all requirements prevent the storage, transport and handling of this information under all circumstances.

For information classified as being Credit Card then we have simply the PCI-DSS standard and all that it would imply.

Personal data requires secure storage and transport as we would expect, but notice the requirements for Safe Harbor provision - this is a good example of where the requirements start crossing between classification structures. To decide the geographical provenance and context of information is specified under the jurisdiction classification, and indeed when constructing the requirements there this will probably be explained again.

This kind of cross-referencing is encouraged from two perspectives, firstly it means that we can clearly see the links between the various aspects of privacy and secondly it probably ends up implying 'too strong' requirements. As we have mentioned, in these cases we can then take a very pragmatic and methodological approach to risk management as the requirements are weakened.

Example Requirements for Further Classification Systems

WE CAN CONTINUE DEVELOPING requirements for each area and here we describe a possible set of policy related requirements for provenance which are a good example of how these requirements refer across to other classification systems and external requirements such as COPPA.

Some requirements such as those related to purpose are fairly generic across all information types and in such cases can be quite easily mapped to just generic information and policy requirement types

Personal Data and Requirements

WE CAN CONTINUE THE requirements specification and development to eventually include the external classification systems and in particular the requirements relating directly to the terms 'personal data' or PII depending upon whichever takes precedence in your local jurisdiction. In table 9 we list example policy level requirement for this class of data. These should be derived as a formalisation of the privacy policy and terms and conditions presented as part of the notice to the users.

As we mentioned earlier we can derive whether data set contain

	Adult	**Child**	**System**	**External**
Collection	Allowed, with consent	As per COPPA, but generally not allowed	Allowed	As per agreements
Storage	Allowed	As per COPPA requirements, encrypted, specific 'authenticated(1)' identity provided. Confidential security classification	Allowed	Allowed as per agreement
Handling	Allowed	Designated personnel only. Not external. Secret security classification	Allowed	Allowed as per agreement
Access Control	Allowed	Designed personnel only	Allowed	Allowed as per agreement
Retention	As per EU standard	As per EU or COPPA whichever is the most restrictive	Allowed	Allowed as per agreement
Disposal	Standard wiping procedures	DoD wipe followed by standard procedures for disposal, or anonymisation through aggregation and sufficient κ-anonymity($>$ 10)	Allowed	Allowed as per agreement
Transport	Allowed	Encrypted. Not to externals	Allowed	Allowed as per agreement
Declassification	Allowed	Not allowed except with parental consent	Allowed	Allowed as per agreement
Audit Trail	As necessary	All actions	As necessary	As defined per agreement

Table 7: Example Policy Level Provenance Classification Requirements

	Primary	Secondary	System Provisioning	Service Provisioning
Collection	With consent	With specific consent	According to Terms and Conditions, see also Identity classifications	Allowed with consent
Storage	Allowed	Allowed if consent given	Allowed, but must be kept separate from other usages	Allowed
Handling	Allowed	Designated personnel only. Not external. Confidential security classification	Allowed	Allowed as per agreement
Access Control	Allowed	Designed personnel only	Only system administrators allowed to log and raw data. Aggregated data is confidential	Owner only. Authority request procedures otherwise for external release
Retention	User account existence plus 2 years	1 week raw, 6 months processed	as Primary data	as Primary data
Disposal	Owner must be informed 6 months prior to deletion. Standard wiping procedures	DoD wipe followed by standard procedures for disposal, or anonymisation through aggregation and sufficient κ-anonymity(> 10)	as Secondary	as Primary
Transport	As for confidential data	As for confidential data. Not to externals	As for confidential data	As for confidential data
Declassification	Not allowed without express owner permission	Not allowed except with express owner permission	As Primary	As Primary
Audit Trail	Logging	All actions	Logging	Logging

Table 8: Example Policy Level Purpose and Usage Classification Requirements

	Personal Data
Collection	Only with consent after presentation of notice. See specific information types for more details, e.g.: location, child, financial, health. Specific sensitive demographic categories only with prior approval and data subject consent and always optional
Storage	Data must be stored securely with file level encryption at a minimum.
Handling	Data must be kept within the company. All personnel must receive data handling training before access
Access Control	Via internal access control systems only. All accesses logged
Retention	Typically 6-24 months after user account removal.
Disposal	Secure wipe of disks/media. Hardware destruction by approved facility
Transport	By secure means: HTTPS as default, encrypted disks/files, removable media must be encrypted. Exceptions on case-by-case basis
Declassification	Not allowed unless data has been sufficiently anonymised
Audit Trail	Access to data and granting of access to be logged.

Table 9: Example Policy Level Requirements for Personal Data

personal data (or PII) from examining the information types and other classifications of data - the relationship is shown in figure 72. For example, if certain characteristics and identifiers are present then the data set is likely to be classed as personal data. Figure 73 previously graphically demonstrates how the granularity of data within each class increases the likelihood of the data revealing personal data. Knowing this relationship can be used to develop and check the requirements developed at a high-level personal data view and at the specific information types.

Given the requirements for two aspects - storage and declassification - for a set of information types and for personal data in particular in table 10 we can demonstrate this cross-correlation and checking between these.

When working with a data set, if that data set is deemed to contain personal data then the *sum* of the individual requirements for the information contained therein should be at least as strong as the requirements for personal data.

Knowing this then allows us to check whether the combination of requirements from the information types and other classification structures do satisfy the requirements for personal data handling and if not where the additional requirements should be introduced. This introduction of additional requirements can be made separately on a case-by-case basis or by updating various combinations of existing requirements.

	Storage	**Declassification**
Personal Data	Data must be stored securely with file level encryption at a minimum	Data must be sufficiently anonymised, κ-anon analysis must be made
Location	If below city level then secured, e.g.: by partitioning/encryption	City level and greater only
Event	Secret classification if containing parameters, else confidential	No parameters or values allowed.
Temporal	n/a	Granularity > 1s
DeviceID	Confidential security classification	Hashed and salted
AppID	Confidential security classification	Allowed
SessionID	No requirements unless combined with a PersonalID or Characteristic	Hashed and salted
PersonalID	encrypted storage, fields encrypted or hashed as necessary. EU data in US see Safe Harbor. Data set partitioning must take place	Not Allowed
Device Address	Confidential or secret as appropriate	Mapped to country level location or hashed and salted

The cases we must now be aware of are as follows

- All requirements together are too strong to admit a system
- The sum of specific requirements are stronger than the high-level personal data (or PII) requirement
- The personal data (or PII) requirement is stronger than the sum of the specific requirements

Table 10: Example Policy Level Requirements for Storage and Declassification of Personal Data and Specific Information Types

In the former case we must weaken or retrench[166] the requirements to specifically admit the features that we wish to implement. This should not be made wholesale but but specifically addressing the required features such as location collection or a specific usage etc. Such retrenchments of the requirements are typical of many systems and each retrenchment should be examined as a risk in its own right.

[166] Richard Banach and Czeslaw Jeske. Simple feature engineering via neat default retrenchments. *The Journal of Logic and Algebraic Programming*, 80(8):453–480, 2011

The second case would be considered the ideal as it means that our high-level policies are set at a suitable level of business risk which then means that the specifics have been constructed in a 'safe' manner. Retrenchment of the specifics can then occur up to the level of the high-level requirements without issue, thought good practice means that each retrenchment here should be investigated. After this point any further weakening of the requirements is as the former case.

The final case suggests that there are serious implementation issues in that the requirements have not been fully developed or that the business is relying too much upon a high-level definition rather than addressing actual system design requirements from the privacy perspective. This is usually seen in immature requirements development processes or where the privacy requirements and system architecture requirements have not been fully communicated or integrated.

Applying Requirements to a Model

TO DEMONSTRATE HOW TO use the requirements we take a fragment of the social camera application's model as shown in figure with all the necessary annotations (conveniently) made. Consider the case in figure 82 where we wish to release the product improvement data not just to the specific owners of that data but to the company in general so that it could be theoretically be used for any *future* usage. For this model we shall explore the storage of data and the declassification for the users of the data in question.

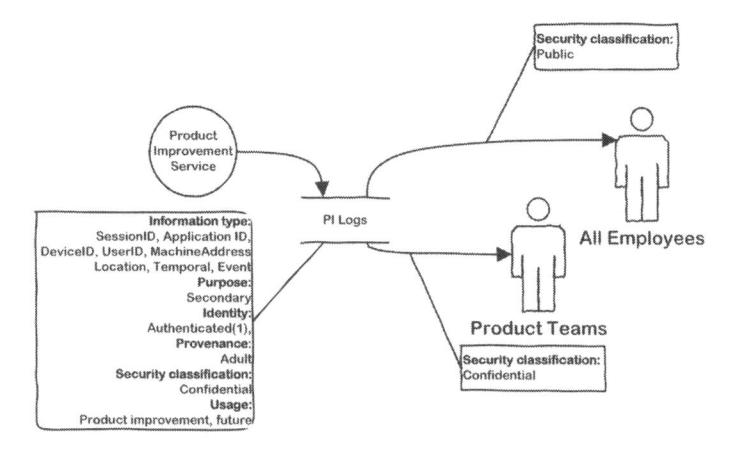

Figure 82: The Release of Personal Data

We have stated in that model that the data contains information of the type: event, location, temporal, machine address and a variety of identifiers: application, session, personal and device. The actual contents of the event we have not presented in detail but we may assume for this exercise that it contains API calls, parameters and their values. It should be fairly clear that this data set contains personal data. Then working with the requirements given earlier such as those in tables 10 and 9, we see that the data store must be secured in some fashion, such as being encrypted or placed in a suitable sandboxed environment.

For most of the requirements the security classification is confidential which implies that encryption of some form must be in place for the storage of this data. The architectural and design requirements take this further to specify the kinds of protection such as file system and database encryption and the algorithms to be used. Let's say that we use TrueCrypt for the file system that the database stores its files on. Does this satisfy or refine the basic requirements that the data be secured? For the architectural and design requirements for personal data - do these conform not only to the policy requirement as expressed earlier but also to the above storage of confidential data?

If we use the above then this satisfies also each of the specific information type requirements *except* for the storage of event data:

> **Event, Policy, Storage** : *Secret classification if containing parameters, else consider this as confidential data. The event field itself may be encrypted rather than the whole record if necessary*

Now we must make an architectural decision of whether to elevate the whole data set to the requirements of the secret classification which will imply more than just adhering to whatever is required for the storage requirement aspect, including retention, handling etc. Fortunately in this case we have an option to specifically deal with one specific case relating to the storage of event type data with these fields being partitioned and encrypted. This might be further architected into the structure of the database through partitioning via a normal form and further protecting those tables containing event data such that access to the main data set only gets a link to the event tables which themselves are protected by another level of access control.

Before we can state whether this is truly enough we must further examine other requirements implied by the secret classification such as access control, retention etc. If our chosen architecture is still not enough then we either continue architecting in more protections or retrench to an acceptable point and accept the inherent risks there. In this case we might decide that the encryption and partitioning suffices to mitigate any additional risk.

The next step is now to decide how to declassify the data such that the relevant parties can obtain their respective data sets. We identify two parties, one being the company or business as a whole and the other being a specific product team. Our business requirements here suggested in figure 82 are that the product team get a set of data which is confidential and the business a set which is public. Table 10 provides policy level requirements here which we are once again required to architect into a solution. One possible refinement of our design is shown in figure 83.

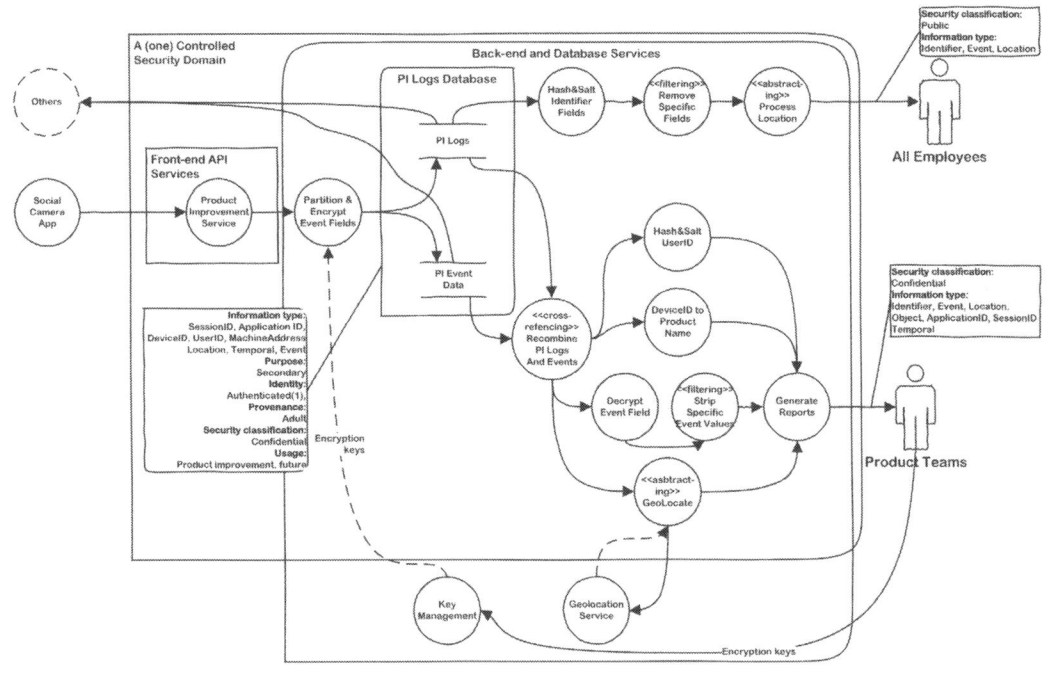

Figure 83: Refined Design for the Release of Personal Data

Here we show not only the partitioning of the database but various architectural and security related partitionings as well as additional processes introduced for the processing of the data from the database.

The model itself only presents and option and highlights the kinds and classification of data in the system. Such a model would - *must* - be backed up with textual documentation including program code and the specification of the processes themselves to fully explain the situation. As we won't go into this detail here but using the model in figure 83 as a basis ask the following questions:

- Is the data set consisting of identifiers (hashed and salted), location (at city level) and a highly stripped event field containing just the event name sufficiently anonymised to be classified as public?

- What are the information content metrics over the above? Is the data sufficiently κ and ℓ-anonymised?

- Is the data set provided to the product teams suitable processed to be classified as confidential? Are the event fields properly processed for example?

- Is the security domain around the database and its processing sufficient or do we need finer grained security to partition the database tables and even the processes?

- What security protections are there between the front-end and back-end services?

- Does adding in key management and geolocation services outside the security domain introduce further data breach risk?

- Who else has access to the data sets? Can they do anything with this?

- Is this a good solution overall?

We can go further and explore further architectural partitioning. For example are the whole report generation processes made by separate systems to the database, for example, do we move these to some analytics service not fully within our control as might be made in some cloudified service?

Summary

CONSTRUCTING A COMPREHENSIVE SET of requirements across abstraction levels, information types and other aspects *and* various requirement aspects is a complex and never ending task, especially as laws and policies vary over time - sometimes in dramatic ways.

Without an overall, comprehensive set of requirements that effectively provides the linkage between lawyer with programmer we cannot construct system that are in any way supportive of information privacy practices in anything other than an ad hoc manner with all the problems that this entails.

Requirements are therefore the foundation of good engineering practice and must never remain embedded in the legal jargon of a privacy policy. Furthermore, if production of such policies is the work of the privacy community then progress in implementing privacy in systems and software will not happen and privacy will remain nothing more than a dogmatic, ivory tower type activity that does little to *support* the business activities.

We have explained in this chapter how requirements can be organised and related to each other - in effect providing a formal link between legal privacy and software engineering privacy.

Risk and Assessment

RISK MANAGEMENT AND ASSESSMENTS are tightly coupled to the set of requirements necessary for the implementation of privacy in any given system. As we have already seen the set of requirements can become quite large and over-constraining[167]. Indeed a system that cannot be built is obviously one that cannot give us any privacy problems. However systems do need to be built and business and customer expectations needs to be met, even if on times these are in conflict with the idea of 'total' privacy.

Ideally we would like to build the system with the strongest possible privacy but with the set of requirements that are the weakest to admit this. Again due to time pressure, money, basic economics[168], business need, customer need this is probably not possible and we must further weaken the requirements to build this system. Each weakening of requirements introduces some risk coming primarily from the compliance and legal side but also from the equally important security, business and customer expectations. We can visualise a simplification of the trade-offs between cost, privacy and risk in figure 84.

For example allowing the sharing of pictures on a social network is a desired feature, but the stripping of meta-data from this type of media is complex from many aspects. If we decide not to strip the meta-data then we are taking a risk that we leak more information than the user expected. However keeping this meta-data is to the user's advantage in that we can enhance the service towards to the user; for example, automatic point-of-interest generation on a map from the picture meta-data. In the model depicted in figure 85 which of the two system is 'best' from a privacy perspective versus system complexity (cost)

[167] Zahid H. Qureshi. A review of accident modelling approaches for complex socio-technical systems. In *Proceedings of the Twelfth Australian Workshop on Safety Critical Systems and Software and Safety-related Programmable Systems - Volume 86*, SCS '07, pages 47–59. Australian Computer Society, Inc., 2007

[168] Kai-Lung Hui and I. P. L. Png. The economics of privacy. In Terrence Hendershott, editor, *Handbooks in Information Systems*, volume 1, chapter 9. Elsevier, 2006

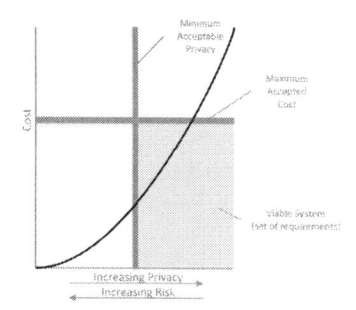

Figure 84: Cost vs Risk and Privacy

versus features.

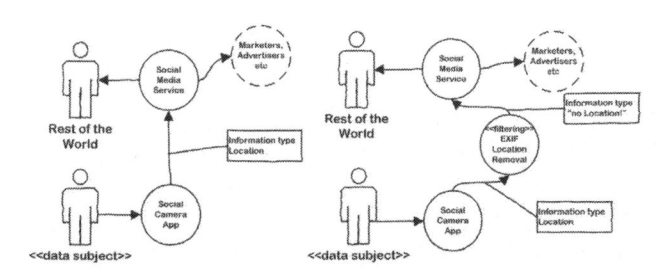

Figure 85: Location Sharing vs EXIF Removal

Therein lies the balancing act between the risk of implementing or not a requirement and the potential consumer and legal problems because that feature was or even was not present. While the example in figure 85 is simple it does show the subtleties that a developer will face. Other cases such as the collection and processing go credit card information is much 'easier' in that the risk and mitigations are obvious[169].

[169] http://www.privacyrights.org/data-breach

There are two basic mechanisms, one forward reasoning based (e.g.: PIA, FMEA etc.) and the other backward reasoning based (e.g.: RCA). We present three basic tools which exemplify these two families of risk assessment reasoning. Customisations to these can be defined as necessary; and if needed the more specific and tailored models can and should be used[170].

[170] N.R. Tague. *The Quality Toolbox, Second Edition:*. ASQ Quality Press, 2005. ISBN 9780873896399

In this section we present how to establish the risk profile of a system through analysing the system and deciding on a set of requirements through privacy impact assessment, threat analysis and also establishing various models of risk and tools for analysing that risk. Furthermore this hopefully reinforces again the necessity of an engineering approach rather than one based solely upon policy[171].

[171] Sarah Spiekermann and Lorrie Faith Cranor. Engineering privacy. *Software Engineering, IEEE Transactions on*, 35(1): 67–82, 2009

A Note on Metrics for Risk

WHILE RISKS CAN BE relatively easily qualified, the quantification of risk in more absolute terms is much harder: Assessing risk is highly subjective[172] and humans are typically remarkably bad at this[173]. There is no absolute scale for risk as such but we can map to a more familiar quantification to assist in this, even if we do lose something of the context. In most cases the mapping to monetary cost is made, for example, by mapping

[172] Bruce Schneier. *Beyond Fear: Thinking Sensibly about Security in an Uncertain World*. Copernicus, September 2003. ISBN 0387026207

[173] Daniel Gilbert. *Stumbling on Happiness Paperback*. Vintage, 2007

number of possible lost records to a monetary value defined in terms of fines, loss of business value etc.

When working with risk metrics it is not necessary, nor often meaningful, to get precise results[174]. Getting a good idea of how much risk even in very coarse terms is acceptable as most of the time we tend to work with terms such as low, medium and high risk which are extremely coarse. The primary aspect here is to get some kind of weighting rather than precise figures. Methods such as FMEA use a number of parameters simply multiplied together to give some kind of metric, though a very uneven and certainly non-linear! While this admits the mathematical definition of a metric (to a point) in that we can take two values and compare them to state that one is greater, or less than another, that is about all we can do.

[174] Joe Peppard and John Ward. Unlocking sustained business value from it investments. 2005

It may have already been noticed that different kinds of data imply differing kinds of risk and an understanding of this can help in generating the metrics or structures necessary for performing risk analyses[175]. For each of our ontologies developed earlier we can map each element in these to a risk profile, and then combine these together to calculate the risk of a particular data set. For example, at each point in a model - element or data-flow - that deal with, say, location data we can assign some kind of 'value' to denote whether processing or transport of location at that point is risky or not. If we combine these risk metric estimates together through some metric function then we can calculate some coefficient that could be applied when performing a more formal risk assessment such as FMEA which uses like values, or, to map to some overall risk value for the entire system.

[175] Michael Stamatelatos, Homayoon Dezfuli, George Apostolakis, Chester Everline, Sergio Guarro, Donovan Mathias, Ali Mosleh, Todd Paulos, David Riha, Curtis Smith, et al. Probabilistic risk assessment procedures guide for NASA managers and practitioners. 2011

Caution should however be once again applied in that we do not spend more time than is absolutely necessary to producing metrics in lieu of actually analysing and understanding the system under review.

The Privacy Impact Assessment

THE POINT OF THE Privacy Impact Assessment (PIA) is to understand the required compliance and inherent risks of a system[176]. It is commonly made at the beginning of a project

[176] Trilaterial Research and Consulting. *Privacy impact assessment and risk management.* Information Commissioner's Office, May 2013

for the purpose of establishing these based set of requirements, though such a review can take place at any time during the course of a project. The content and focus of the PIA will change and become more 'technical' as the development work proceeds. A PIA made the end of a project is effectively an audit.

Any attempt to *precisely* define the content and scope of the PIA can not be done but an overall template for a PIA is possible and is given below:

- What is the system and what does it do?
- Who are the data subjects, controllers and processors?
- What data is collected and contained within the system?
- What are the purposes, usages, provenances, and level of identity of the data collected, stored and processed?
- Who are the users of the data?
- Who has external access to data?
- What is the access control to the data?
- What are the assessment and prioritisation of the risks to the system?

Defining what the system is and does is critically important but often left inadequately done - though some of this can be blamed on poor project management, 'agile' processes, scope creep and so on. If any these factors are present, then addressing the scope of the assessment and properly understanding the system becomes even more important.

As part of the PIA we should be able to obtain some model (expressed using the data flow notation) of the system regardless of the status of development - at worst we can rely upon a very basic, top-level rendering which should be constructible from even the most early of system ideas. If not, then this would rather suggest a problem with the whole definition of the work.

Systems do interact with other systems and often with those that are outside of our direct control. Typically amongst these are those that share information such as social media providers, cloud storage etc., but also systems for financial or tax calculation, payment processing and a host of other externalised services are also found. Each contributes to the overall risk inherent in the system and establishing whether this is risk is induced due to contractual - business to business - or user means has to be identified and assessed. For example, a system with a single type of user, no interaction with 3rd parties and more-or-less completely sandboxed is of an overall lesser risk than, say, a system that collects credit card information, health data, stores this in the cloud and interacts publicly with social media providers; PCI data, medical data, public sharing, loss of control of physical storage location just to name a few issues that arise.

In summary understanding the system allows us to address the scope and obtain some kind of coefficient to our measurement of risk. Note also how we can already construct a generic data flow model from this information provided here; doing so will be invaluable in further and more specific discussions later and even may provide significant insights into the workings of the system to the team developing that system!

As privacy is always about information and its use, directly addressing the kinds of content, identification levels and provenance are always to be made as part of a PIA. Note that our classification systems already give us some idea of the questions we need to ask. For example:

- Does the system collect:
    - User identifiers, Device identifiers, etc.?
    - Location data? At what level of detail: lat/long, POI etc.?
    - Financial data? Receipts, credit card data etc.?
    - etc...
- Does the system collect data from:
    - Identified and logged-in adults
    - 'Anonymous' or 'pseudo-anonymous' adults
    - Children
    - 3rd parties (for cross-referencing)
    - etc...
- Does the system use the data for:
    - Advertising

- Direct marketing
- etc...

It is important that this questioning does not turn into a listing by rote of various data types and usages but a conversation about the status and plans for the system. It is also crucially important never to ask the question *'do you collect personal data/PII?'* The answer to this question will be invariably *'no'* as teams try to avoid what is perceived as an effort to stifle develop with excessive privacy demands. As we start to obtain a more detailed understanding of data collection and storage. The more data we obtain here the more we can identify issues precisely. Though, if questions can not be answered or the answers are too generic then these act as warnings in their own right. Often this means the system has not been well defined regardless of the current status of development - this is always an implicit risk.

Answers that suggest that data from children, excessive personal data collection, secondary data collection and work with 3rd parties with particular interest in data such as marketers etc contribute significantly to the risks inherent in the system.

Establishing access control boundaries is necessary from both the technical and human sides. While we can rely upon good security to protect our systems it is often the human factors which cause the problems. This is often a very good time to cross-reference with any security checks being made on the system.

Security is out of scope for the the PIA[177] we concentrate more on the human factors which typically revolve around who has access to the data. More specifically for whom is access relevant and what mechanisms we can build that reduce the overall risk from human based data breaches.

Access control mechanisms both technical and procedural to limit access to certain users are the most general and widespread. Any reference to access control mechanisms is also an implicit requirement to explore the 'human' aspects within the system[178]. This happens to be probably one of the most critical and oft neglected areas to investigate.

Many organisations employ siloed teams and work in an agile environment where management of such access is made in a

---

[177] But an absolutely necessary part of any privacy assessment or information governance programme!

[178] James Reason. Human error: models and management. *British Medical Journal*, 320(7237):768–770, March 2000. ISSN 0959-8138

highly-localised and ad hoc manner. The major issue here is the process for admitting access, keeping an audit trail and most importantly managing the removal of access when no longer needed. This of course then feeds into the wider aspect of data handling which we have already outlined in the requirements section earlier and where most of the human related issues have direct impact[179].

As we have already seen when calculating the set of requirements we can obtain too many or a set of overconstraining requirements. The scope of the PIA can assist in deciding which requirements are unnecessary in the context of the given system

Failure Mode and Effects Analysis

FAILURE MODEL AND EFFECTS ANALYSIS (FMEA) describes a wide family of techniques for assessing risk[180] some of which are more specifically tailored for differing situations such as the use of SWIFT [181] or DRBFM [182]. FMEA is specifically forward reasoning in that from the identification of a risk the questions of what can happen and how can these be mitigated are asked.

The basic premise of FMEA is each *identified* area of concern is ranked according to its severity (S), probability (P) and detection (D) by its Risk Priority Number (RPN) score. The RPN is simply calculated as $RPN = S \times P \times D$, where the higher the score the more critical the risk. The values for S, P and D are usually on a scale of 1 to 10, which is not necessary linear in nature, ie: 4 is not necessarily twice as severe/probable/detectable as 2 and care must be made to properly map these to real world values as much as possible. For example it is common to relate severity with some monetary value such as the hit that the company profits would take based upon loss of brand value, fines, etc.

Ultimately and regardless of the actual values chosen we obtain an ordering between the potential faults where we can clearly see which are the most critical against those of lesser concern. This at least drives some form of prioritisation viz. the project as a whole or against specific requirements and features. In table 11 we show the various failure modes and a quick analysis of the effects, causes and detection for the user sharing their current location to the wider public via our social camera application:

[179] I might need some of this data, but just in case I'll copy it all to this USB stick...which'll be safe in my pocket...

[180] R. McDermott, R.J. Mikulak, and M. Beauregard. *The Basics of FMEA*. 2nd edition, 1996. ISBN 9780527763206

[181] A J Card, J R Ward, and P J Clarkson. Beyond FMEA: the structured what-if technique (SWIFT). *Journal of Healthcare Risk Management*, (31):23–29, 2012

[182] Robert Schmitt and Carsten Scharrenberg. Approach for improved production process planning by the application of quality gates and DRBFM. In George Q. Huang, Kai-Ling Mak, and Paul G. Maropoulos, editors, *DET*, volume 66 of *Advances in Intelligent and Soft Computing*, pages 1089–1100. Springer, 2009. ISBN 978-3-642-10429-9

ID	Effect	S	Cause	P	Detection	D	RPN
1.1	User suffers monetary loss	8	Device GPS on	7	Check GPS status before share	1	56
1.2			App privacy settings incorrect	4	Check app settings	2	64
1.3			Soc.Med. privacy settings incorrect	8	Not detectable	9	576
2.1	User suffers personal embarrassment	3	Device GPS on	7	Check GPS on before share	1	21
2.2			App privacy settings incorrect	4	Check app settings	2	24
2.3			Soc.Med. privacy settings incorrect	8	Not detectable	9	216

Table 11: Example FMEA for Location Sharing

Examining these results we see that the major problem that the user suffers some monetary loss is the greatest risk and this primarily comes from not being able to check the privacy settings of the social media provider and similarly with the personal embarrassment that might come from sharing location.

While the FMEA can tell us where our greatest potential risks are, it can not tell us which are the easiest to defend against other than in a very crude sense by examining the detection metrics. For example, detecting the user's privacy preferences on a variety of social media site - from the analysis above - is very difficult, and it therefore might be deemed too expensive to defend against. There are other arguments here of course such a whether *we* should have the responsibility for this or not.

Of course these are only two cases from many that need to be examined. To find these cases we can systematically examine each data flow path through the model from the data subject to particular end points. In the case above we simply took the flow as shown in figure 86 in the context of information of the Location information type.

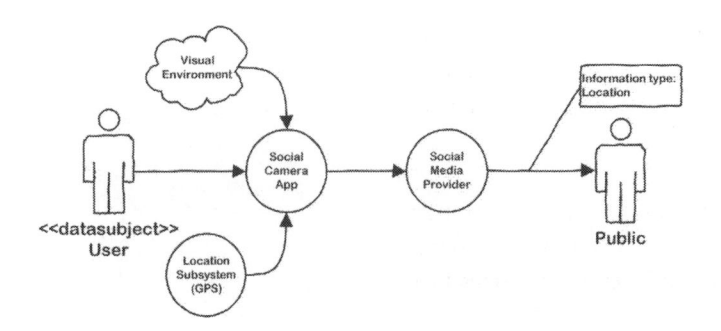

Figure 86: The Chosen Data Flow for FMEA of Location Data via Social Media Provider

We might continue this exercise by looking at other information types or flows of particularly sensitive data classification. The table of degree of identification of various kinds of information type previously in figure 73 can be used as a further metric for sorting these.

For each identified entry in the FMEA, we are required to produce a set of recommended actions such as those listed in table 12 based upon the identified risks in table 11.

ID	Recommended Actions	Actions Taken	New S	New P	New D	New RPN
1.1	Warn user using a warning icon	Icon added	4	4	1	16
1.2	Warn user using a dialog box for certain providers	Dialog added	2	3	2	12
1.3	No action	n/a	-	-	-	-
2.1	As 1.1	As 1.1	4	4	1	16
2.2	As 1.2	As 1.2	2	3	2	12
2.3	No action	n/a	-	-	-	-

Table 12: Example FMEA Recommended Actions for Location Sharing

An alternative method of using FMEA is to make a very broad and high-level analysis based upon the general risk and vulnerability categories shown previously in figure 77 and their particular semantics with respect to the threats they classify.

As we can see in the example in table 13 the risks of monitoring of the system and then of collection, aggregation and identification of the system are the primary risks - this is probably what we should expect from any system at this level of risk abstraction. While it seems that we consider monitoring overall as a risk to the system, specific surveillance is much less of a worry - what the reasoning for this is needs to be investigated and probably lies with the fact that specific, targeted surveillance is considered less detectable and therefore difficult to defend against. The low values for the insecurity, disclosure and confidentiality breaches probably reflect good internal security and privacy practices.

As with all FMEA reviews, the figures given for the S, P and D criteria are always imprecise and subject to review over time. In this respect FMEA is not a precise tool for risk metrics but provides focus on specific risks.

Effect	S	Cause	P	Detection	D	RPN
Monitoring	2	Secondary data collection, system over-logging	7	Whistleblowing, employee monitoring	5	140
Surveillance	8	External factors, spying, company espionage	5	Not possible reliably	1	40
Surveillance	8	Internal factors, employee factors	2	Intrusion analysis, monitoring	3	40
Collection	5	Over collection of data, poor data minimisation	7	Data set analysis, architectural practices	8	280
Aggregation	7	Poorly managed analytics, poor data quality	8	Data set analysis	8	448
Identification	6	Poorly managed analytics, no data minimisation	4	Data set analysis	8	192
Insecurity (Overall)	3	Training, coding practices, poor sys admin.	3	Code reviews, architectural reviews, etc	7	63
Insecurity (Storage)	3	Database management practices, architecture	2	Config. reviews, Monitoring	8	40
Insecurity (Transmission)	2	Non-secure transport protocols, keys	1	Code review, architectural reviews	9	18
Disclosure	1	Agreements and legal issues, untrusted c/p's	2	Review and monitoring	4	8
Confidentiality Breach	2	Data breach with severe economic impact	2	Customer complaint, media	5	20

Table 13: Example FMEA for High-Level Risk Categories

Root Cause Analysis

WE USE ROOT CAUSE ANALYSIS (RCA) as the prototypical backward reasoning tool which seeks to assist in understanding why a particular accident occurred. Its use in the PIA is therefore limited to a degree in that at the early stages of development specific privacy failures might not be obtainable. However if particular, specific concerns are identified then RCA can be used here to understand how that accident and therefore risk mitigated.

RCA[183] takes an identified, actual failure then repeated decomposition of the possible causes of that failure from various perspectives are made until a set of underlying causes are identified.

[183] ABC Consulting. *Root Cause Analysis Handbook: A Guide to Effective Incident Investigation.* Rothstein Associates Inc., 2nd edition, 2005

To assist in this various techniques have been developed and in particular the fishbone diagramming or Ishikawa Diagramming technique is used. Root cause analyses can be analysed from any number of perspectives, for example the following categories are used (with suggested descriptions of our context) in the manufacturing industry - known as the 6M's - and suffice for example when dealing with development failures.

People : who are involved with the process, eg: system administrators, users, operations staff etc

Methods : how was the development performed and what policies, rules, regulations etc were used in the derivation of requirements and architecture

Machines : what tooling was used to accomplish the work; was a PIA sufficiently made, were the data-flow diagrams analysed etc

Materials : what equipment was used to accomplish the work; addressing not just hardware and software (operating systems, libraries, encryption techniques) but also development tools

Measurements : what metrics were captured, in particular what risk analysis was made and what were the results?

Environment : what is the team/company culture, deadlines, process (agile, formal, ad hoc, agile-in-name-only-but-we-hacked-it), team competences, degree of interaction with relevant professionals (eg: privacy, security etc)

In other environments such as health care where the RCA is used to deal with particular specific emergencies then a differing or additional set of categories in used to reflect that including for example detection of incident, contributory factors etc. Such a formulation is useful is response to 'accidents' such as privacy breaches or loss of confidentiality.

Given that the contents of an RCA will vary depending upon the situation being investigated it is good practice to develop a library of categories which can be used. If these categories are overlapping in their scope then this should not be considered a problem as it will provide a more thorough analysis overall. In all RCA reports the scope of the incident, the persons (and systems) affected, details of the root cause and recommendations are always present. Table 14 shows an example root cause analysis based on an incident that might occur from the flow described in figure 85. In this example RCA report the relationship between the categories here and the 6M categories above should be apparent even if the naming has changed for this particular situation.

	Root Cause Analysis Report
Incident Date:	14 May 2014
Report Date:	25 May 2014
Author:	A.Other
Risk Classification:	Disclosure, Confidentiality Breach, Aggregation
Severity:	Low
Summary and Scope:	User reported a data breach due to their location being leaked to the public via a social media provider. The scope of this investigation was to plot only the movement of location data from the user/application to the boundary of our control, ie: where the data left the the device to the social media provider. We do not consider any flow other than from the user to public.
Chronology	provided in separate report
Additional Documentation	Ishikawa Diagram provided in separate report. User emails detailing original complaint.
Persons Affected	An end user of the social camera application and a public audience via the social media provider
Components	The default settings in the social camera application warn about over-sharing of location data which might be present in the picture. This notice is presented with the option to consent or not each time the picture is shared. The components involved are the mobile device, camera, location subsystem (GPS), social camera application sharing component
Risk Analysis	A risk analysis for this situation was performed and inclusion of a notice presenting this was deemed sufficient. An option to include EXIF stripping was included in the original design but inclusion was out of scope for the current release. The user has the option to switch location capture off from the device setting itself.
Root causes	User misunderstanding of the possibility of over-sharing and 'clicking-through' the warning notice given. User's privacy settings on the social media provider set to share information publicly
Recommendations	Increase education to users of the possibilities of oversharing via other means, eg: company blog etc. Rework text in location oversharing notice on application and increase priority of location suppression option in next version.

Table 14: Example RCA Summary Report

Fault Tree Analysis

FAULT TREE ANALYSIS (FTA) is used for analysing and evaluating routes or paths to failure in a system. It additional provides a visual mechanism for displaying these as well. The origins of FTA date back to the 1960's and it has been extensively used, especially is manufacturing and industrial system development[184].

The basic method employed is to identify top-level risks and

[184] Clif Ericson. Fault tree analysis - a history. In *Proceedings of The 17th International System Safety Conference*, 1999

then formally construct using logic symbols a graph of faults culminating in the reasons that generate those fault. The use of 'logic symbols or gates' allows one to specify and, or, not, xor type choices for the faults or reasons that occur at lower levels.

This tree is then augmented with probabilities for each reason, choice and failure while provides a calculation on the approximate probability of a particular top-level fault occurring and the probabilities of each path through the tree. Also as faults can occur in multiple places this provides cross-referencing of faults across the system and an understanding of how for a seemingly simple reason, multiple faults and errors can occur. For example, the failure of a single component might trigger multiple and even conflicting errors, or worse two failures might have the effect of negating one out or being confused with a different scenario causing the wrong assessment to be made when observing the system under operation.

Threat Assessment

ORIGINATING FROM THE SECURITY domain we have a number of established threat assessment models[185] which are all applicable to some degree with terminological and focus changes to privacy. These exist at different levels of complexity and abstraction. Some are therefore more suited to the PIA level of assessment while other at the architectural or high-level data flow, and further again at the code level. As is typical, no one threat assessment model is suitable for all circumstances and all levels of development and a combination of techniques and tools must be applied to obtain proper due diligence and coverage.

[185] A. Shostack. *Threat Modeling: Designing for Security*. Wiley, 2014. ISBN 9781118809990

We have presented the STRIDE threat assessment technique earlier as a classification structure of risk. This can be easily applied to the data flow modelling we have seen earlier and indeed is in the Microsoft SDL approach to modelling security aspects of a system. STRIDE can be applied at both element and data flow level as necessary. For example we consider the case presented in figure 87 with the element analysis being presented in table 15

For each of these we can then perform further analyses as

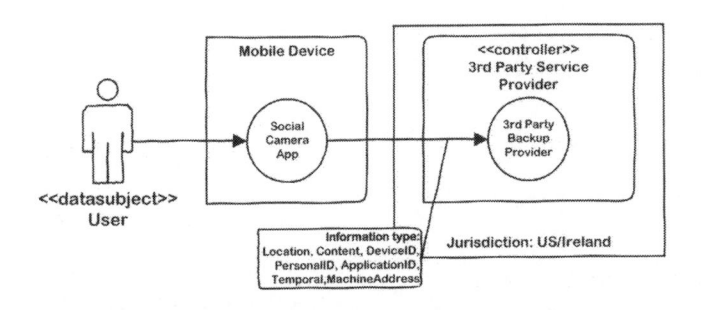

Figure 87: 3rd Party Backup Data Flow for STRIDE Analysis

Element	Interaction	S	T	R	I	D	E
Social Camera App	Sends data to another process	•			•		
	Sends data to external or untrusted process	•		•	•		
	Processes location data				•	•	
3rd Party Backup Svc	Receives data from many unknown sources	•	•	•	•		
Soc Cam-3rd Party Data Flow	Sends personal data	•	•	•	•	•	
	May leak traffic data	•	•		•	•	•
	Crosses device boundary		•		•	•	
	Crosses controller boundary	•			•	•	•
	Crosses geographical jurisdiction				•	•	•

Table 15: Example STRIDE Analysis

necessary to drive the requirements, or, ensure that our existing requirement set mitigates against these threats as necessary.

There are many methods for enumerating such threats including known threat libraries[186] and techniques such as brain-storming, use case analysis, etc. These can be combined with deep analysis of specific threats identified through FMEA for example.

[186] OWASP Top 10 Project - includes both security and privacy threats is a good place to start.

Gap Analysis

THE USE OF A 'GAP ANALYSIS' is a management technique to both plot out the course between some current or initial state and some final or desired state *and* to concretely specify the actions required to get there. Its use in privacy engineering and especially in the derivation of requirements and their subsequent implementation is useful to properly understand which risks are not being sufficiently mitigated in the current state.

While no formal, general, well-defined process for executing a gap analysis exists, though some specific versions tailored for a more high-level view of privacy can be used[187] as well as other specific areas such a medical privacy and information quality[188].

[187] Kim Bustin. Conducting a privacy gap analysis: A primer for privacy officers. October 2011

[188] Yang W. Lee, Diane M. Strong, Beverly K. Kahn, and Richard Y. Wang. Aimq: a methodology for information quality assessment. *Information and Management*, 40(2):133–146, 2002

One mechanism that can be helpful in a gap analysis is when looking at the total set of requirements is examining how many of the deeper levels of engineering abstraction have the required level of detail for implementations. The more implementation requirements missing the greater the degree of 'gap' between your privacy policies and engineering requirements. Furthermore in deciding which areas to target we can look at the various risk areas and then which of those are most critical in the current business environment.

Risk Register

IT IS LIKELY THAT during the course of an audit many issues will be found and these will have to be defended against. The issues will vary in sensitivity and may or may not cause the system being audited to pass or fail. Indeed it is very common to allow a system that has failed an audit to go-live or continue development on the condition that the issues discovered will be addressed.

Such issues fall into two broad categories

- Those that constitute a major risk and must be dealt with before any progress can be made

- Those that constitute an acceptable risk and should be dealt with at some future time

The recommendations and results from an audit that is not completely successful will become a political and business risk game in assigning these risks to one of the two above categories. In either case it is critical that a record of such findings be kept. This record can then be used as evidence of non-compliance, part of any gap-analysis in internal capabilities, a description of current business risks and a statement of the overall privacy maturity level.

A register must be kept[189,190] of such findings and risks should include the following fields - though these of course vary by local business needs and practices:

- Risk categorisation, eg: as in figure 77
- Description of the findings
- Assigned risk metric, eg: low, medium, high etc
- System affected
- Audit details, such as dates, times, auditors, management etc
- Result of risk, future tasks, go/no-go etc
- Management sign-off

[189] Project Management Institute. *A Guide To The Project Management Body Of Knowledge (PMBOK Guides)*. Project Management Institute, 2004. ISBN 193069945X, 9781933890517

[190] Jeff Reed. *Project Management with PRINCE2 Best Practice Handbook: Building, Running and Managing Effective Project Management - Ready to Use Supporting Documents Bringing PRINCE2 Theory into Practice*. Emereo Pty Ltd, London, UK, UK, 2008. ISBN 1921573104, 9781921573101

This then constitutes a record of business decisions and importantly the escalation and management sign-off on acceptance or otherwise of the risk. Getting any kind of higher management sign-off is critical in ensuring that non-compliance is dealt with and that the audit team has successfully demonstrated its work. In the case where sign-off of the risks can not be made due to a myriad of issues then a full and detailed record of all communication of that risk must be included; this ensures that the audit team has made its necessary due diligence and communicated its results. If a privacy breach happens then this to some degree should ensure that the audit team is 'in the clear'.

Summary

WE HAVE INTRODUCED A number of specific techniques and the generic nature of a privacy impact assessment to understand the risks inherent in a system and from these suggest additional requirements to that system[191]. One must also ensure that if the same risks occur and the same requirements be suggested then these should be reflected back in an update to the overall set of requirements. In some circles such occurrences are known as patterns - regardless of terminology these are the

[191] Renata Vieira, Douglas da Silva, and Tomas Sander. Representation and inference of privacy risks using semantic web technologies. *CEP*, 90619:900, 2010

same in that we need to utilise the results to better construct our requirements and reviews to mitigate privacy risks.

No one review or assessment technique is sufficient in all cases and even then some techniques require customisation in their use to the local environment[192]. For example, an FMEA review in one system might be very detailed while in another very light using metric values such as low, medium and high. The main point here is that it is critical to make a review but time should be spent on generating meaningful results from the review and not worrying about the precise application and subtleties of the review technique itself.

Note that in all investigations we can and should refer back to the earlier defined risk taxonomies (viz.figures 77 and 76) in order to provide additional scope and formality to the risks being investigated and identified.

[192] Shari Lawrence Pfleeger. Risky business: what we have yet to learn about risk management. *Journal of Systems and Software*, 53(3):265–273, 2000

Notice and Consent

BEFORE DATA CAN BE collected or sent to or from any party there must be agreement between the parties involved over the type and scope of data. These agreements are often expressed as the terms and conditions and/or privacy policy that a user needs to accept before using a system. There are also agreements of an implicit form such as when browsing a web site.

The presentation of these agreements can be in many forms such as a paper document or block of text presented on a webpage or via an application's first-time usage screen. The actual consent similarly can be made using good, old fashioned pen, or by clicking on some button or check-box element in a user-interface. Information systems of the kind we are addressing here, the notice is presented to the end user through electronic means and the consent gained or not typically by explicit action via some user-interface element. We may understand the relationship between the terms of agreement, notice, consent as depicted in figure 88.

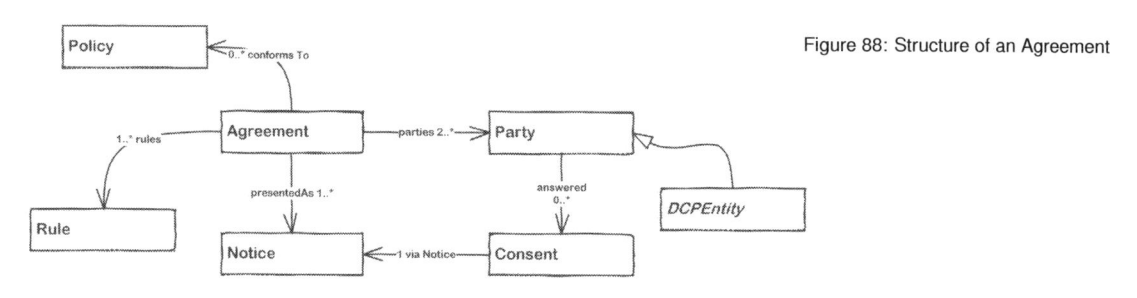

Figure 88: Structure of an Agreement

Note the correspondence with the notions of controller, processor and data subject from figure 69 which are the kinds of the parties we are particular interested in identifying with regards to privacy. At any point in time there are many agreements between a user and the provider of a service in effect - some of these are implicit, some explicit and all exist monotonically.

In this chapter we will describe the nature of an agreement, in particular the consent and notice parts and how the contents of these can be derived from the information contained with a data flow model of an information system. We will also describe how particular choices can affect the data flows within a system by inducing additional use cases for particular consent scenarios, and finally we will describe how the generic agreement case can be constructed and represented as a policy.

We will avoid any discussion of the implementation of policies or rules using a policy language. There are a number of languages already existing such as P3P, XACML, EPAL and so on, which all can be used for such purposes. We do not and cannot take any stand on which is best for a particular organisation or system due to the subtle variances in business and engineering practices that might come into play. The most important aspect here is that the method of implementation admits the agreement in such a manner that it does have an effect as stated in the agreement not just of the initial data collection but the whole data flow as necessary.

It is worth mentioning the role of policies and their place with regards to the whole agreement structure. Policies themselves are no more than agreements but take on a more general role or aspirational role and define the scope of particular decisions within a business environment. In effect they define the overall limits and rules by within which a business operates and derives particular agreements from. In many cases the privacy agreement between a business and its customers are reiterations on the internal privacy policy anyway.

Notice

A NOTICE RELATES TO how an agreement is presented in a form which can be understood, ostensibly by a human in most cases. Included in here will eventually be the actual implementation and physical or virtual form of that notice, for example, some modal dialog box with hundreds of lines of legal text and a single 'agree' button at the end. Other more 'friendly' forms can include informal presentation of a vague description of what services an application might use on a mobile device when presented to the user in a app store environment; or as a checkbox graphical element stating whether marketing material is wanted or not, and so on.

Notices are the points where a user is able to make a choice of whether to consent or not to the agreement to a service. They may be presented to a user many times during the use of an application or system. Figure 89 shows a few of the notices presented to a user over this usage life, along with a demonstration that a number of notices may be grouped together to be dealt within a single interaction on occasion. It is good practice to ensure that notices are clear from the user's perspective and not grouped in such a way that a single consent is for multiple, excessive agreements. The presentation of a notice may be either a one-off notice or may be revisitable through the application or service settings as the user's preferences to data collection and processing change.

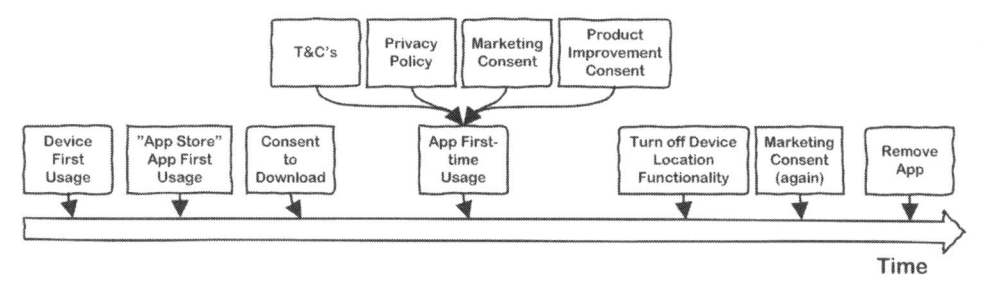

Figure 89: Examples Notices over the Usage Life of an Application

The contents of a notice for most cases when interaction with human users are a natural language representation of the rules that the agreement represents. These rules pertain to the handling of the various kinds of data, their usages etc. For example, the statement:

> We collect personal information from you when you register an account with us and when using services that require this facility to function. We also collect information such as your IP address and other relevant details when accessing our services. We may use this information for the purposes of monitoring and running our services and for providing our products and services.

which may be an representation of rules constructed from our classification systems. For example, given the data flow model in figure 90 we show information passing from a data subject to a controller for a two particular usages: service provisioning and system provisioning. The data collected in total includes the machine address (IP address), photo (JPEG/PNG, including EXIF), password (hopefully encrypted) and personal identifiers (username).

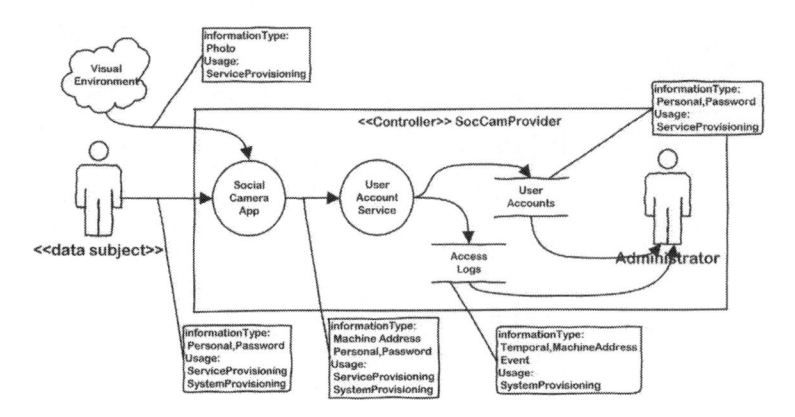

Figure 90: Example System and Service Provisioning Data Flows

If the model represents the actual implemented situation then we see that for this part of the service does appear to agree with the statement presented to the user. Furthermore it is explicit in this model which parts of the data collected are used for what and where they flow to - in this case some 'human' system administrator. We also note that not all data is passed, for example, the Photo data with any embedded meta-data such as location.

The model also shows the limits of the usage of the data, that is the user account data can only be used for providing the service - we can use this information (at least not with the agreement above and not in the context of the model) for generating marketing lists or for further cross-referencing beyond what is necessary for that social camera service. Similar constraints apply to the data contained in the access logs.

Within a data flow model, a single element such as our administrator does not necessarily represent one person but to persons who have this role. It may be, and here we would require some refinement to the model to accurately see - that there are two administrators whose roles regarding their access to data does not intersect. The data contained in the two stores have very specific usages which gets more complex when both of these are passed to the administrator who may have the capability and possibility to cross-reference this data as shown in figure 91. This highlights both the limits of an agreement in and a very human problem in information system design and would need to be considered in any risk assessment.

We can also work 'backwards' can calculate the agreement rules and thus a natural language representation for the notice from the model. So again using the model in figure 90 we can construct 'rules'[193] such as:

- Temporal, Machine Address and Event data can be used for system provisioning within the context of the controller.

- Personal identifiers and passwords can be used for service provisioning within the context controller.

- No data (in the context of this model) will flow outside the controller's context

Typically there are as many rules as there are individual paths through the data flow from the data subject, plus a rule to explicitly state the frame[194] in which we are working. If these rules for processing of data conform to the natural language statement then all is correct. Natural language of course has its own issues with ambiguity and the style language in which notices are written in which is usually a form of legalese will add much complexity and debate to this. However having a set of common classifications and their semantics, plus a very specific context in which to work will ease this significantly.

Indeed performing both processes above - checking the rules *against* the model and recalculating those rules *from* the model - can highlight inconsistency with the agreement *and* the implementation and should form part of good practice when developing such systems.

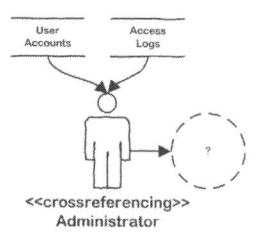

Figure 91: Agreement Limits and Humans

[193] Shayak Sen, Saikat Guha, Anupam Datta, Sriram K Rajamani, Janice Tsai, and Jeannette M Wing. Bootstrapping privacy compliance in big data systems. In *Proceedings of the 35th IEEE Symposium on Security and Privacy (Oakland)*, 2014

[194] John McCarthy. Circumscription - a form of non-monotonic reasoning. *Artificial intelligence*, 13(1):27–39, 1980

Consent

A CONSENT IS A DECLARATION of the choice made by a user with regards to the agreement being presented through a notice. When a consent is made we must consider how the consent needs to be recorded, what needs to be recorded and at what level of identification the consent needs to be recorded at[195].

[195] Owen Sacco, Alexandre Passant, and Stefan Decker. An access control framework for the web of data. In *Trust, Security and Privacy in Computing and Communications (TrustCom), 2011 IEEE 10th International Conference on*, pages 456–463. IEEE, 2011

In our social camera application we consider (at least) three places where a consent is made by the user:

- when the application is downloaded
- when the application is run for the first time
- when the use opts-out/in of secondary data collection

In the first case the agreement is actually between the user and the application store or download provider. The agreements here are more of the form that the user is allowed to download and the data collected little more than an identity of who downloaded which can include a machine address and/or user identifier depending upon the level of identification provided, an application identifier and time stamp; additionally we might have record of some financial information such as a receipt. At this point we have little more than a consent to download and record that information.

The second case we have an option to record information that the application was started and the user has consented to actually using the application. At this point it is necessary to present any terms and conditions of use including a privacy policy along with an option to agree to those or not. This notice might be combined with notices of other agreements as the developer sees fit (or is willing to risk). We might choose to record the user's reaction here to better understand whether they actually started the application or not; such a scenario is shown in figure 92.

Note the amount of information we can collect in addition to the Event that describes the user's response[196]. This actually causes some issues for any agreement between data subject and the controller where the agreement now needs to take into account this data flow. This might even be the case where a user does not actually use the application and we wish to record this.

[196] We could easily add Location to this as well without relying upon the geolocation later!

It is quite interesting here to note the alternative which would be to cross-reference between the application first-time usage logs and the application store downloads - such a data flow is shown in figure 93. In this model it is even now possible

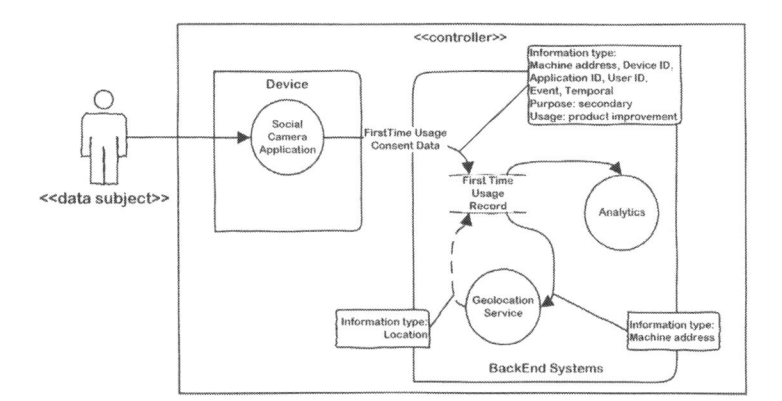

Figure 92: First Time Usage Consent Data Flow Model

that we don't collect any information in the case where the user declines the agreement at the application first-time usage stage - we could infer this by searching for events such as application downloaded and never used within a given period of time. If we layer on the possible controller and processor relationships over this the complexity of managing the agreements and data flows becomes very apparent.

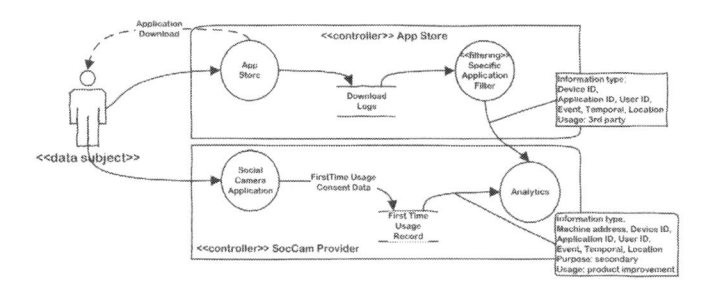

Figure 93: Cross-referencing First Time Usage Consent Information

Referring back to the construction of the notices we have a notice for the app store which requires the allowance of personal data to be shared with a 3rd party and then for the application itself a notice for the collection of such consent information. Furthermore we have a data flow between two controllers which itself would need to be agreed upon between those parties.

Finally the location of the storage of the consent needs to be considered. In the model in figure 93 we only hinted to the physical partitioning. To express this when considering all the data flowing from an element, it is good practice to decompose the data flows so specific channels of communication carrying consents can be isolated and examined in isolation.

Cross-Referencing Identification in Consents

THE LEVEL OF IDENTIFICATION of the user making a consent can be made indirectly or directly depending upon the level of authentication the user has provided. In some cases we must allow for the fact that the user might not wish to be identified such, as when entering false account details to create an 'anonymous account' or alternative persona[197]. Even if no details are directly passed then identification can be made via traffic data and correlating with IP addresses. In the extreme case we could even fingerprint the interactions to deduce the identity. In the case of a first-time usage notice, there might be no explicit recording of the consent as just getting past the presentation of notice to use the application is enough.

[197] JohnR. Suler. Identity management in cyberspace. *Journal of Applied Psychoanalytic Studies*, 4(4):455–459, 2002

If we work with strongly identified users where we have to assume that the user providing the credentials is the user in question. Dealing with the possibility that they have logged in to a system on behalf of someone else can not easily nor effectively be addressed current technology in any satisfactory manner. This is especially the case when dealing with services that might be used by minors or children and where the authorisation has been provide via an account belonging to an adult or where the characteristic and demographic details can not be verified, such as stating date of birth. For most systems the requirements of KYC would be excessive to say the least.

Consideration must also be given in cases where the identifier associated with the consent is not personal but related with an object identifier and its subtypes. Here we can only indirectly associate this with a unique human being and is often the case working with device first usage scenarios. This also occurs when seemingly unique identifiers become obfuscated, for example particularly in the case of IP addresses 'suffer' from obfuscation via network address translation, DHCP and proxies.

Furthermore in trying to identify a user that has not authenticated in the case where we do receive such an identifier we might additionally rely upon some form of cross-referencing. For example, if a user has registered a device, but this introduces the problem that reidentification of a user in this context may not be permissible unless explicitly agreed upon by the user; let alone questions regarding the reliability of this.

Implementation of an Agreement

WHEN IMPLEMENTING AN AGREEMENT we need to consider the following aspects:

- the mechanisms of displaying the notice to the user
- the mechanisms by which the consent is captured
- the mechanisms by which the consent is stored and/or transported to a storage page
- the mechanisms that use the value of the consent
- the mechanisms by which the rules are enforced
- the control points of the enforcement

Notice Display and Consent Capture, Content and Store

THE USUAL METHOD OF displaying a notice is by some user-interface element, which can be presented upon application first usage, title screen (as in figure 94) or some other suitable modal dialog box for example. It is not unknown to use modeless dialog boxes when presenting some agreements such as those for cookie acceptance on web pages. We are also required to decide how many notices are combined together in this user-interface element when displayed; it is not unusual to find notices all presented together with multiple choice user interface elements having to be set all at the same time. This is done for the convenience of the user so that everything can be dealt within one action.

Once a notice has been presented we have a number of ways of obtaining the user's answer to the agreement. Other than the usual acceptance or decline we must also consider the case where no answer is given due to application termination, web page close or even ignoring the agreement as might be possible in some cases. The control flow in figure 95 is typical of the case where acceptance must be obtain before continuing.

Figure 94: Social Camera First Time Usage Screen with Notice

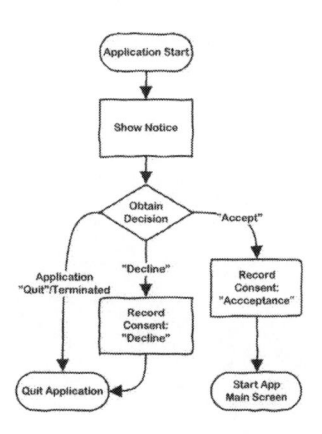

Figure 95: Control Flow for Modal Notices and Consent

Where a modeless mechanism of interaction is employed then we see a different situation where we are left in a state where interaction with a service can continue without an explicit answer as in figure 96. In these cases the legal aspects can vary on whether an agreement has been *implicitly* consented to or not.

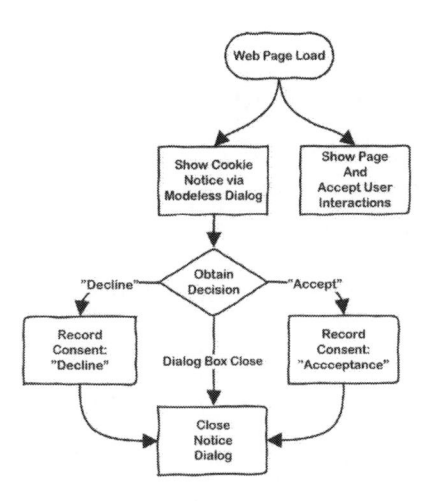

Figure 96: Control Flow for Modeless Notices and Consent

Furthermore the ability for the user to change their mind regarding a particular agreement needs also to be considered as may be the case with agreements related to marketing and secondary data collection and that default values for a consent need to be expressed. Figure 97 shows a typical and revisitable notice for consenting to such agreements. There are differences between European and US privacy laws regarding whether certain agreements should be opt-out or opt-in by default.

The actual contents of a consent if recorded should only contain that data which is necessary to ascertain the decision, who made the decision and when the decision was made. The classification

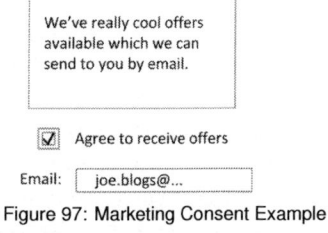

Figure 97: Marketing Consent Example

of such data would be Event, Identity (User Identity) and some Temporal information. Figure 93 shows a data flow containing much more information than this; all of which may be valid if we are trying to track over multiple different kinds of devices, user-interfaces, locations and so on. Again we are required to ensure that this is suitably presented in the notice and have performed data minimisation - which may or may not be in accordance with actual needs.

The location of storage of the consent can obviously vary from local storage in some configuration file to being stored as part of the user's account profile. Either is valid depending upon the features we wish to provide to the consumer. Obviously in cases such as those found on mobile devices where not only is network connectivity and bandwidth an issues, but also whether applications are written without further supporting infrastructure, versus, say a major cloud infrastructure and application ecosystem provider, there are going to be many other business, performance and feature requirements at play.

When modelling, once a suitable level of refinement is reached it is good practice to separate any consent flows from other flows, even though the same channel of communication and protocols might be being used. Figure 98 shows a simple example of how this might look when modelled.

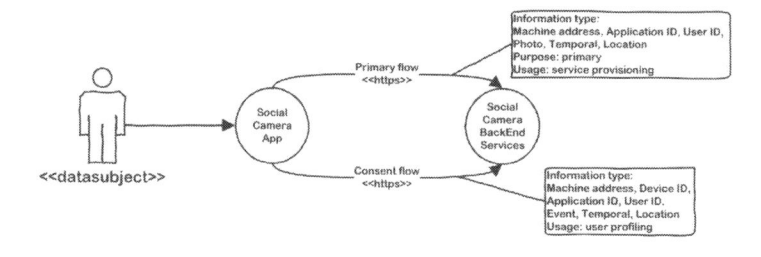

Figure 98: Consent Data Flow

Control Points

THE POINT AT WHICH an agreement is enforced was in the above examples relatively simple in that the user was presented with a simple choice of acceptance and continuing to use the application or not. For many agreements that the user is faced with this is not so simple and we continue here with the latter two points of implementing agreements relating to the mechanisms by which the rules are enforced and the control points where they are implemented.

Consider the case where a user is presented with the option to receive marketing material through a notice such as that in figure 97; figure 99 depicts all the data flows that run between a user and marketing via various other places of data collection.

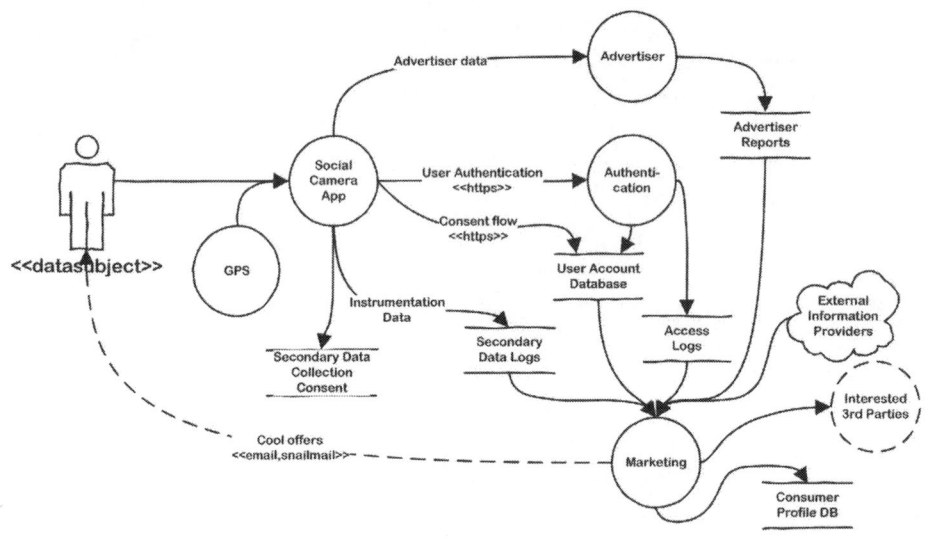

Figure 99: Marketing Data Flow

We assume that we have implemented our notice in the social camera application itself and allow the user to provide his or her consent to marketing as desired *and* made the decision to store the consent value in the user account data base. Furthermore a notice for secondary data collection is also implemented in a similar manner except that consent is stored locally to the application. There also exists the capability for the application to obtain the device's current location by utilising GPS. This gives us the following agreements to consider:

- Access to device location API or GPS subsystem(s)
- Secondary Data Collection
- Advertising
- User Account
- Marketing Consent

Access to location can be controlled in one of two ways: either by requesting that the application does or does not do this, or, by actively preventing the application providing location data through operating system features. The implementation of the latter is out of our control and the former simply made by providing a mechanism to turn this feature off from the application's context. The control point here is expressed by the data flow from the GPS subsystem to the Social Camera Application.

Secondary data collection can be controlled in a similar manner depending upon the platform and the implementation used by the application writer - both even might coexist on the same device. The control point here is the data flow between the social camera application and the secondary data logs. It is however important to note that there might even exist two separate use cases for when no consent to collection is made: no information flow and a restricted, 'anonymous' flow of data.

The advertising flow's agreement is controlled actually through the usage of the application. It is quite normal for applications to be supported through advertising and implicit consent to this is made by actually running the application; though the notice might only be presented on the first-time usage and on demand via some help screen.

It is a business decision whether users have to the logged in to use a service or not and there are many factors for and against this. The main aspect here is that if a user is logged in then we have a strong identity provided. This can and usually is particularly important when constructing a user profile. The control point here is on the user authentication flow but has repercussions regarding how the data from the consent flow is processed.

Finally the consent for marketing flow controlled from the notice in figure 97 provides us with at least seven data flows over which a control flow can be constructed. Just because a user opts-out of marketing does not mean that a user profile for marketing data is not constructed. At its weakest an opt-out of this particular agreement means we place our control point on the 'cool offers' flow from marketing back to the user, meaning that they would no longer receive such marketing material.

We could be more sophisticated and proactive towards the user's personal data by modifying the flows into the marketing process which may infer that marketing does not take place due to insufficient information or poor data quality; this might also be in addition to the control point mentioned above.

Furthermore an opt-out of marketing might also imply that we no longer construct the user's entry in the consumer profile database nor provide it to other interested 3rd parties. This latter case, while it may not be directly tied to marketing but the whole agreement between the data subject and controller, *feels* like marketing to the user of the system. Then we must also be very aware of the possibilities of information being passed around both inside and externally to the system with data about the user appearing in unexpected places. This has two effects, firstly that users become aware that their data is not nicely contained inside some monolithic, black-box system that just provides the services for their applications but also that some of the internal workings of the system start becoming visible[198].

[198] Uwe Aßmann. *Invasive software composition*. Springer, 2003. ISBN 978-3-540-44385-8

Clients and Servers

BECAUSE NEARLY ALL SYSTEMS have client (front-end) and a server (back-end) processing most product development tends to split the two. This is especially the case when systems are being called upon to provide APIs to developers so that someone else takes responsibility for system integration and constructing additional client applications. For client applications which have a user interface the presentation of notices and collection of consents is fairly straightforward. Either they do this or their application is generally considered to be non-compliant with privacy laws.

For server installations which do not provide user-interface this is somewhat problematical; doubly so for client application developers who might not see a full view of what that server-side is actually doing. Wrapping controller-controller and controller-processor agreement rules together to present to a user is fraught with difficulties for the average client application developer.

As we have explained, we can calculate the rules of an agreement from summing together the usages, purposes and information types of the sinks of information. By tracing these back to the partition between client and server and relating these with the individual data flows we can construct what the agreement that a client should show would look like, even if we only construct the rules and not the notice text itself.

Taking the model in figure 99 as the start, for the average application developer it would appear as in figure 100 where each flow would correspond to an API or part of an API provided by the back-end systems. For each of these flows the back-end system developers could calculate the agreement rules and present these to the client application developer.

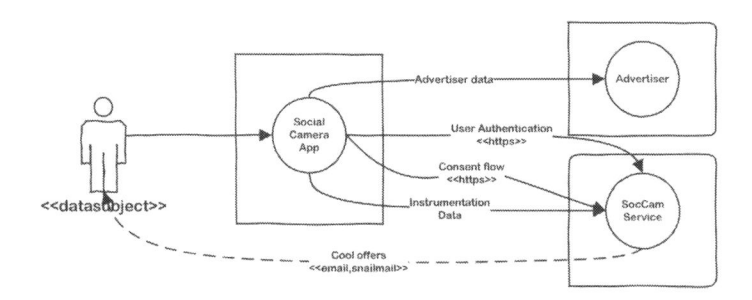

Figure 100: Simplified Client-Server Data Flows For Agreement Calculation

This actually also has an important use when auditing back-end systems where such a calculation of the agreement rules can become part of the documentation of that system for presentation to client developers and used in their own auditing and development activities.

Summary

UNDERSTANDING THE AGREEMENT BETWEEN the controllers and processors of information and the data subject and how this is applied is one of the major challenges in any information system dealing with any kind of information and especially that of personal data. While there can be much argument about the contact of the agreement itself and whether this is fair to the data subject is a major philosophical subject in itself. Even in so-called zero-sum situations where both parties obtain something from the agreement the information asymmetry between the parties can be so overwhelming to even make this argument meaningless at best. Information systems that develop privacy as an inherent property, regardless of this argument, need to ensure that the information they capture is handled with utmost care so that there can exist user trust in the system; this is primarily an economic argument from the point of view of the business providing the service via that system.

The actual implementation of an agreement itself generates many requirements outside that of privacy pertaining to the basic structure of the system. This we understand through the data flow model and its contents which themselves need to be cross-referenced with the other kinds of architectural models and requirements.

Privacy Enhancing Techniques

THE TERM PRIVACY ENHANCING TECHNOLOGY (PET) covers a very broad category of work specifically aimed at better protecting the customer's or user's privacy through, ostensibly, technological means. Proposed definitions of the term PET has been stated in reports by the UK's Information Commissioner's Office[199] and the European Commission[200] and can be traced back to earlier work by the Information and Privacy Commissioner of Ontario, Canada with the Dutch Data Protection Authority[201]. Despite this the term PET can be used to apply to both techniques employed during the construction of information systems and to those technologies used by users. The definition which we will work from is[202]:

> "a technology whose sole purpose is to enhance privacy"

We do not consider technologies for the security of a system, for example firewalls etc., but our focus to those technologies which directly act upon the information content and not the transportation of that information nor protection of the channel of communication. We present here a number technologies or techniques[203] for manipulating and measuring information for the purposes of enhancing privacy which can and should be applied together as required to architect a solution.

> A technique is a method of doing things, whereas technology is the application of that method (scientifically): application of techniques forms a technology.

Many techniques can be considered privacy enhancing or privacy preserving and there exists much research on these[204].

[199] *Privacy by Design: An Overview of Privacy Enhancing Technologies*. The Information Commissioner's Office (UK), November 2008

[200] *Privacy Enhancing Technologies (PETs)*. European Commission, Brussels, memo/07/159 edition, May 2007

[201] Ann Cavoukian. *Moving Forward From PETs to PETs Plus: The Time for Change is Now*. Information and Privacy Commissioner of Ontario, Canada, January 2009

[202] Jason Cronk. Thoughts on the term "privacy enhancing technologies". Via blog, 2013

[203] Peter Langendörfer, Michael Maaser, Krzysztof Piotrowski, and Steffen Peter. *Privacy Enhancing Techniques: A Survey and Classification*. Information Science Reference, 2008

[204] Charu C. Aggarwal and Philip S. Yu. A general survey of privacy-preserving data mining models and algorithms. In Charu C. Aggarwal, Philip S. Yu, and Ahmed K. Elmagarmid, editors, *Privacy-Preserving Data Mining*, volume 34 of *The Kluwer International Series on Advances in Database Systems*, pages 11–52. Springer US, 2008

Here we will outline a number of particular categories of privacy enhancing technologies.

Hashing

A HASH FUNCTION IS a function that takes a set of data - string, value, stream - and transforms this into typically a fixed length representation. They find uses in associative data structures, cache management etc. They conform to a set of properties including determinacy meaning that for any given input the output is always the same, variability of output in that for minor changed in the input, major changes in the output are seen, as well as a number of others. Hash functions are also typically one-way functions such that computing their inverse is computationally expensive or mathematically hard.

The particular for of hash we are interested in are the cryptographic hash functions which we can used to change the representation of data in such a way that the inverse function is not (practically) computable and the input is not derivable by other means from the output. We use this to take a block of data, transform it into a fixed sized representation and without the need to decrypt the data. For example using the SHA-256 hashing function[205] some of these properties are shown below. Note in this first example the output with a trivial difference of the end punctuation mark:

[205] Henri Gilbert and Helena Handschuh. Security analysis of SHA-256 and sisters. In Mitsuru Matsui and Robert J. Zuccherato, editors, *Selected Areas in Cryptography*, volume 3006 of *Lecture Notes in Computer Science*, pages 175–193. Springer, 2003

```
SHA256('The quick brown fox.') →
42e25dd386eb55b56db34af535fab5231db8cf1b588af95bc9c32ef849507fc5

SHA256('The quick brown fox!') →
0452ba1c161cc328e963fb7620324ef53ce1ee60b6455edd424450fbd7fe59b4
```

And demonsrtating the length of the input does not matter with regards to the output:

```
SHA256('The fox') →
a5a61814056e3c3fb0a541eb997b60caff734b1f49ed31c7e38b3cc4eb6777eb

SHA256('The quick brown fox jumps over the lazy dog') →
d7a8fbb307d7809469ca9abcb0082e4f8d5651e46d3cdb762d02d0bf37c9e592
```

For privacy, hashing functions are used to obscure fields with a data set. For example given the following (truncated and summarised) log file containing amongst others a machine address in the form of the IP address:

```
10.192.43.6 10/Dec/2013:00:12:44:16 "GET /index.html HTTP/1.0" 200 "Mozilla/5.0"
10.192.43.6 10/Dec/2013:00:12:44:26 "GET /upload.html HTTP/1.0" 200 "Mozilla/5.0"
10.192.43.6 10/Dec/2013:00:12:45:03 "GET /index.html HTTP/1.0" 200 "Mozilla/5.0"
192.167.221.141 10/Dec/2013:00:12:45:12 "GET /personal.html HTTP/1.0" 200 "Mozilla/5.0"
78.19.1.1 10/Dec/2013:00:12:45:22 "GET /naughty.html HTTP/1.0" 200 "Mozilla/5.0"
10.192.43.6 10/Dec/2013:00:12:45:58 "GET /secret.html HTTP/1.0" 200 "Mozilla/5.0"
127.0.0.1 10/Dec/2013:00:12:46:07 "GET /index.html HTTP/1.0" 200 "Mozilla/5.0"
```

we can use hashing to obscure the IP address so that the source can not be traced thereby reducing the amount of personal data in the set such that the IP address are as follows:

```
4559f7191f3d978ab89a320628cac466739ac506f42abba8a244fb38e496a7b7 ...
4559f7191f3d978ab89a320628cac466739ac506f42abba8a244fb38e496a7b7 ...
4559f7191f3d978ab89a320628cac466739ac506f42abba8a244fb38e496a7b7 ...
076e9ce5a5e1236c9af723c799f3d3c4f24cc2c16e5c01547999769c35eac821 ...
055e06068d0ef1b786e1c95c4941dc8b5163edfc5590446fee93af7afdca0ab5 ...
4559f7191f3d978ab89a320628cac466739ac506f42abba8a244fb38e496a7b7 ...
12ca17b49af2289436f303e0166030a21e525d266e209267433801a8fd4071a0 ...
```

Note that we have only changed the representation of the information and not the information content. The information type of the IP address field is Machine Address, and after hashing it is *at best* an Identifier, though whether the address is recoverable is another matter.

It is actually the recoverability of hashing that is the problem. To reverse a hashing is extraordinarily difficult, though with improvements in computing power this is possible but there are alternatives. The most popular technique is the precompute the hashes and then match the output of a hash against these tables - this is known as a rainbow table attack. In the above we could simply compute all IPv4 addresses[206] and generate a table of hashed forms of these, when we then see a hashed form we can simply search this table to reconstruct the original text.

[206] There are approximately 4.3×10^9 IPv4 and 3.4×10^{38} IPv6 addresses and even in this latter case a rainbow table is possible for certain, important subsets

deSHA256('4559f7191f3d978ab89a320628cac466739ac506f42abba8a244fb38e496a7b7') →
10.192.43.6

The solution here is to use a 'salt' which is a set of *sufficiently* random data used as additional input into the hashing function, for example a UUID4 string. This is the primary mechanism by which we can defend against rainbow table attacks as shown above - depending upon the unguessability of the salt. There are three considerations here: the first being the notion of sufficiently random, the second dealing with the amount of time over which the salt remains consistent and thirdly where the salt is stored or coded.

The second issue to more related to fingerprinting of the data to enable re-identification[207]. If the salt remains constant over a sustained period of time, or even permanently then other fields could be used as quasi-identifiers and fingerprinting could be applied to recover at last patterns of behaviour. Once patterns are identified then the possibilities of cross-referencing, even by statistical means, could re-identify personal content. This means that salts should be considered in much the same way as keys would be with encryption functions.

[207] Lukasz Olejnik, Claude Castelluccia, Artur Janc, et al. Why Johnny can't browse in peace: On the uniqueness of web browsing history patterns. In *5th Workshop on Hot Topics in Privacy Enhancing Technologies (HotPETs 2012)*, 2012

When working with data sets containing many fields care must be taken that the data set isn't its own rainbow table. Examination of the diversity of the data contained within the fields when cross-referenced against each other must be made so that even if one field is hashed, other fields do not act as potential inverses to this. For example consider the fields below extracted from some data-set containing a Machine Address and Device Identifier:

```
10.192.43.6 - 32 18050X 495464 1
1b0ad6a24d281093abec0e735d5029db - 32 18050X 495464 1
10.192.43.6 - 38d7069b684671024e195b44bbe851c4
```

Under various circumstances certain identifiers are hashed for anonymity reasons such as whether the user has consented to some secondary data collection agreement or not. What happens here is as we can see above that fields with the same IMEI number have both hashed and unhashed IP addresses associated with them. It is unreasonable to infer that there is a bijection between IP address and IMEI.

Even in the above case it can easily be demonstrated that with salts we can trace identifiers and infer bijections between them over other kinds of data present in the files. For example using temporal data, spatial data, accesses to particular objects and so on. Use of hashing even with salts does not guarantee anonymity!

Encryption

ENCRYPTION IS PROBABLY THE best known of any technology for the protection of information and one that is mainly used in the security aspect rather than privacy. However as privacy does not come without security it is therefore important to understand what encryption is, the rationale behind its use and its application to privacy. Encryption itself does not necessarily provide privacy, but it does provide a means for hiding the contents of a message.

Encryption[208] is simple a process of encoding messages such as that no unauthorised parties can read that message. A message here being practically everything from a communication between parties, a field in a database or an entire dataset itself. The basics of encryption can be summarised such that we have a messages M and C where the latter is the former in its ciphered form, two functions E and D to encrypt and decrypt messages respectively and a set of keys $K_1, K_2, \ldots, K_n$ where:

$$\begin{aligned} E_{K_1}(M) &= C \\ D_{K_2}(C) &= M \\ D_{K_2}(E_{K_1}(M)) &= M \end{aligned}$$

[208] Bruce Schneier. *Applied Cryptography (2Nd Ed.): Protocols, Algorithms, and Source Code in C*. John Wiley & Sons, Inc., New York, NY, USA, 1995. ISBN 0-471-11709-9

In symmetric encryption systems the keys used by E and D are the same, while in asymmetric systems[209] they are different. There are also variations in how the algorithms process the data, either as a stream of bits where they are known as stream ciphers, or as blocks of data with the appropriate name of block ciphers. The choice between symmetric and asymmetric algorithms depends upon the computing resources and how the key management will work. Symmetric algorithms are simpler in construction but require a longer, single key; asymmetric require multiple keys and have a greater demand upon computing resources.

[209] also called public-key systems

From a privacy point of view we are primarily concerned with the following:

- Strength of encryption algorithm

- Symmetric versus asymmetric

- Key management

- Application of encryption

Encryption algorithms come in various strengths based on their internal functioning and based on the key sizes used. The particular choice will depend upon local policy however at the time of writing the AES algorithm[210] which has been standardised by NIST along with a 256-bit key remains as the most favourite of the recommended algorithms[211]. It should be noted that there are questions about nearly all encryption algorithms with regards to whether they contain back doors or have been secretly broken by 'government organisations'. While there is much discussion on this[212] any confirmation or otherwise will probably remain conjecture for a very long time. This particular concern also applied to cryptographic hashing functions too.

If encryption is used then there will be the necessity to use or construct a mechanism for managing and distributing keys. Key management will then form a significant part of any information system[213]. Much of key management outside of the technical implementation will concern key lengths, longevity of keys and key rotation - how long are keys valid for. These are primarily security concerns and we refer the reader to the afore cited publication for more information on this.

The application of encryption for privacy tends toward the security perspective rather than privacy. Encryption of data transport (SSL etc.), datasets and file systems especially when exporting data outside of known systems (or even inside!) and then even more when dealing with cloudified systems is the norm.

Field level encryption of data sets is rarely used but does have its uses especially when data is required to be recovered from the encrypted form, unlike hashing where this is not possible. This however suffers from similar problems to hashing in terms of re-identification and behaving as an identifier, but does find its use in certain access control and content protection situations. Field-level encryption may also require the necessity to utilise multiple keys or encryption schemes within the same data set.

[210] J. Daemen and V. Rijmen. *The Design of Rijndael: AES - The Advanced Encryption Standard.* Information Security and Cryptography. Springer, 2002. ISBN 9783540425809

[211] Twofish, Blowfish, TripleDES are others to name just a few.

[212] https://www.schneier.com/blog/archives/2013/09/the_nsa_is_brea.html

[213] Elaine Barker, William Barker, William Burr, William Polk, and Miles Smid. Recommendation for key management - part 1: General. In *NIST Special Publication 800-57, August 2005, National Institute of Standards and Technology,* 2005

This obviously increases the complexity of processing the data and of managing keys.

Finally the position of the encryption of the data in the data flow between user and storage and processing has an effect on the viability of encryption as a privacy protecting mechanism. For example, if database field-level encryption is used then all the processing stack before the application of encryption is potentially at risk from a data breach.

Dataset Partitioning

A COMMON CASE FOR access to a dataset is seen in figure 101 where two or more clients have access to a single database or datasets. It is common to construct a database as a single entity with many tables corresponding to many use cases from different users. Access control can vary significantly in granularity from records, tables to the whole database. Partitioning of a database can be made according to its internal access control mechanisms, from external points such as might be made in an API, operating system level access control as well as physical partitioning.

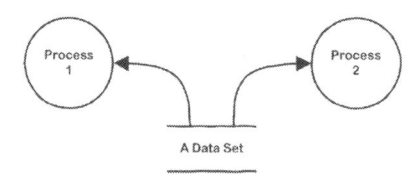

Figure 101: Two Clients, One Database

The main danger of any store of data, be it DMBS, file system or text file, is the amount of data that can be obtained under an access control failure situation. The notion of failure here includes where identifiers or quasi-identifiers are combined external to the database.

Partitioning the storage of a dataset reduces the risk that all the data becomes accessible, but does not necessarily reduce the leakable of information such as identifiers. Performing this does require use of relational theory[214] to properly match partitioned records together between tables or structures when required. This will be true regardless whether a 'traditional' or 'schema-free' data structure is used! Figure 102 shows how we might

[214] C. J. Date. *An Introduction to Database Systems (7th Ed.)*. Addison-Wesley Longman Publishing Co., Inc., Boston, MA, USA, 1999. ISBN 0-201-38590-2

model the partitioning of a data set (in any form).

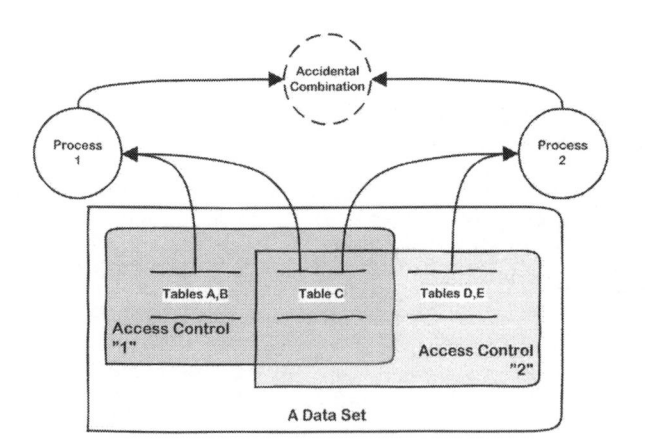

Figure 102: Two Clients, One Partitioned Database

In this model there are two particular features that occur in such systems. The first is that there may exist tables or other structure which share information that can be used to link data sets together. If the data can be combined then this information might be used to restore the linking between the data sets. This might occur in situations where the identifiers (including those structures that act as quasi-identifiers) in one data set are obfuscated by one means and in another data set by other means; then there might exist tables that effectively demonstrate the bijection between these! As we can see in figure 102 the inclusion of a flows to some data breach process should always be included so that a proper risk analysis of this flow be made!

Tokenisation and Randomisation

RATHER THAN HIDING OR obfuscating the original form of the data we can also transform the data such that it contains less information content but remain useful for other processing purposes. For example if we wish to understand from where users are accessing our systems geographically it is generally not necessary to work at the accuracy that co-ordinates provided by GPS attain; for the most part city or country level is sufficient. Similarly for most purposes an accurate date of birth is unnecessary whereas just the year suffices. The category of functions providing this ability are known by the terms of fuzzing, randomisation and tokenisation.

Another common example expressed of a tokenisation function is specified below for mapping the date of birth to an age range:

$$tokenize_{DoB}(DoB, today) := \begin{cases} < 10, & \text{if } 0 \leq years(today - DoB) < 10 \\ 10 - 20, & \text{if } 10 \leq years(today - DoB) < 20 \\ 20 - 25, & \text{if } 20 \leq years(today - DoB) < 25 \\ 25 - 30, & \text{if } 25 \leq years(today - DoB) < 30 \\ 30 - 50, & \text{if } 30 \leq years(today - DoB) < 50 \\ > 50, & \text{if } years(today - DoB) \geq 50 \end{cases}$$

A similar case can be seen with the transformation of a device or object identifier to data which in that context can be considered so generic as not to warrant a specific information type; for example mapping device names to manufacturer:

$$tokenize_{Device}(d) := \begin{cases} \text{"Nokia"}, & \text{if } d \in \{Lumia925, Lumia930, Lumia1020 \ldots\} \\ \text{"Apple"}, & \text{if } d \in \{iPhone4, iPhone5, \ldots\} \\ \text{"Samsung"} & \text{if } d \in \{Galaxy4, \ldots\} \\ \vdots \\ \text{"Unknown"} & \text{else} \end{cases}$$

Other cases can be seen in the processing of financial data such as credit card numbers[215] where storage of a card number and CVC information is if not prohibited then extremely restricted, but the storage of partial information or related tokens permissible.

[215] PCI Security Standards Council Scoping SIG, Tokenization Taskforce. *Information Supplement: PCI DSS Tokenization Guidelines*, August 2011

In the cases above, we reduce the identifiability of the information but increasing the set of unique persons that combination of data refers to, for example, the set of persons born on 26 July 2014 who own Lumia1020 devices is much more identifiable than the set of Nokia device owners in the age range of 10 to 20 years. The basic premise here is that we can no longer use the fields mentioned in the above examples as quasi-identifiers over that data set.

Another technique to protect privacy in a similar manner to tokenisation is to introduce random data or more specifically to perturb the existing data such that inferences about a specific individual can not be made, but preserve the average over the whole set of data.

Randomization of data is performed when accurate values might cause additional problems. For example to reduce the information content of individual date of birth records we might add or subtract a random amount consistently over the data set. While this obviously ruins the individual record's information content it does not change the overall averages and distribution of data. This technique is commonly seen in traffic management systems which record the speeds of individual vehicles but then perturb the data such that the individual vehicle's speed can not be used for, say, enforcement of traffic laws, but the overall average speed of vehicles on that stretch of road is accurate. Of course the distribution properties and size of the random function used need to be controlled such that too small or too large values for either will retain too much individual information or ruin the data respectively.

For example to introduce a degree of uncertainty into the ages of individuals in a data set we might compute the following

$$randomizedAge(DoB, today, \delta) := years(today - DoB) + random_{int}(-\delta \ldots +\delta)$$

Given that the value δ is appropriate and sufficient; in the above case we might perturb the date by ± 3 years. The *mean* age will remain the same given a large enough data set; this is one of the considerations of using this technique.

Furthermore, it must be noted that given enough data then the randomisation values can be inferred. This might occur when working with location data for example where data collected over a period of time might provide information about this. For example, if we collect a user's location at a high-level of accuracy often then we might end up with a series of plots describing a wide area but with the original co-ordinates inferred as the centre of the set of randomized points. Additionally while individual locations or ages or similar might be randomized, tends over time such as the vector of travel will likely be easy to calculate.

κ-Anonymity

WHEN RELEASING A DATASET the process of anonymising that data normally needs to take place, especially if that set is being declassified or rendered in some state where it contains enough information for useful processing but not personally identifiable or personal information. One important technique is that of κ-anonymity which provides both a method by which data is removed and a measure of assessing the degree of uniquely identifiable records in that set[216]. It has found relatively widespread usage in anonymising medical data sets[217,218] for example.

Consider a simple marketing information data set from our social camera application' example; this might contain data as expressed in table16 which describes the amount of uploads a particular has made over a particular time frame.

[216] V. Ciriani, S. Capitani di Vimercati, S. Foresti, and P. Samarati. κ-anonymity. In Ting Yu and Sushil Jajodia, editors, *Secure Data Management in Decentralized Systems*, volume 33 of *Advances in Information Security*, pages 323–353. Springer US, 2007

Email	Name	Date of Birth	Primary Device	1 day	1 week	1 month
a@y.z	Alice	13 June 1966	Lumia1020	4	10	20
b@y.z	Bob	10 July 1856	Lumia930	40	200	600
e@y.z	Eve	26 March 1913	iPhone4	1	2	3
c@y.z	Carol	11 May 1918	iPhone4	3	6	290
d@y.z	Dan	28 March 1928	iPhone3	30	35	39
f@y.z	Frank	28 June 1941	iPhone2	22	140	297
m@y.z	Mabel	17 Oct 1956	Lumia820	75	88	99
o@y.z	Oscar	9 Sept 1941	iPhone7A	11	15	28
s@y.z	Sybil	7 Feb 1941	Lumia999	146	2110	2540
w@y.z	Wendy	7 Nov 1939	Nokia1100	46	784	1120

Table 16: Raw Example Marketing Data Set

We might now wish to release this data set publicly for additional analytics which are outside of the scope of the current marketing department's remit. For example, we might wish that someone makes a correlation between device, age and trend in photo uploads over time. To κ-anonymise a data set it is necessary to reduce the amount of unique records in such a way that the value of the data set is not too compromised and that it becomes *difficult* to match any single record against any unique or identifiable human. A data set where for each record there is a possible choice of 2 uniquely identifiable persons is said to have a κ-anonymity of 2 and so on. This is achieved through a combination of field suppression and tokenisation. Any number of these might be chained together to create a more anonymised data set as shown in figure 103.

[217] Latanya Sweeney. κ-anonymity: A model for protecting privacy. *Int. J. Uncertain. Fuzziness Knowl.-Based Syst.*, 10(5): 557–570, October 2002. ISSN 0218-4885

[218] Khaled El Emam and Fida Kamal K. Dankar. Protecting privacy using κ-anonymity. *Journal of the American Medical Informatics Association : JAMIA*, 15 (5):627–637, 2008. ISSN 1527-974X

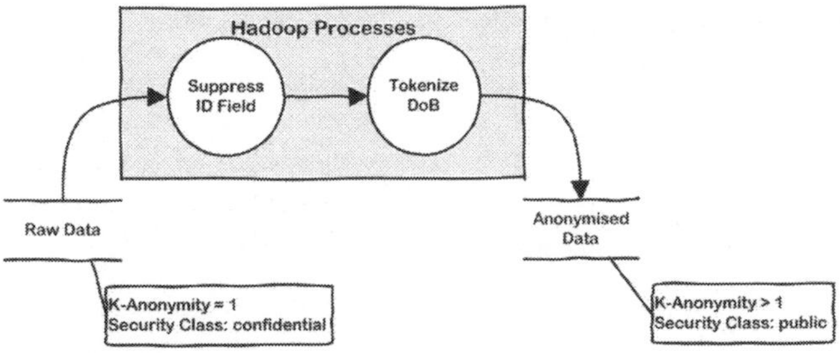

Figure 103: Data Flow for an Example κ-Anonymisation of a Data Set

Field suppression is simple in that we suppress the values in a particular field by replacing those fields with some information-less value or removing those fields from the resultant new data set. For example we might suppress the email and name fields in table 16 to prevent linking back to the original data. Suppression must not be confused with ignoring a field; for example the fields denoting the amounts of uploads might be ignored from the analysis rather than being suppressed. If we further tokenise the date of birth and device fields in the manner described earlier then we might obtain the resultant data set as in table 17.

Email	Name	Date of Birth	Primary Device	1 day	1 week	1 month
*	*	1950-1969	Nokia	4	10	20
*	*	1850-1869	Nokia	40	200	600
*	*	1910-1929	Apple	1	2	3
*	*	1910-1929	Apple	3	6	290
*	*	1910-1929	Apple	30	35	39
*	*	1930-1949	Apple	22	140	297
*	*	1950-1969	Nokia	75	88	99
*	*	1930-1949	Apple	11	15	28
*	*	1930-1949	Nokia	146	2110	2540
*	*	1930-1949	Nokia	46	784	1120

If we ignore the record with the date of birth in the range 1850-1869, the κ-anonymity of table 17 is 2; meaning that for any record in the set there is at least one other record that is identical and therefore indistinguishable from any other. If however we include the one records with the date of birth 1950-1869 then the κ-anonymity is back to one.

Table 17: κ-anonymised Example Marketing Data Set

This latter case actually highlights one of the problems with this mechanism in that it can be extremely difficult to remove unique records, despite them being to all purposes anonymous. Furthermore, as we have here, this record is quite an outlier in the data set which itself increases the changes of reidentification. If the number of such records are low then these could be suppressed or further tokenised[219].

[219] Arik Friedman, Ran Wolff, and Assaf Schuster. Providing κ-anonymity in data mining. *The VLDB Journal*, 17(4):789–804, July 2008. ISSN 1066-8888

Over very large data sets it can become useful to use κ-anonymity in a more statistical sense to calculate the average and standard deviations which can be used to provide a crude metric on the data set.

Finally one can observe in the above set that the upload figures themselves could contribute to reidentification; for example, one particular user has an extremely high number of uploads, while another shows a huge deviation in uploads. Even here it might be necessary to provide tokenisation and even randomisation of values even though these are not taken into account when calculating the κ-anonymity.

Beyond κ-anonymity

κ-ANONYMITY HAS A NUMBER of weaknesses and to address this further tools such as ℓ-diversity[220] and t-closeness[221] are required. One of the major weaknesses is the diversity of data present and an attack on the data known as a homogeneity attack where given enough background knowledge inferences can always be made.

[220] Ashwin Machanavajjhala, Johannes Gehrke, Daniel Kifer, and Muthuramakrishnan Venkitasubramaniam. ℓ-diversity: Privacy beyond κ-anonymity. *2013 IEEE 29th International Conference on Data Engineering (ICDE)*, 0:24, 2006

[221] Ninghui Li and Tiancheng Li. t-closeness: Privacy beyond κ-anonymity and ℓ-diversity. In *In Proc. of IEEE 23rd International Conference on Data Engineering (ICDE'07*, 2007

The technique of ℓ-diversity involves partitioning fields within the data set such that within each grouping there exists a balanced representation. In the example we provided earlier in table 17 we noted due to the outliers the κ-anonymity was compromised, even though it appears that the data overall was fairly anonymous. Actually this data set because of this precise reason would be stated to have poor ℓ-diversity. That is certain ranges of tokenised values have internally a poor representation of values. A refinement of ℓ-diversity is t-closeness which addresses the range of values within some class of data.

We have already introduced the notion of adding noise and random values to the data; the technique of differential privacy[222] formalises this and provides metrics on the effectiveness of introducing that noise. This kind of processing is more sophisticated than presented earlier and has applications in location data

[222] Cynthia Dwork. Differential privacy: A survey of results. In *Theory and Applications of Models of Computation*, volume 4978 of *Lecture Notes in Computer Science*, pages 1–19. Springer Verlag, April 2008

sets where relatively few data points can identify an individual[223] and very large data sets where statistical inferences can be drawn as was the case where the Netflix recommendation engine training set was cross-referenced with external, publicly available information[224].

The major disadvantage of differential privacy at the current time is the complexity of application of the algorithm and general knowledge about the technique.

[223] Yves-Alexandre de Montjoye, César A. Hidalgo, Michel Verleysen, and Vincent D. Blondel. Unique in the Crowd: The privacy bounds of human mobility. *Scientific Reports*, 3, March 2013b

[224] Arvind Narayanan and Vitaly Shmatikov. Robust de-anonymization of large sparse datasets. In *Proceedings of the 2008 IEEE Symposium on Security and Privacy*, SP '08, pages 111–125, Washington, DC, USA, 2008. IEEE Computer Society. ISBN 978-0-7695-3168-7. DOI: 10.1109/SP.2008.33. URL http://dx.doi.org/10.1109/SP.2008.33

Summary

NO ONE TECHNIQUE CAN be employed to ensure anonymity of data and all techniques have their advantages and disadvantages. All data sets are required to be processed through any combination of the techniques presented here and the many variations thereof. Furthermore there are restrictions even on releasing anonymised data set depending upon the environment from which and to which they are released[225].

In all cases the following should be ensured from a technical standpoint at a minimum:

[225] *Anonymisation: Managing Data Protection Risk Code of Practice*. The Information Commissioner's Office (UK), November 2012

- Identifiers are suitably obfuscated

- Content, Characteristic and Demographic data is appropriately removed, obfuscated, tokenised as necessary

- Location and Temporal data are processed to minimise fingerprinting of data

- Key and salt management are appropriate and properly implemented

- Metrics, such as κ-anonymity, ℓ-diversity are calculated and understood

- Data sets are partitioned accordingly with respect to identifiers and quasi-identifiers

Auditing and Inspection

THE AUDITING AND INSPECTION programme is the key component to ensuring that the information systems being developed are both internally compliant and externally with regards to the business. The information gathered during any auditing exercise is not just for the benefit or even persecution of the project being audited but must be used more widely across all projects. It is not in the scope of this section to describe the minutiae detail of an audit but to give a structure from which local auditing procedures can be developed. Specifics can be found by examining quality standards such as CMM[226], SPICE[227], the ISO27000 and ISO29100 series and of course prior experiences[228].

One of the best examples of the benefits of auditing comes if the auditing team have the ability to see horizontally across an organisation. This given additional insights into the whole workings of an organisations and provides opportunities, if they are willing to be accepted, to facilitate common data semantics, deduplication and sharing of information between systems and developments as well as facilitating communication and integration across disciplines such as security, performance and so on.

As auditing carries with some onerous connotations it must be made clear that the point of an audit is *not* to prevent or block the development of a system but to proactively, or interactively, ensure compliance, find solutions to (in our case) privacy issues and assist the development team in working forward towards a complete and successful product.

[226] CMMI Product Team. CMMI for systems engineering, software engineering, integrated. product and process development, and supplier sourcing. cmu/sei-2002-tr-011. Technical report, Software Engineering Institute, Carnegie Mellon University., Pittsburgh, Pennsylvania, 2002

[227] Fabio Bella, Klaus Hörmann, and Bhaskar Vanamali. *From CMMI to SPICE - Experiences on How to Survive a SPICE Assessment Having Already Implemented CMMI*, volume Product-Focused Software Process Improvement of *Lecture Notes in Computer Science*, pages 133–142. 2009

[228] Miguel A. Martínez, Joaquín Lasheras, Eduardo Fernández-Medina, José Ambrosio Toval Álvarez, and Mario Piattini. A personal data audit method through requirements engineering. *Computer Standards & Interfaces*, 32(4):166–178, 2010

The Audit Process

FOR ANY PROJECT THERE is a multiple, interleaving of individual processes with various effects and interactions upon each other. The auditing process is just another parallel suite of tasks that interacts with the software development. Ultimately it is not whether one process stops to allow the other to run or whether they run in parallel but how the results of both are used to better the overall quality[229] of the system being constructed[230]. One possibility of organising the work is shown in figure 104 which involves continuous assistance from privacy experts with a scheduled audit taking place as development approaches completion.

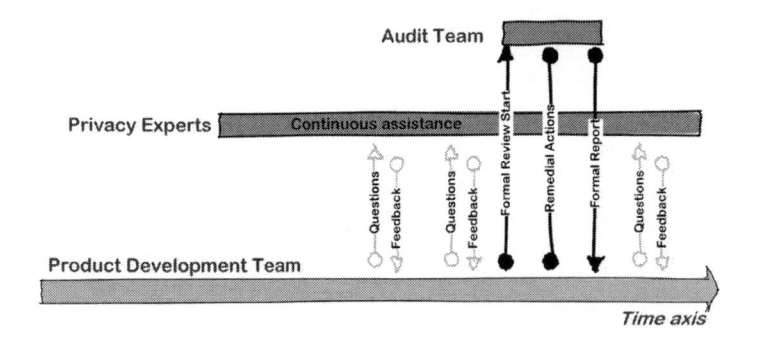

[229] R.M. Pirsig. *Zen and the Art of Motorcycle Maintenance: An Inquiry Into Values.* Bantam Books: Nonfiction. Vintage, 1974. ISBN 9780099786405

[230] J. Guaspari. *I Know It When I See It.* AMACOM BOOKS, 2004. ISBN 9780814473931

Figure 104: One Method of Organising Audits in the Software Development Process

When planning or running an audit it is always necessary to decide who is responsible for the audit and how much inspection is going to be performed. Audits can be run by the development team responsible for the construction of the system as a self-audit, though this must be balanced against possible self-interest and over-familiarity with the system. Similarly an auditing team independent of the development team need not be a faceless group of bureaucrats but can and should integrate themselves within the development team.

When it comes to how much of an inspection or audit then we must take into consideration the current state of the development: is it at the concepting stage versus deployment? An audit at the concepting stage can not be used as the criteria to approve a system but rather act more as a basis for requirements unless the system is absolutely set in stone regarding its requirements and development procedures. An audit at the end of the development process may actually report after development has been completed and therefore its recommendations only applied to a later version of the system, leaving the current version potentially in a non-compliant state. The development processes itself must be understood and the audit organised within the context of this. A single, large audit will probably not work well in an agile environment and similarly lots of small audits not in a waterfall process.

Contents of an Audit

WHILE THE CONTENTS AND procedures employed might vary greatly, a common base from which to pick and choose the required information is always necessary. The following areas are proposed as a *basis* for constructing the audit contents:

- Data Modelling
    - Data Flow Modelling and Aspects
        * Basic generic models and necessary use cases
        * Logical and physical architectural partitioning
        * Data classification: security, information type, provenance etc.
        * Data subject, Controller and Processor identification
        * Jurisdiction
    - API Descriptions
- Legal
    - Policy Conformance
    - Agreements: Notice, Consent and Control Points
    - Additional Necessary Compliances, e.g.: PCI-DSS, COPPA etc.
- User Interface and Experience
- Procedural Controls and Human Factors

These would be coupled together with three broad categories of report[231]:

- Audit Scope

[231] While we note that there are three broad reports, this is not necessarily an indication on how the documentation should be written but rather a way of partitioning the various reports in some logical manner

- Audit Work

- Audit Results

The Work of an Audit

DEPENDING UPON CONTEXT ADDITIONAL or even a subset of the above may be employed. Furthermore, the above may be part of a larger suite of integrated audits covering areas such as security, performance etc., or, be themselves split over other audits. In these cases actually including these, even though they are not explicitly performed, provides a cross-check and thus an integration point between audits. As we shall see later, it is often good practice to cross-reference a privacy audit with any existing, on-going or planned security audit(s).

The core of any audit will derive its questioning and investigation from the state of the data flow models and individual use cases of the system. A well organised development team should be able to present these in a formal form along with crossreferences to program code if necessary. For critical components a detailed code review should be performed in addition to any static checking of code and APIs that has already been made.

The data modelling activity will require that each of the various layers of model be presented, especially those involving controller and processor partitions. A data classification will reveal if personal data possibly being used and the levels of security and privacy protection being applied to that. The major issue seen in audits is the denial that personal data is being used with an oft excuse involving hashing and anonymisation. An audit will need to consider and reveal traffic data as well as interesting cross-referencing processes, not to mention how the storage and been distributed and partitioned.

Legal aspects of the system under audit mainly concern which consents are required to process data in the manner required. This then involves understanding any privacy policies, terms and condition and any application or service specific extensions and how the user provides their consent. It is also common to see wider legal aspects[232] such as Sarbanes-Oxley[233], PCI-DSS[234], various trade compliances etc. in some systems,

[232] Constantine Gikas. A general comparison of FISMA, HIPAA, ISO27000 and PCI-DSS standards. *Information Security Journal: A Global Perspective*, 19(3):132–141, 2010

[233] United States Code. Sarbanes-Oxley Act of 2002, PL 107-204, 116 Stat 745. Codified in Sections 11, 15, 18, 28, and 29 USC, July 2002

[234] *Payment Card Industry (PCI) Data Security Standard: Requirements and Security Assessment Procedures.* PCI Security Standards Council, version 3.0 edition, November 2013

especially those utilising financial data as might have been discovered through the data modelling exercise.

Given that there are generally two kinds of systems, those with a user-interface and those without, we could expect that in the latter case we do not deal with notice and consent. This is true, except that in the latter case, which are the 'back-end' systems it will always be required to derive what an 'ideal' notice and consent would be for using that system. This gives the requirements to anyone utilising that system to what policies, notices, consents etc. should be put in place before use[235]. Obviously in the former case we are required to investigate the actual user-interface and experience itself.

User interface and user experience are exceptionally important in any consumer facing system and are the site of many privacy failures, especially when presenting suitable options, opt-outs, opt-ins and consent to any data collection and processing activities. When working with the user-*interface* we are required to understand the specific screens, what information is displayed, how it is displayed, input validations in the interface etc. Here it is especially useful to list the screens and the particular orders in which they can be accessed.

When dealing with user-*experience* we are more concerned with how everything is presented to the user from even the initial purchase and browsing via an app store, or discovery through some web interface for example, to how screens are presented and whether the content is being presented in a manner that allows the user to effectively see the privacy and data collection choices. At minimum here the auditors need to ensure that the notices and consents and related opt-in/out controls are effectively presented at the correct times in the application lifecycle. It is also necessary at this point to cross-check the user-interface with the actual functionality and other data collection processes at that point.

Finally we deal with procedural controls and human factors which specifically refers to the procedures employed in the running and management of the system under audit. Often overlooked but the very real human problems of access control and data handling need to be investigated. One of the major points of data breach in any system is accidental loss of data because of how the system and business processes are administered.

[235] Aaron K. Massey, Paul N. Otto, Lauren J. Hayward, and Annie I. Anton. Evaluating existing security and privacy requirements for legal compliance. *Requirements Engineering*, 15(1):119–137, 2010. ISSN 0947-3602

Reporting

WE NOTED THAT THERE are three broad reports, one to scope and initiate the audit, one documenting the work and the final report. Of these the first two would remain internal to the audit and only the latter would be presented to the owners of the system being audited.

Scoping is critical to any successful audit; if the boundary of work is not specified early then either the audit will miss areas of concern or that the audit will follow a path taking it outside of the immediately system under audit. The scope of any audit does not necessarily even necessarily conform to the system boundaries of the system being audited. For example it may be the case that only certain components and certain interactions are necessary to audit at this point in time.

There are dangers here in that specifying too small an audit scope may not reveal the more interesting features of a system from a privacy perspective. In this respect we advocate that for any given scope, an audit must deliberately step outside of that defined scope for completeness. This scoping report must contain enough information that any auditor can obtain a high-level view of the system under audit, the personnel responsible for each part of the system (i.e.: architects, business owners), priorities and timescales. Furthermore any information pertaining to previous audits including security, performance, business continuity etc. must be summarised.

It is useful in the scoping report to include ideas of the primary risks of the system and an evaluation of these. This can be made as formal as necessary, for example, in a system that deals with very little personal data then an information risk assessment be made, while in one dealing with health or financial information then an accordingly detailed risk analysis be made. Tools such as FMEA described later can be used here.

Once the scoping report is complete or complete enough such that work can start in earnest then everything made must be documented as work of the audit. The form of this will largely depend upon the audit team and local procedures for documentation. This must be sufficiently detailed such that it is possible to return to this documentation at any point a be able to trace the work of the audit team, the information received from the owners of the system under audit and all recommendations and decisions made. It is in this report that the models of the system, classifications and work on the legal, procedural and user-interface aspects will be recorded.

Note that many of the aspects of the scoping report will be formalised and worked on in detail in the audit. For example, if a quick risk assessment was made in the scoping report then this should be followed up with a more detailed, formal risk assessment once the work of the audit team has started in earnest.

The final report of any audit is a formal document to the owners of the system under audit clearly stating what is required of the system to pass inspection. It is rare that systems pass an audit without any recommendations, though care must be made that recommendations aren't made for the sake of making recommendations. An example structure for such a report can be seen below:

Summary Section describing the nature of the audit and including:

- Name of the System Audited
- The System Owner
- List of reviewers and auditors
- Dates of the audit
- Date of final report
- Result of the audit

Findings providing a textual summary of the system and the audit results

Recommendations providing a formal list of recommendations each containing the following information:

- An identifier for the recommendation (e.g.: numeric identifier or link to a bug or requirements system identifier)
- Description of the work necessary
- Priority of the work
- Timescale and/or deadline for completion of the work
- Name of person responsible (from the system development team, not an auditor!)

Follow-up procedures may be necessary depending upon the overall result which may range from a success to 'success with recommendations' to outright failing the audit. How the follow-up is made is largely outside the scope of the audit, though local procedures might dictate that once all high priority recommendations are fulfilled then this would constitute completion of the follow-up.

Checklists for Auditing Activities

THE CHECKLIST[236] IS A well known tool for organising work and is exemplified by the archetypal aviation checklists. The history[237] of the checklist and its use in other areas of work is well known, for example, in medical situations the checklist is an invaluable tool[238]. The checklist is the list of things that *should* have been completed or ascertained at a particular point in time.

The checklist is *not* a tool for measuring the progress of any process, nor is it a description of any process, but rather a set of, possibly broad, criteria that should have been fulfilled at particular milestones in a process. If the term 'checklist' is problematical or has too many process connotations then the term **aide-mémoire** can be used as a synonym.

Whether a point in a checklist is completed when the checklist is run or completed is *not* necessarily indicative of whether the process should continue or not, but rather a note that *something* is probably amiss. For example, in the checklist in figure105 the simple question of asking whether a security check has been made or not can provide an alert to the reviewer of the existence or not of necessary documentation, or the need to bring in additional experts etc.; rather than a stop to the process.

We use a number of checklists for different purposes within the auditing and inspection work. These have been developed from local practice, experience and in presentation based upon the WHO Surgical Safety Checklist[239,240]. The reasoning here is that the format here is simple and open to local and agile practices; whereas prior experience with aviation style checklists lead to a situation of 'tick boxes mentality'. Note that all checklists are

[236] Atul Gawande. *The Checklist Manifesto*. Profile Books, 2011

[237] P.S.Meilinger. When the fortress went down. *Air Force Magazine*, pages 78–82, 2004

[238] Peter Pronovost, Dale Needham, Sean Berenholtz, David Sinopoli, Haitao Chu, Sara Cosgrove, Bryan Sexton, Robert Hyzy, Robert Welsh, Gary Roth, Joseph Bander, John Kepros, and Christine Goeschel. An Intervention to Decrease Catheter-Related Bloodstream Infections in the ICU. *New England Journal of Medicine*, 355(26):2725–2732, 2006

[239] *Implementation manual WHO Surgical Safety Checklist*. World Health Organization, 2008. WHO/IER/PSP/2008.05

[240] http://www.who.int/patientsafety/safesurgery/ss_checklist/en/index.html

designed to be customised as local conditions require.

Auditing Team Checklist

FOLLOWING ON FROM THE contents of a privacy audit described earlier, we present in figure 105 a checklist to assist in assessing the status of each stage of the privacy review.

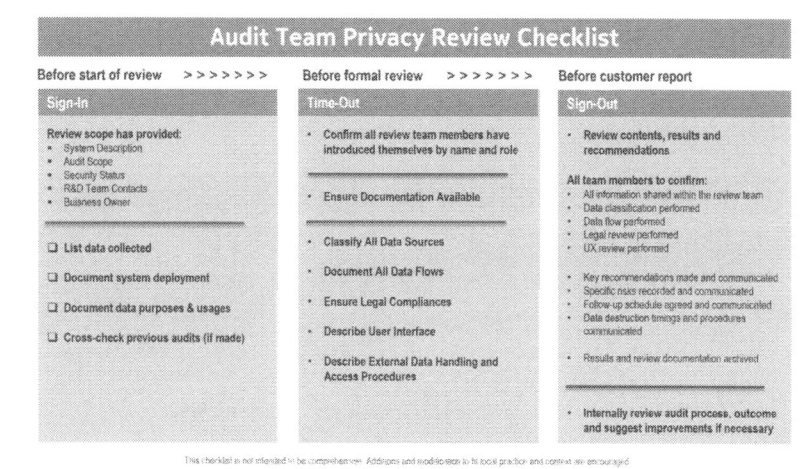

Figure 105: Audit Team Checklist

This particular checklist is divided into three sections (cf: WHO Surgical Safety Checklist) corresponding to the initiation or scope, work of the audit and final reporting. Each section is denoted as follows:

Sign-In is where the audit team becomes aware of the task at hand and understands the overall nature of the system being audited. This checklist is typically only run once and it is likely that not every point here will be completed sufficiently.

Time-Out actually refers to taking a pause. This particular checklist may be repeated numerous times as necessary or wanted during the work of the audit. It is used to ascertain which parts of the audit have been covered, but does not measure the degree of completeness or quality of the audit work.

Sign-Out is the point where the audit work is finished and the term sign-out can refer to the act of the auditor signing the final report before release. This checklist may be run numerous times as the wrapping up and writing of the final report takes place.

A point to note, as described in the sign-in description above, is that it is likely that not every point will be completed sufficiently. This does not indicate a failure in the process or failure to complete work but rather as pointers to areas of concern. For example, if the audit scope is not completed then this means more care must be taken when starting the audit work itself. Similarly if the more technical aspects such as the overviews of data collection, deployment and data usage are not sufficiently completed then this is a similar risk indicator. The risks here being that either the information is unknown, the wrong people are involved or that the system is in a too incomplete state for an audit.

Development Team Pre-Review Checklist

IT IS USEFUL TO forewarn development teams about audits and again a checklist can help in that team better preparing for said audit. Figure 106 shows an example pre-review checklist than can be used for this.

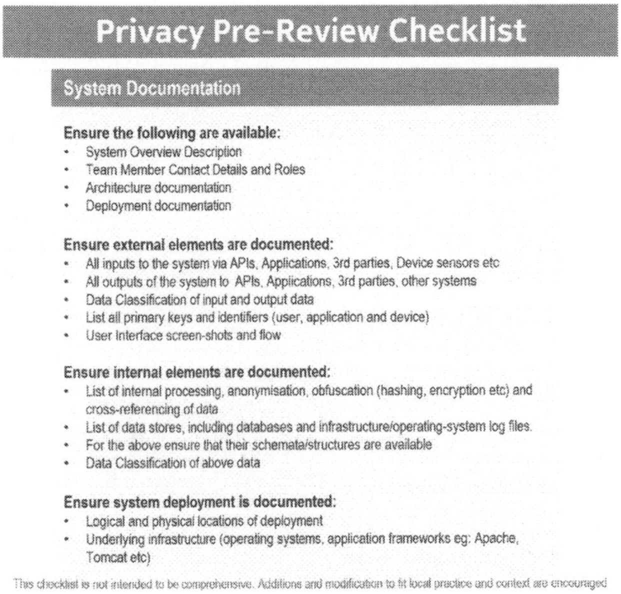

Figure 106: Development Team Pre-Review Checklist

Privacy Pre-Review Checklist

System Documentation

Ensure the following are available:
- System Overview Description
- Team Member Contact Details and Roles
- Architecture documentation
- Deployment documentation

Ensure external elements are documented:
- All inputs to the system via APIs, Applications, 3rd parties, Device sensors etc
- All outputs of the system to APIs, Applications, 3rd parties, other systems
- Data Classification of input and output data
- List all primary keys and identifiers (user, application and device)
- User Interface screen-shots and flow

Ensure internal elements are documented:
- List of internal processing, anonymisation, obfuscation (hashing, encryption etc) and cross-referencing of data
- List of data stores, including databases and infrastructure/operating-system log files.
- For the above ensure that their schemata/structures are available
- Data Classification of above data

Ensure system deployment is documented:
- Logical and physical locations of deployment
- Underlying infrastructure (operating systems, application frameworks eg: Apache, Tomcat etc)

This checklist is not intended to be comprehensive. Additions and modification to fit local practice and context are encouraged.

The main points of this checklist are as follows:

- Ensure that all documentation is available and the correct people to answer both business and technical questions are made known to the audit team and are aware that an audit will be taking place.

- Ensure that the external interfaces to the system are documented.

- Ensure that specific internal workings are documented. This is especially true of the data stores and their data schemata and any processing such as anonymisation or cross-referencing of data. Note that here is the first reference to data classification; this is made so that development teams become more aware of the necessity to properly document, classify and model their data and its flows.

- Ensure that details on the system deployment are made. This is especially true with the move towards cloud based solutions where the actual location, both in geographical and physical terms, may induce additional analysis, for example as might be seen with international data transfers etc.

The emphasis on documentation is well-founded in that many systems rely upon their code to act as documentation or the internal knowledge of the engineering who built the system[241,242]. In both cases this means that information will be lost, especially if personnel move jobs, and if information is lost then that section of the system can not be audited properly for any necessary compliances.

[241] Eric Allman. Managing technical debt. *Communications of the ACM*, 55(5):50–55, 2012

[242] Philippe Kruchten, Robert L. Nord, Ipek Ozkaya, and Joost Visser. Technical debt in software development: from metaphor to theory report on the third international workshop on managing technical debt. *ACM SIGSOFT Software Engineering Notes*, 37(5):36–38, 2012

Development Team Post-Review Checklist

THE DEVELOPMENT TEAM POST-REVIEW checklist shown in figure 107 can be used by the development teams in conjunction with working through an audit's final report to guide the team through the requirements as presented earlier.

This checklist is in two parts:

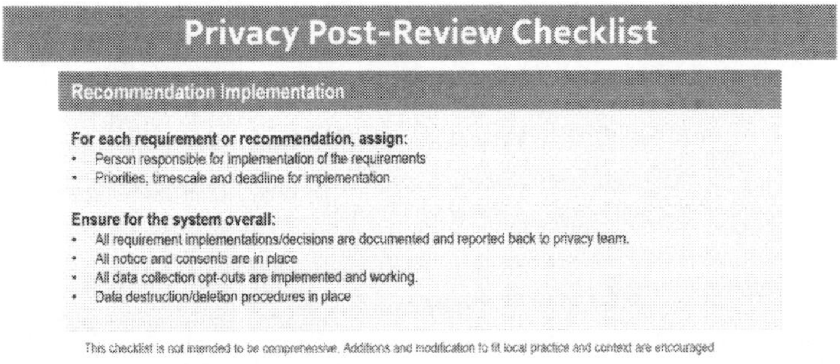

Privacy Post-Review Checklist

Recommendation Implementation

For each requirement or recommendation, assign:
- Person responsible for implementation of the requirements
- Priorities, timescale and deadline for implementation

Ensure for the system overall:
- All requirement implementations/decisions are documented and reported back to privacy team.
- All notice and consents are in place
- All data collection opt-outs are implemented and working.
- Data destruction/deletion procedures in place

This checklist is not intended to be comprehensive. Additions and modification to fit local practice and context are encouraged

Figure 107: Development Team Post-Review Checklist

For the requirements this lists the set of aspects that must be decided upon by the development team, ie: the priorities, persons responsible etc. This might be in addition to or a modification of what is already specified in the requirements by the audit team, for example, if the priorities of the development team are different to that of the audit team.

For the system as a whole this is a set of reminders for the development team on specific points.

Especially in the first case, but obviously involving the second, if there are point of contention between the development team and the audit team, for example in the case of priorities and deadlines, then these must be decided by discussion between the groups.

Development Team Checklist

AS WELL AS THE use in auditing and audit preparation and follow-up, a development team can also be provided with a checklist that they can apply independently of any audit. Such a checklist can be divided as before into sections to be made at project start, relevant milestones and at release readiness stages. An example of this checklist is provided in figurer 108.

Again it must be emphasised that such a checklist is not a measure of progress or a declaration of any process but rather a set of criteria that should be ascertained at particular places in the development flow.

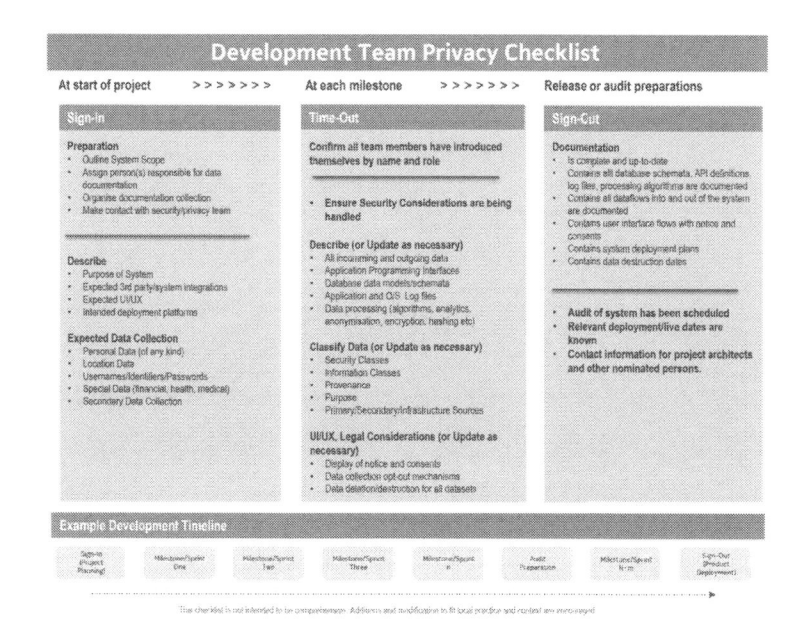

Figure 108: Development Team Checklist

Metrics for Audits

AUDITS AND THEIR RESULTS are an excellent source of metrics from both the management and engineering perspectives. We obviously obtain information about the overall state of the systems under development and also of the audit process itself. For any audit it is good practice to gather metrics detailing the amount of time an audit takes and the level of risk estimated or calculated in the system. Plotting time against risk establishes the relationship between risk and time - which is not necessarily linear, viz. figure 109 - and can be later user to estimate the duration of future audits and therefore their optimal timing with regards to when an audit should take place.

The inverse relationship can also be calculated, that is risk from audit duration. If this figure does not match the expected risk of a system from a privacy impact assessment then this suggests a possible problem in the understanding of risk inherent in the system being audited or usually potential flaws in the emerging specification of the system.

The recording of the start and end times is practically a given in all cases; measuring the effort being placed in terms of number

Figure 109: Audit Complexity Metric

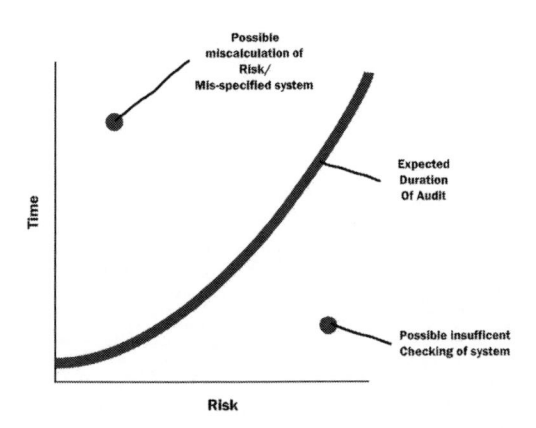

of persons involved, the amounts of emails and other communications shared and even some kind of indication of the difficulties encountered is invaluable in understanding some very deep aspects of company, management and engineering culture.

All of these management metrics can be obtained from any suitable documentation system which should record the start and end times, updates and other meta-data as required.

A further interesting set of management metrics can be collected after the audit has been completed. The amount of recommendations to the development team and the time to implement those recommendations can be used to ascertain the degree to which audit results are being taken into consideration and the importance placed upon this. If few recommendations are being acted upon and/or the time is excessive then this suggests that there are competence, managerial and organisational problems with the development team itself. One possibility that should always be considered is that such results might also point to problems with the quality of the audit and recommendations.

From an engineering perspective there are a number of metrics than can be derived from the data flow model and annotations contained therein. Such metrics as cyclomatic complexity[243] or data flow complexity[244] can be plotted against estimated risk to establish again the relationship between these. Suitable coefficients to the complexity metrics of the diagrams must be chosen to ensure that detailed diagrams do not skew the results versus complex diagrams. The basic maxim is that complex and numerous data-flows, many interacting components or a wide

[243] Thomas J. McCabe and Charles W. Butler. Design complexity measurement and testing. *Communications of the ACM*, 32(12):1415–1425, December 1989

[244] Kuo-Chung Tai. A program complexity metric based on data flow information in control graphs. In *Proceedings of the 7th International Conference on Software Engineering*, pages 239–248. IEEE Press, 1984

variety of data then risk substantially increases.

Summary

ALONG WITH COMPREHENSIVE AND relevant requirements, the audit and inspection practices are critical to the overall compliance of any software system being constructed. Care must be taken that the auditing processes do not exist to block development of any system but rather to ensure systems *are* properly built. While there do exist circumstances where the auditing process will have to block development, these should be taken as points more of reflection in the architecture and possibly routes to innovation in the design and implementation of the system.

Developing a Privacy Programme

To ENABLE SUCCESSFUL INTRODUCTION of privacy into our engineering processes we must construct the structure which allows all of this to be bound together. A basis for this structure which we term an information privacy programme is made by drawing on techniques from systems theory[245,246] and from other disciplines such as medical and aviation[247] in particular. There are many ways of structuring the activities and responsibilities of such a programme and here we propose a structure to an information privacy programme as being in two parts: the activities and programme elements, and the knowledge base as shown in figure 110.

[245] L. Von Bertalanffy. *General System Theory: Foundations, Development, Applications*. The international library of systems theory and philosophy. Braziller, 2003

[246] Peter Checkland and Sue Holwell. *Information, Systems and Information Systems: Making Sense of the Field*. John Wiley & Sons, Inc., 1998

[247] R Wood. *Aviation Safety Programs*. Jeppsen, 3rd edition edition, 2003

Figure 110: Information Privacy Programme Structure

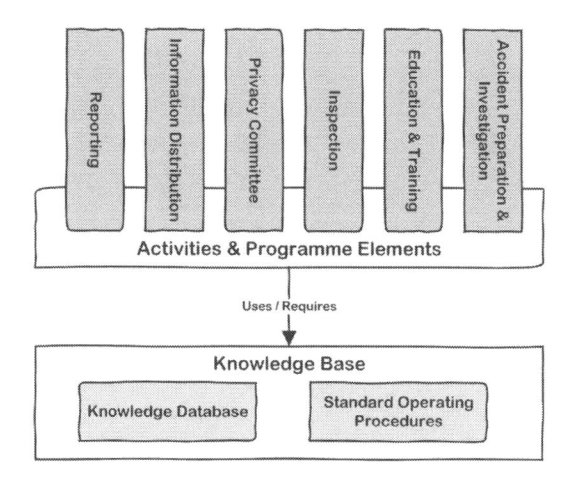

The activities and programme elements are the 'visible' aspects of the programme when viewed by an outsider. It is via these parts that the whole programme is actually run and organised. While each of the activities may interact with the others - this is a necessity - they are each required to develop the knowledge based and standard operating procedures as a common reference and good practice for all. The list of activities is of course subject to revision and extension as local needs dictate. Along with the knowledge base, these activities are discussed in the following sections.

The knowledge data consists of all 'static' knowledge and information such that it can be used as an encyclopaedic reference to theoretically any privacy question. The standard operating procedures (SOP's)[248] refer to how activities such as auditing, incident handling, escalation etc. are processed and handled such that each and every activity is properly completed and with a suitable level of discipline.

[248] T. Kern. *Flight Discipline*. McGraw-Hill Education, 1998. ISBN 9780071503204

The work of the inspection programme will not be discussed in this chapter in detail and leave this to the auditing and inspection chapter. This however does cover many aspects of understanding how privacy is being implemented in the systems being used and constructed in the business environment. This may be achieved through multiple, simultaneous means such as auditing, mentoring, coaching and consultancy. It needs to operate in both proactive and reactive mode as the business and software development requires. This area constitutes the bulk of the work of the information privacy programme and will require deep involvement in the software engineering processes and skill-set to properly succeed.

The rest of the activities and programme elements will be discussed in the following sections.

The Reporting System

THIS IS A MECHANISM by which people both inside and outside the organisation can bring to attention issues, problems, notification of data breaches and other privacy related queries such as authority requests to attention. It may not necessarily exist nor be implemented as an integrated system with a common front-end, but as a number of individual *channels* that together to effectively provide a single point of collection of such issues. It is therefore also the clearing house for any queries to the programme and its activities *and* acts as front-end to any kind of issue and/or ticket management system.

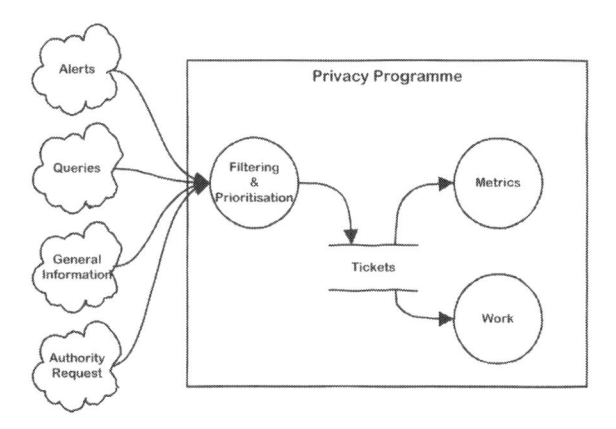

Figure 111: Dataflow in a Reporting System

Let us then examine four typical kinds of inputs to the system and the kind of data that needs to be recorded:

- Alerts

- Queries

- General Information

- Authority Request

Alerts are specific notifications of a privacy problem such as notification of a data breach, a 'whistleblowing' activity, etc. These are privacy's equivalent of the kinds of emergency alerts that one might find in security. Alerts can be generated automatically if such tooling exists as in the case with intrusion detection systems employed in securing inbound and outbound data through a firewall. Such alerts needs to be tackled at a high-level of priority.

The bulk of the information fed into any reporting system is going to be a general query nature such as requests for assistance from development teams. Anything collected under this categorisation must be examined to ascertain whether this is a simple one-off query or the start of something more major such as the request for an audit or a system decommissioning. Via this route one can also integrate notifications from outside processes such as those that might be used by the development teams, for example, it can be useful to record via this route notification of a project start for example. Typically queries via this route tend to be of a medium priority.

General information constitutes all those low priority notifications such as externally published data such as communications from authorities regarding changes in legislations or a particular news item. This actually does turn out to be quite a fruitful route for discovering issues and new ideas as well as being the route by which new legislation is brought to the programme. If opened up to a wider audience it encourages more general participation from outside the information privacy programme members.

The final category are those which require particular handling and this mainly pertain to requests from authorities for data access. While one could argue that this might be a sub class of a query[249], the nature of such a request as this normally demands very sensitive handling involving a number of parties including significant legal support.

[249] and it might be depending upon your local procedures and taxonomy for these things

Any reporting mechanism should allow anonymous contributions and in this respect could be compared to the aviation related programmes CHIRP and CHIRP-MEMS[250]. Reporting systems of this nature can invite many irrelevant comments of varying nature so any use of the reports made must be filtered. If anonymity can be achieved then this can become quite an effective tool in understanding much of an organisations culture and many underlying development problems, particular those related to project management.

[250] CHIRP and CHIRP-MEM are confidential reporting systems for aviation and maritime professionals to report safety issues, concerns, near accidents and the like

As a number of related reports can be received for one overall problem, we must be careful in how we construct the reporting metrics and not rely on the number of reports received a proof that privacy problems exist. Indeed receiving a number of reports early in the development of the privacy programme is normal with an expected decrease in numbers but with an associated increase in quality of the reports as the programme and knowledge of privacy in the organisation increases.

For each request it will be necessary to record what kind of request, the priority of that request - possibly derived from the type of request, sufficient timestamping and the source if not anonymous. This is the usual minimum for many ticketing systems and audit trails. As work progresses on that ticket then suitable procedures must be in place to handle updating of the tickets, merging, decomposition, escalation and closing. An example ticket flow is presented in figure 112.

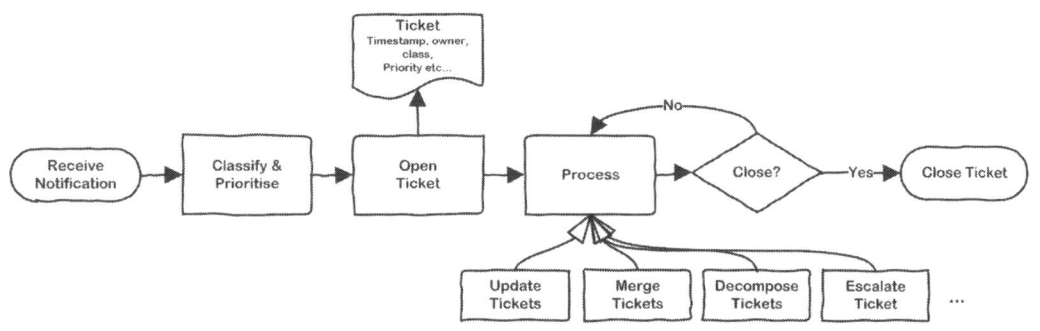

Figure 112: Reporting System Ticket Process

Particular care must be taken to **sufficiently and unambiguously define the closing criteria** of a ticket. Reopening a ticket is problematical and especially so when in the context of management and quality standards. We recommend that reopening of a ticket actually means creating a new ticket with reference back to the old to explain the situation. Reopening a ticket can indicate some deep seated problems in the work of the information privacy programme and/or the overall management of the organisation, and therefore in all cases should be further investigated to understand why a ticket was reopened. In some cases it might even be prudent to consider a reopening of a ticket within the accident preparation and investigation activity.

Such a reporting system provides a very clear look at the current workload, the types of queries being request of the information privacy programme and the length of time it takes to resolve an issue. With suitable subclassification we can break down tickets, especially things of a query and alert nature, to gain quite detailed insights and metrics on how the organisation as a whole is working. The reporting system therefore should be used to drive much of the work of the information privacy programme.

The Information Distribution System

THIS IS A MECHANISM by which privacy related topics can be communicated to interested parties outside of the information privacy programme. Such information might be of the "interest" variety, e.g.: notification of new laws or relevant news articles, to the critical such as a notification of an information breach or threat which must be acted upon by all receiving parties.

Effectively communicating privacy issues to an organisation relies upon that communication being directly targeted to the audience that should consume that information. Generic privacy advice is fine but too much should be avoided as this tends to get ignored by more technical or knowledgeable personnel. All information should be practical in nature to the audience and this is especially the case when working with very technical personnel in that they do require relevant and implementable answers to the problems they face during development.

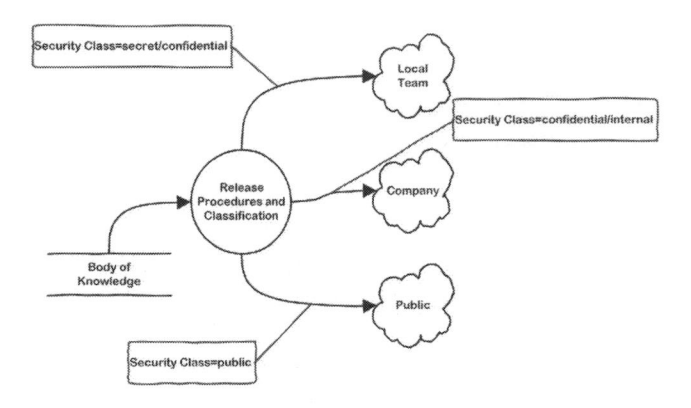

Figure 113: Dataflow in an Information Distribution System

In effect we are communicating our body of knowledge about privacy to both internal and external audiences. Most organisations have communications departments dedicated to handling external communications who will need to liaise with the privacy programme; though the only times this seems to happen is when a data breach unfortunately occurs. When preparing any communication it will be necessary to ensure suitable authorisation procedures are in place whether internal or external in nature.

If something bad such as a data breach does take place then it is the information distribution system that will be placed under great demand as different parts of the organisation require information. Testing this with a well-defined procedure of work is essential and should be made part of any disaster recovery or business continuity programme.

The Privacy Committee

THIS IS THE ONE are fraught with political difficulties, but a small group from a *cross-section of technical and non-technical roles* within the company. This is where many programmes fail because of overloading this committee with management or non-technical staff. Most privacy professionals work on a continuum from legal to engineering and it is necessary to respect a good balance of skills as depicted in figure 114 without too many skills gaps and too wide semantic gaps such as those that exist between lawyers and software engineers. Such classifications as presented earlier such as the information types, purpose, usage, identity etc., significantly help in this semantic gap by fixing the terminology and enabling communication and translation between the disciplines.

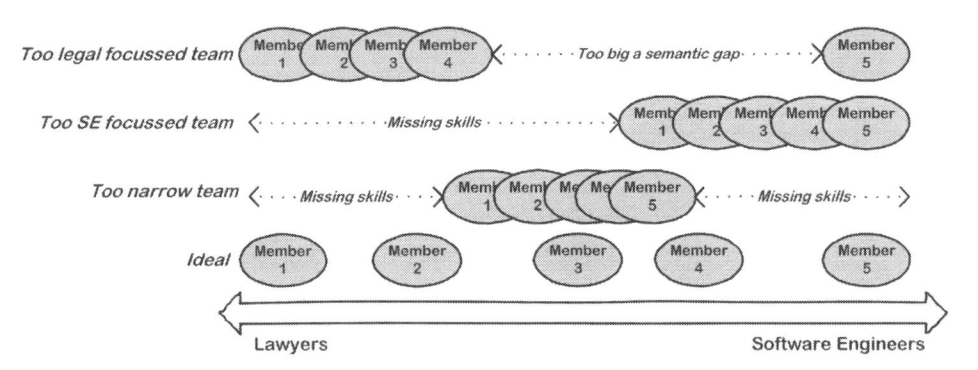

Figure 114: Privacy Committee Skills Continuum

[251] sometimes called a 'leadership team' - the actual title is relatively immaterial

The privacy committee[251] has the responsibility to act and set the overall policy of the business and the work of the information privacy programme, that is to set the bounds, methods of operation and handle any escalations which may arise. To management outside of the privacy programme they can act as a first point of call and furthermore in this respect then act as the official source of metrics and strategy for the programme overall.

Their duties will include their own self-assessment and therefore act to improve the ways of working of the information privacy programme as a whole. The committee must also act to bring on board both internal and external expertise such as that from specific engineering disciplines, research and design, legal etc. as necessary and in a timely manner. The committee should not see itself as infallible nor as setters of dogma; this latter point must be avoided at all costs else the committee and whole programme will become mired in politics and not address the real work at hand.

The chair of such a group should be **both** legally and technically competent and have a good understanding of the business and the risks that the business wishes to take with respect to privacy and information handling. The size of the team can vary but smaller is more manageable and agile - in most cases 5 to 7 persons is ideal. The size however should reflect the number of major divisions within a company.

The authority by which any committee operates is grounded in its relationship to supporting executive management and the business. It will be found that the information privacy programme cannot preside over the information governance, good practice and safety of the business if it can not allow the business to progress and develop.

Education and Training

EDUCATION AND TRAINING IS always critical but often badly done (if at all). Developing relevant training for the external parties is critical to long-term success and accident avoidance. Most if not all privacy programmes tend to concentrate only on high-level awareness training which although has a wide audience it has relatively very little impact in that the content tends to be skewed towards more compliance and legal handling of data rather than the deeper technical issues. Another reason awareness training is often ignored is that it contains very little information on how to implement the ideas being conveyed.

Again we have the reactive versus proactive argument here in that we have to decide whether the training is mandated or optional and whether it is instigated by the information privacy programme or requested upon demand. Both have their advantages and disadvantages such as optional training is usually more effective but rarely taken because of time demands, while mandated training is often considered a chore.

One of the main difficulties of any education and training programme are the metrics generated through the amount of trainings taking place. For example, mandated high-level awareness training will have a very high take-up, often approaching 100%, but very little impact, whereas focused training to very select audience will have a major impact but be limited due to its small audience. There are a number of ways to effectively deal with this: one is to force people to take exams and gain qualifications - this can be timely and costly and the provider of the certification must be chosen carefully. Another is to tie the taking of a course with material benefits such as bonuses and personal responsibility etc.

One argument that might come up is that an employee who has taken training actively disregards the message in that training during his or her work is then in breach of company policy with all that might entail. However an employee doing the same work without the training can always use the fact that they have not taken the training as an excuse. We can offer no overall good advice here other than to base the decision on how to handle these situations on local company culture.

Training should be integrated with any other providers of training across the company. For example, if training is provided in, say, web development then this can act as a link to any privacy training. Such a situation might occur when training about the effects of, say, SQL injection, we could both integrate the security and privacy concerns thus making the latter more relevant whilst bolstering the former. Similar things can be made with skills such as database design, developing web forms linked with aspects of data minimisation and so on. All this helps to put what is often too stand-alone training on a much firmer and more contextually relevant basis.

Training should not just be focussed on the development teams but also directed to the privacy committee and personnel working in this area. This can be coupled with the privacy committee's own self-assessment as required earlier or as a stand-alone module in its own right. While targeting technical and legal areas is the primary target, emphasis should also be placed on intra- and inter-team communication and the non-technical skills. Frameworks such as ANTS[252] can be modified to assist in this process to ensure that the levels of teamworking, communication and overall preparation for any forthcoming privacy incident, accident or just 'normal' work are kept at a high-level. Worth highlighting here are the four areas of the

[252] Scottish Clinical Simulation Centre. *Anaesthetists' Non-Technical Skills (ANTS) System Handbook: Framework for Observing and Rating Anaesthetists' Non-Technical Skills.* University of Aberdeen, June 2012

ANTS systems which are generally applicable: Team Working, Task Management, Decision Making and Situational Awareness.

Accident Preparation and Investigation

HOPEFULLY A DATA BREACH or similar incident will never happen, however even in the best kept systems we can find some surprising bugs such as the now infamous Heartbleed bug in OpenSSL. Having procedures to deal with these incidents *and* tools and techniques for understanding *why* the accident occurred are critical to a good solution and outcome[253]. Likewise, a good investigation procedure which not only traces down the causes but provides solutions is also critical in such situations.

[253] Zahid H. Qureshi. A review of accident modelling approaches for complex critical sociotechnical systems. Technical Report DSTO-TR-2094, Australian Government Dept. of Defence: Command, Control, Communications and Intelligence Division, January 2008

We look now as three aspects of this

- Preparation
- Investigation
- Cross-Referencing

Preparation for a privacy accident requires that a communications network and process between relevant personnel and departments is already in place. This ranges from very operational aspects such as 24-hour on-call telephone numbers being available, suitable conferencing facilities etc. to more procedural aspects as knowing who will be in charge and what the chain of command (escalations) will be. It is similarly critical to ensure that procedures are well-defined and followed from the moment an accident happens. This ensures that no errors are made in what information needs to be gathered, who needs to be contacted, what needs to be documented etc. If in the event that such an incident leads to an external legal response then it is imperative that the information privacy programme has already ensured that due diligence in case of an accident has been made[254].

[254] R.H. Wood and R.W. Sweginnis. *Aircraft Accident Investigation.* Endeavor Books/Mountain States Litho, 2006. ISBN 9781892944177

Preparation also includes practice in that it must be part of an organisation's business continuity testing and procedures[255]. While a data breach might not be seen as exciting as loss of networks or fire or some other unfortunate, more visible accident,

[255] J.T. Reason. *Managing the risks of organizational accidents.* Ashgate, 1997. ISBN 9781840141054

the consequences of being unprepared as just as great. Practice of the accident response will also show where there exist errors in procedure or where the difficulties might lie.

Investigation of an accident occurs partially as the accident happens but mainly after the event. As an accident happens it is of course necessary to understand what is happening but is relatively minimal in that we just need to gather information about the scope and overview of the effects and possible causes.

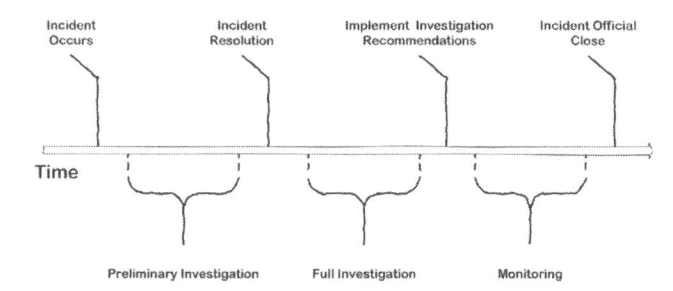

Figure 115: Accident Investigation Timeline

A full investigation generally starts after the resolution of the accident procedures and will go into more depth in order to produce a final report with recommendations. Note that any recommendations should be communication using the above mentioned mechanisms. Such an investigation will of course rely upon previously gathered information from audits and relevant data gathered via the reporting system. If as we have alluded to there is an external investigation it is imperative that procedures have been followed and due diligence made. The core of any accident report will be a root cause analysis.

It can be argued that performing this and especially the investigation constitutes a large amount of work. Reports, including analyses such as RCA and FMEA, can be as short and terse as necessary and the recommendations might actually be simple in nature. Without any of this there can be no learnings made from an accident and without learnings then the possibilities of a similar or even the same accident occurring again is just as great, if not greater, than it was before.

Cross-referencing refers to the integration, interplay and communication between different aspects and departments within an organisation. At minimum a privacy incident is going to require assistance of legal, communications, security and management. As soon as a privacy incident is known then all four (at least) must be communicated with and a relevant person made responsible within the information privacy programme to handle the overall management of the incident appointed. It is critical that the information privacy programme takes responsibility for handling the incident and acts as the central point of contact; if management of an incident is outsourced then the focus of the incident and the response will be within the context of the outsourcing. For example, if a data breach occurs and management of the incident is given to, say, operational security, then the incident will be framed in that context and not in a privacy context.

Ultimately any information privacy programme must ensure information safety and practices through communication, leadership, vigilance and ensuring that situations where data breaches of any kind might occur are investigated through proper proactive and reactive means[256].

[256] Robert L Helmreich. On error management: lessons from aviation. *British Medical Journal*, 320(781), 2000

The Knowledge Base

WITHOUT A COMMON BODY of knowledge any information privacy programme will not work. If members of the privacy group each keep their own expertise and knowledge to themselves then there can be no progress in consistent application of privacy rules and ideas into the organisation and its products. If there is no consistency then the chances of accident are greatly increased. Furthermore the reputation of any information privacy programme will be severely compromised from the point of view of any users of that programme such as the development teams.

The knowledge base itself need not be anything formal or implemented in the sense that it is not a specific database application, but rather a collection of tools, techniques, documents, policies, procedures, ticket results and learnings that can be accessed and applied consistently by all privacy programme members. In some cases automation of these might be available such as a ticketing database, metrics generation or even a standardised requirements database.

The term tools and techniques can be used in a very wide sense to include all things that are directly relevant to the running of the privacy programme and also externally available to the users of the privacy programme such as the development teams. Such tools might or will include checklists, ontological structures, taxonomies etc. Included here are also the standard operating procedures relating to the activities of the privacy programme.

The knowledge base should never sit just as a repository but be actively presented, discussed and updated. Regular or formal meetings of the members of the privacy programme, which might additionally contain interested 3rd parties from other places in the organisation, should have input into this. One method that has proven successful in many cases is the active input through directed research activity into the knowledge base; one member might have a particular interest in encryption algorithms and so might contribute this way, another might be more legally inclined and keep track of the progress of government legislation and present this to all team members. The main point here is that the knowledge base must be both deep and wide and contain input from both legal and engineering perspectives.

Having a knowledge base and standard operating procedures however does not ensure that everything does go well and care must be taken to ensure that these standard procedures do not interfere or undermine existing expertise[257]. Furthermore such procedures can not be constructed to foresee all possible future scenarios but should always act as a base for due diligence in such situations.

[257] Charles L Bosk, Mary Dixon-Woods, Christine A Goeschel, and Peter J Pronovost. Reality check for checklists. *The Lancet*, 374(9688):444–445, August 2009

Within a knowledge base must always exist the current set of base documents, which tend to be of a legal nature, defining the policies, annexes, terms and conditions, 3rd party policies etc. from which the requirements for handling of personal data and its categories can be derived. This means that we have all of these in two forms: the legal text and the derived set of requirements such as those listed in table 9 along with their refinements to architectural, design and other deeper levels as necessary.

Summary

MUCH EMPHASIS MUST BE placed on getting a functional and effective information privacy programme running. While the constituent parts of the program will vary as to what has been presented here, the work of the programme is still the same: to promote proper handling of data and information with the aim to properly protect users' privacy.

The most critical part of any programme is the knowledge base, without which there can be not common reference point for any aspect of privacy such as modelling techniques, procedures and terminology.

Finally the information privacy programme's relationship with other programmes to promote, for example, architectural and design practices, security, compliance etc. must be ensured. No programme of any nature can exist as a sole entity nor can it serve only itself - via this route lies only dogma and political infighting in its various forms destructive to the business.

Conclusions

WE HAVE PRESENTED IN this book a number of tools and techniques including data flow modelling, FMEA, RCA, threat analysis, etc. for the understanding and analysis of the privacy aspects of, theoretically, any information system. We have additionally presented structuring mechanisms for requirements, agreements, notices and consent, assessments and even of the overall privacy programme.

We have deliberately not insisted on the use of all of these in any greater formal structure; indeed forcing a structure or suite of tools and techniques on a project without allowing that project to utilise what is really required is likely to be a disaster at best. We prefer and recommend that what is presented here to be considered a toolkit with advice on which tools can be used when and for what purpose. The correct and wider use of these tools then comes from direct experience and education.

The complexity of information systems varies greatly and in some cases even a single, simple data flow model with just a few processes and a single path from data subject to consumer of the data might provide just as much complexity as a large, multi-faceted cloudified system. It might even be that in the former case we have to use many use cases, formal specification, FMEA, RCA, STRIDE and other analysis techniques. The applicability of any tool and technique should be the most important factor rather than that tool or technique's dogmatic existence. However using the tools is the only way to achieve understanding and experience in those tools and ultimately of the information system being constructed! Just having the toolkit without any attempt to use it does not help the correct development of the system.

Of particular importance to the engineers, lawyers, other privacy professionals and other disciplines is the terminology and establishing a common framework which allows disparate teams of people to communicate. This is especially so in privacy which spans a less explored area between the legal and software engineering professions.

Enforcing common terminology, even if it differs in syntactical content from what is presented here, is essential in any business or system. Even if a team internally uses their own *language*, a common terminology between teams acts as a lingua-franca that might just prevent a massive misunderstanding severely compromising the integrity and compliance of system.

From a user point of view, privacy is a growing and very serious concern and unless we can actively demonstrate that the systems we are constructing that collect and utilise their data, not just personal data, but all data and its transformation into information, knowledge and even possibly wisdom, then user trust will be eroded with economic consequences in its various forms[258].

Furthermore, steps to understand the system from a privacy perspective in the manner explained here will result in benefits in the security, performance and other non-functional domains and assist in bringing practitioners in those domains into a closer working union.

Finally, it must be once again emphasised that leaving privacy just as high-level policies does not and will never produce systems with privacy as an inherent property. Privacy **must** be engineered according to engineering principles. To reach this, privacy as a discipline must embrace the wide semantic gulf between engineering and legal and neither can or should dominate if we are really to reach the goals of systems that truly respect and enhance the consumer experience.

[258] Lothar Fritsch. The clean privacy ecosystem of the future internet. *Future Internet*, 5(1):34–45, 2013

Bibliography

Daniel Abril, Guillermo Navarro-Arribas, and Vicenç Torra. On the declassification of confidential documents. In *Modeling Decision for Artificial Intelligence*, pages 235–246. Springer, 2011.

Alessandro Acquisti. The economics of personal data and the economics of privacy, 2010.

US Administration. Executive order 13526 - classified national security information. Technical Report Section 1.4, US Government, 2009.

US Administration. Executive order 13556 controlled unclassified information. Technical report, US Government, April 2010.

Steve Adolph, Alistair Cockburn, and Paul Bramble. *Patterns for Effective Use Cases*. Addison-Wesley Longman Publishing Co., Inc., 2002. ISBN 0201721848.

Charu C. Aggarwal and Philip S. Yu. A general survey of privacy-preserving data mining models and algorithms. In Charu C. Aggarwal, Philip S. Yu, and Ahmed K. Elmagarmid, editors, *Privacy-Preserving Data Mining*, volume 34 of *The Kluwer International Series on Advances in Database Systems*, pages 11–52. Springer US, 2008.

George A. Akerlof. The market for lemons: Quality uncertainty and the market mechanism. *The Quarterly Journal of Economics*, 3(84):488–500, 1970.

Eric Allman. Managing technical debt. *Communications of the ACM*, 55(5):50–55, 2012.

Annie I. Antón and Julia Brande Earp. A requirements taxonomy for reducing web site privacy vulnerabilities. *Requirements Engineering*, 9(3):169–185, 2004.

Annie I. Anton, Julia B. Earp, Colin Potts, and Thomas A. Alspaugh. The role of policy and stakeholder privacy values in requirements engineering. In *Proceedings of the Fifth IEEE International Symposium on Requirements Engineering*, pages 138–145, 2001.

Uwe Aßmann. *Invasive software composition*. Springer, 2003. ISBN 978-3-540-44385-8.

Thomas H. Austin, Jean Yang, Cormac Flanagan, and Armando Solar-Lezama. Faceted execution of policy-agnostic programs. pages 15–26, 2013.

Franz Baader, Diego Calvanese, Deborah L. McGuinness, Daniele Nardi, and Peter F. Patel-Schneider, editors. *The description logic handbook: theory, implementation, and applications*. Cambridge University Press, New York, NY, USA, 2003. ISBN 0-521-78176-0.

Ralph J. Back and Joakim Wright. *Refinement Calculus: A Systematic Introduction (Texts in Computer Science)*. Springer, April 1998. ISBN 0387984178.

Richard Banach and Czeslaw Jeske. Simple feature engineering via neat default retrenchments. *The Journal of Logic and Algebraic Programming*, 80(8):453–480, 2011.

Richard Banach, Michael Poppleton, Czeslaw Jeske, and Susan Stepney. Engineering and theoretical underpinnings of retrenchment. *Sci. Comput. Program.*, 67(2-3):301–329, 2007.

Michael Barbaro and Tom Zeller Jr. A face is exposed for AOL searcher no. 4417749. *The New York Times*, Aug 9, 2006.

Elaine Barker, William Barker, William Burr, William Polk, and Miles Smid. Recommendation for key management - part 1: General. In *NIST Special Publication 800-57, August 2005, National Institute of Standards and Technology*, 2005.

J. Barwise and J. Seligman. *Information Flow: The Logic of Distributed Systems*. Cambridge Tracts in Theoretical Computer Science. Cambridge University Press, 1997. ISBN 9780521583862.

Kent Beck, Mike Beedle, Arie van Bennekum, Alistair Cockburn, Ward Cunningham, Martin Fowler, James Grenning, Jim Highsmith, Andrew Hunt, Ron Jeffries, Jon Kern, Brian Marick, Robert C. Martin, Steve Mellor, Ken Schwaber, Jeff Sutherland, and Dave Thomas. Manifesto for agile software development, 2001.

Khalid Belhajjame, James Cheney, David Corsar, Daniel Garijo, Stian Soiland-Reyes, Stephan Zednik, and Jun Zhao. PROV-O: The PROV Ontology. Technical report, W3C, 2012a.

Khalid Belhajjame, Helena Deus, Daniel Garijo, Graham Klyne, Paolo Missier, Stian Soiland-Reyes, and Stephen Zednik. Prov model primer. Technical report, W3C, 2012b.

Fabio Bella, Klaus Hörmann, and Bhaskar Vanamali. *From CMMI to SPICE - Experiences on How to Survive a SPICE Assessment Having Already Implemented CMMI*, volume Product-Focused Software Process Improvement of *Lecture Notes in Computer Science*, pages 133–142. 2009.

Charles L Bosk, Mary Dixon-Woods, Christine A Goeschel, and Peter J Pronovost. Reality check for checklists. *The Lancet*, 374(9688):444–445, August 2009.

Kim Bustin. Conducting a privacy gap analysis: A primer for privacy officers. October 2011.

A J Card, J R Ward, and P J Clarkson. Beyond FMEA: the structured what-if technique (SWIFT). *Journal of Healthcare Risk Management*, (31):23–29, 2012.

Ann Cavoukian. *Moving Forward From PETs to PETs Plus: The Time for Change is Now*. Information and Privacy Commissioner of Ontario, Canada, January 2009.

Ann Cavoukian. Privacy by Design: A Primer, September 2013.

Centers for Medicare and Medicaid Services. The Health Insurance Portability and Accountability Act of 1996 (HIPAA), 1996.

Scottish Clinical Simulation Centre. *Anaesthetists' Non-Technical Skills (ANTS) System Handbook: Framework for Observing and Rating Anaesthetists' Non-Technical Skills*. University of Aberdeen, June 2012.

Gayathri Chandrasekaran, Tam Vu, Alexander Varshavsky, Marco Gruteser, Richard P. Martin, Jie Yang 0003, and Yingying Chen. Tracking vehicular speed variations by warping mobile phone signal strengths. In *PerCom*, pages 213–221. IEEE, 2011.

Peter Checkland and Sue Holwell. *Information, Systems and Information Systems: Making Sense of the Field*. John Wiley & Sons, Inc., 1998.

V. Ciriani, S. Capitani di Vimercati, S. Foresti, and P. Samarati. κ-anonymity. In Ting Yu and Sushil Jajodia, editors, *Secure Data Management in Decentralized Systems*, volume 33 of *Advances in Information Security*, pages 323–353. Springer US, 2007.

CMMI Product Team. CMMI for systems engineering, software engineering, integrated. product and process development, and supplier sourcing. cmu/sei-2002-tr-011. Technical report, Software Engineering Institute, Carnegie Mellon University., Pittsburgh, Pennsylvania, 2002.

Benjamin Coifman and Michael Cassidy. Vehicle reidentification and travel time measurement on congested freeways. *Transportation Research Part A: Policy and Practice*, 36(10):899 – 917, 2002. ISSN 0965-8564.

European Commission. European Commission's press release announcing the proposed comprehensive reform of data protection rules, 25 January 2012.

USA Congress. Public Law 107 - 56 - Uniting and strengthening America by providing appropriate tools required to intercept and obstruct terrorism (USA PATRIOT ACT) act of 2001, 2001.

ABC Consulting. *Root Cause Analysis Handbook: A Guide to Effective Incident Investigation*. Rothstein Associates Inc., 2nd edition, 2005.

What is CUI? Controlled Unclassified Information Office, National Archives and Records Administration.

ChristopherJ. Cowton. The use of secondary data in business ethics research. *Journal of Business Ethics*, 17(4):423–434, 1998.

Jason Cronk. Thoughts on the term "privacy enhancing technologies". Via blog, 2013.

J. Daemen and V. Rijmen. *The Design of Rijndael: AES - The Advanced Encryption Standard*. Information Security and Cryptography. Springer, 2002. ISBN 9783540425809.

Fida Dankar, Khaled E. Emam, Angelica Neisa, and Tyson Roffey. Estimating the re-identification risk of clinical data sets. *BMC Medical Informatics and Decision Making*, 66, 9 July 2012.

C. J. Date. *An Introduction to Database Systems (7th Ed.)*. Addison-Wesley Longman Publishing Co., Inc., Boston, MA, USA, 1999. ISBN 0-201-38590-2.

John Day. The (un)revised OSI reference model. *SIGCOMM Comput. Commun. Rev.*, 25(5):39–55, October 1995. ISSN 0146-4833.

Yves-Alexandre de Montjoye, César A. Hidalgo, Michel Verleysen, and Vincent D. Blondel. Unique in the crowd: The privacy bounds of human mobility. *Scientific Reports*, 2013a.

Yves-Alexandre de Montjoye, César A. Hidalgo, Michel Verleysen, and Vincent D. Blondel. Unique in the Crowd: The privacy bounds of human mobility. *Scientific Reports*, 3, March 2013b.

Bart De Win, Riccardo Scandariato, Koen Buyens, Johan Grégoire, and Wouter Joosen. On the secure software development process: CLASP, SDL and Touchpoints compared. *Information and software technology*, 51(7):1152–1171, 2009.

Mina Deng. *Privacy preserving content protection*. PhD thesis, Katholieke Universality, Belgium, 2010.

Li Ding, Jie Bao, JamesR. Michaelis, Jun Zhao, and DeborahL. McGuinness. Reflections on provenance ontology encodings. In DeborahL. McGuinness, JamesR. Michaelis, and Luc Moreau, editors, *Provenance and Annotation of Data and Processes*, volume 6378 of *Lecture Notes in Computer Science*, pages 198–205. Springer Berlin Heidelberg, 2010. ISBN 978-3-642-17818-4.

E. U. Directive. 95/46/EC of the European Parliament and of the Council of 24 October 1995 on the Protection of Individuals with Regard to the Processing of Personal Data and on the Free Movement of such Data. *Official Journal of the EC*, 23, 1995.

Merlin Dorfman. System and software requirements engineering. In *IEEE Computer Society Press Tutorial*, pages 7–22. IEEE Computer Society Press, 1990.

Cynthia Dwork. Differential privacy: A survey of results. In *Theory and Applications of Models of Computation*, volume 4978 of *Lecture Notes in Computer Science*, pages 1–19. Springer Verlag, April 2008.

Peter Eckersley. How unique is your web browser? Technical report, Electronic Frontier Foundation, 2009.

Khaled El Emam and Fida Kamal K. Dankar. Protecting privacy using κ-anonymity. *Journal of the American Medical Informatics Association : JAMIA*, 15(5):627–637, 2008. ISSN 1527-974X.

Khaled El Emam, Emilio Neri, and Elizabeth Jonker. An evaluation of personal health information remnants in second-hand personal computer disk drives. *Journal of medical Internet research*, 9(3), 2007.

Japan Electronics and Information Technology Industries Association. JEITA CP-3451 exchangeable image file format for digital still cameras: EXIF version 2.2, 2002.

Dag Elgesem. The Structure of Rights in Directive 95/46/EC On the Protection of Individuals with Regard to The processing of Personal Data and the Free Movement Of Such Data. *Ethics and Inf. Technol.*, 1(4):283–293, February 1999. ISSN 1388-1957.

Khaled Emam, Fida Dankar, R+'egis Vaillancourt, Tyson Roffey, and Mark Lysyk. Evaluating the risk of re-identification of patients from hospital prescription records. *The Canadian Journal of Hospital Pharmacy*, 62(4), 2009.

Clif Ericson. Fault tree analysis - a history. In *Proceedings of The 17th International System Safety Conference*, 1999.

EU. 2000/520/EC: Commission Decision of 26 July 2000 pursuant to Directive 95/46/EC of the European Parliament and of the Council on the adequacy of the protection provided by the safe harbour privacy principles and related frequently asked questions issued by the US Department of Commerce (notified under document number C(2000) 2441) (Text with EEA relevance.), 2000.

EU. Directive 2002/58/EC of the European Parliament and of the Council Concerning the Processing of Personal Data and the Protection of Privacy in the Electronic Communications Sector, 2002.

EU. Opinion 4/2007 on the concept of personal data. article 29 data protection working party, June 2007.

EU. Opinion 15/2011 on the definition of consent. article 29 data protection working party, 2011.

Privacy Enhancing Technologies (PETs). European Commission, Brussels, memo/07/159 edition, May 2007.

Handbook on European Data Protection Law. European Union Agency for Fundamental Rights, April 2014.

Ian Farquhar. Engineering security solutions at layer 8 and above. *RSA Speaking of Security Blog*, 7 December 2010.

R. Fielding, J. Gettys, J. Mogul, H. Frystyk, L. Masinter, P. Leach, and T. Berners-Lee. RFC 2616, Hypertext Transfer Protocol – HTTP/1.1, 1999.

Roy T Fielding. *Architectural Styles and the Design of Network-based Software Architectures*. PhD thesis, University of California, 2002.

Roy T. Fielding and Richard N. Taylor. Principled design of the modern web architecture. *ACM Trans. Internet Technol.*, 2 (2):115–150, May 2002.

International Organisation for Standardisation. Open systems interconnection - basic reference model: ISO/IEC 7498-1, November 1994.

Martin Frické. The knowledge pyramid: a critique of the DIKW hierarchy. *J. Information Science*, 35(2):131–142, 2009.

Arik Friedman, Ran Wolff, and Assaf Schuster. Providing κ-anonymity in data mining. *The VLDB Journal*, 17(4):789–804, July 2008. ISSN 1066-8888.

Lothar Fritsch. The clean privacy ecosystem of the future internet. *Future Internet*, 5(1):34–45, 2013.

Erich Gamma, Richard Helm, Ralph Johnson, and John Vlissides. *Design Patterns*. Addison-Wesley, 1995. ISBN 0201633612.

Atul Gawande. *The Checklist Manifesto*. Profile Books, 2011.

Constantine Gikas. A general comparison of FISMA, HIPAA, ISO27000 and PCI-DSS standards. *Information Security Journal: A Global Perspective*, 19(3):132–141, 2010.

Daniel Gilbert. *Stumbling on Happiness Paperback*. Vintage, 2007.

Henri Gilbert and Helena Handschuh. Security analysis of SHA-256 and sisters. In Mitsuru Matsui and Robert J. Zuccherato, editors, *Selected Areas in Cryptography*, volume 3006 of *Lecture Notes in Computer Science*, pages 175–193. Springer, 2003.

Ian Avrum Goldberg. *A pseudonymous communications infrastructure for the internet*. PhD thesis, University of California, 2000.

Cesar Gonzalez-Perez and Brian Henderson-Sellers. A powertype-based metamodelling framework. *Software and Systems Modeling*, 5(1):72–90, 2006. ISSN 1619-1366. DOI: 10.1007/s10270-005-0099-9.

I. J. Good. Studies in the History of Probability and Statistics. XXXVII A. M. Turing's statistical work in World War II. *Biometrika*, 66(2):393–396, 1979.

Glenn Greenwald, Ewen MacAskill, and Laura Poitras. Edward Snowden: the whistleblower behind the NSA surveillance revelations. *The Guardian*, 10 June 2013.

Michael Gregg. OSI: Securing the Stack, Layer 8 – Social engineering and security policy. *TechTarget*, 1 May 2007.

J. Guaspari. *I Know It When I See It*. AMACOM BOOKS, 2004. ISBN 9780814473931.

Seda Gürses, Carmela Troncoso, and Claudia Diaz. Engineering privacy by design. In *Conference on Computers, Privacy and Data Protection (CPDP)*, 2011.

Munawar Hafiz. A collection of privacy design patterns. In *Proceedings of the 2006 Conference on Pattern Languages of Programs*, PLoP '06, pages 7:1–7:13, New York, NY, USA, 2006. ACM. ISBN 978-1-60558-372-3. DOI: 10.1145/1415472.1415481.

Qingfeng He, Annie I Antón, et al. A framework for modeling privacy requirements in role engineering. In *Proceedings of REFSQ*, volume 3, pages 137–146, 2003.

Robert L Helmreich. On error management: lessons from aviation. *British Medical Journal*, 320(781), 2000.

M. Howard and S. Lipner. *The security development lifecycle: SDL, a process for developing demonstrably more secure software*. Microsoft Press Series. Microsoft Press, 2006.

Kai-Lung Hui and I. P. L. Png. The economics of privacy. In Terrence Hendershott, editor, *Handbooks in Information Systems*, volume 1, chapter 9. Elsevier, 2006.

Rebecca Iglesias, Rob Nicholls, Anisha Travis, and Webb Henderson. Private clouds with no silver lining : Legal risk in private cloud services. *Communications and Strategies*, 84(1), 2012.

Information Commissioner. *Data Protection Act 1998 Legal Guidance: a reference document for organisations and their advisers that provides a broad guide to the Act as a whole*. Information Commissioner's office, September 2009.

Privacy by Design: An Overview of Privacy Enhancing Technologies. The Information Commissioner's Office (UK), November 2008.

Anonymisation: Managing Data Protection Risk Code of Practice. The Information Commissioner's Office (UK), November 2012.

Direct Marketing: Data Protection Act Privacy and Electronic Communications Regulations. The Information Commissioner's Office (UK), 24 November 2013. Version 1.1.

Ponemon Institute. 2013 cost of data breach study: United kingdom, May 2013.

Project Management Institute. *A Guide To The Project Management Body Of Knowledge (PMBOK Guides).* Project Management Institute, 2004. ISBN 193069945X, 9781933890517.

RFC 791 Internet Protocol - DARPA Internet Programme, Protocol Specification. Internet Engineering Task Force, September 1981.

ISO29100: Information technology - Security techniques - Privacy framework. ISO/IEC, 29100:2011(e) edition, December 2011.

Christos Kalloniatis, Evangelia Kavakli, and Stefanos Gritzalis. Addressing privacy requirements in system design: the PriS method. *Requirements Engineering*, 13(3):241–255, 2008.

T. Kern. *Flight Discipline.* McGraw-Hill Education, 1998. ISBN 9780071503204.

Gregor Kiczales. Towards a new model of abstraction in the engineering of software. *IMSA'92 Proceedings (Workshop on Reflection and Meta-level Architectures)*, 1992.

Anya Kim. Position paper building privacy into the semantic web: An ontology needed now, 2002.

Martin Kost, Johann Christoph Freytag, Frank Kargl, and Antonio Kung. Privacy verification using ontologies. In *ARES*, pages 627–632. IEEE, 2011. ISBN 978-1-4577-0979-1.

Gerald Kotonya and I. Sommerville. *Requirements engineering: processes and techniques.* Worldwide series in computer science. J. Wiley, 1998. ISBN 9780471972082.

Philippe Kruchten. The frog and the octopus: a conceptual model of software development. *CoRR*, abs/1209.1327, 2012.

Philippe Kruchten, Robert L. Nord, Ipek Ozkaya, and Joost Visser. Technical debt in software development: from metaphor to theory report on the third international workshop on managing technical debt. *ACM SIGSOFT Software Engineering Notes*, 37(5):36–38, 2012.

Philippe Kruchten, Robert L Nord, Ipek Ozkaya, and Davide Falessi. Technical debt: towards a crisper definition report on the 4th international workshop on managing technical debt. *ACM SIGSOFT Software Engineering Notes*, 38(5):51–54, 2013.

Butler W. Lampson. A note on the confinement problem. *Communications of the ACM*, 16(10):613–615, October 1973.

Peter Langendörfer, Michael Maaser, Krzysztof Piotrowski, and Steffen Peter. *Privacy Enhancing Techniques: A Survey and Classification*. Information Science Reference, 2008.

Peter Gorm Larsen, Nico Plat, and Hans Toetenel. A formal semantics of data flow diagrams. *Formal Aspects of Computing*, 3, 1994.

Ora Lassila, Mika Mannermaa, Marwan Sabbouh, and Ian Oliver. Aspect-oriented data. In *W3C Workshop on RDF Next Steps*, June 2012.

Yang W. Lee, Diane M. Strong, Beverly K. Kahn, and Richard Y. Wang. Aimq: a methodology for information quality assessment. *Information and Management*, 40(2):133–146, 2002.

Lawrence Lessig. *Code and other laws of cyberspace*. Basic, New York, 1999.

Lawrence Lessig. Code is law: On liberty in cyberspace. *Harvard Magazine*, Jan-Feb 2000.

D. K. Lewis. *Convention: A Philosophical Study*. Oxford: Blackwell, 1969.

Ninghui Li and Tiancheng Li. t-closeness: Privacy beyond κ-anonymity and ℓ-diversity. In *In Proc. of IEEE 23rd International Conference on Data Engineering (ICDE'07*, 2007.

Barbara Liskov. Keynote address - data abstraction and hierarchy. In *Addendum to the Proceedings on Object-oriented Programming Systems, Languages and Applications (Addendum)*, OOPSLA '87, pages 17–34. ACM, 1987a. ISBN 0-89791-266-7.

Barbara Liskov. Keynote address - data abstraction and hierarchy. *SIGPLAN Not.*, 23(5):17–34, January 1987b. ISSN 0362-1340.

Chang Liu and Kirk P. Arnett. An examination of privacy policies in fortune 500 web sites. *American Journal of Business*, 17(1):13–22, 2002.

Panagiotis Louridas. Some guidelines for non-repudiation protocols. *SIGCOMM Comput. Commun. Rev.*, 30(5):29–38, October 2000.

Gus Lubin. The incredible story of how Target exposed a teen girl's pregnancy. *Business Insider*, February 16 2012.

Ashwin Machanavajjhala, Johannes Gehrke, Daniel Kifer, and Muthuramakrishnan Venkitasubramaniam. ℓ-diversity: Privacy beyond κ-anonymity. *2013 IEEE 29th International Conference on Data Engineering (ICDE)*, 0:24, 2006.

Shah Mahmood and Yvo Desmedt. Two new economic models for privacy. *SIGMETRICS Performance Evaluation Review*, 40(4): 84–89, 2013.

Robert A. Martin and Sean Barnum. Common weakness enumeration (CWE) status update. *Ada Lett.*, XXVIII(1):88–91, April 2008. ISSN 1094-3641.

Miguel A. Martínez, Joaquín Lasheras, Eduardo Fernández-Medina, José Ambrosio Toval Álvarez, and Mario Piattini. A personal data audit method through requirements engineering. *Computer Standards & Interfaces*, 32(4):166–178, 2010.

Aaron K. Massey and Annie I. Antón. A requirements-based comparison of privacy taxonomies. In *Proceedings of the 2008 Requirements Engineering and Law*, RELAW '08, pages 1–5, Washington, DC, USA, 2008. IEEE Computer Society. ISBN 978-0-7695-3630-9.

Aaron K. Massey, Paul N. Otto, Lauren J. Hayward, and Annie I. Anton. Evaluating existing security and privacy requirements for legal compliance. *Requirements Engineering*, 15(1): 119–137, 2010. ISSN 0947-3602.

Thomas J. McCabe and Charles W. Butler. Design complexity measurement and testing. *Communications of the ACM*, 32(12): 1415–1425, December 1989.

Erika McCallister, Timothy Grance, and Karen A. Scarfone. SP 800-122. Guide to Protecting the Confidentiality of Personally Identifiable Information (PII). Technical report, NIST, Gaithersburg, MD, United States, 2010.

John McCarthy. Circumscription - a form of non-monotonic reasoning. *Artificial intelligence*, 13(1):27–39, 1980.

R. McDermott, R.J. Mikulak, and M. Beauregard. *The Basics of FMEA*. 2nd edition, 1996. ISBN 9780527763206.

Michael Mealling and Ray Denenberg. Uniform Resource Identifiers (URIs), URLs, and Uniform Resource Names (URNs): Clarifications and Recommendations. Internet RFC 3305, August 2002.

Thomas Finneran Michelle Finneran Dennedy, Jonathan Fox. *The Privacy Engineer's Manifesto: Getting from Policy to Code to QA to Value*. Apress, 2014.

Richard Mitchell, Jim McKim, and Bertrand Meyer. *Design by Contract, by Example*. Addison Wesley Longman Publishing Co., Inc., Redwood City, CA, USA, 2002. ISBN 0-201-63460-0.

Rajeev Motwani and Ying Xu. Efficient algorithms for masking and finding quasi-identifiers. In *Proceedings of the Conference on Very Large Data Bases (VLDB)*, 2007.

Arvind Narayanan and Vitaly Shmatikov. Robust de-anonymization of large sparse datasets. In *Proceedings of the 2008 IEEE Symposium on Security and Privacy*, SP '08, pages 111–125, Washington, DC, USA, 2008. IEEE Computer Society. ISBN 978-0-7695-3168-7. DOI: 10.1109/SP.2008.33. URL http://dx.doi.org/10.1109/SP.2008.33.

J.F. Nash. *Non-cooperative Games*. Princeton University, 1950.

NIST Special Publication 800-53: Security and Privacy Controls for Federal Information Systems and Organizations. National Institute of Standards and Technology, April 2013.

Helen Nissenbaum. Will security enhance trust online, or supplant it? In R. Kramer and K. Cook, editors, *Trust and Distrust Within Organizations: Emerging Perspectives, Enduring Questions*, pages 155–188. Russell Sage Publications, 2004.

Helen Nissenbaum. *Privacy in Context: Technology, Policy, and the Integrity of Social Life*. Stanford University Press, 2010. 9780804752367.

Helen Nissenbaum. A contextual approach to privacy online. *Daedalus*, 140(4):32–48, Fall 2011.

OECD. Development of policies for protection of critical information infrastructures, 2007.

US Dept of Defence. *National Industrial Security Program Operating Manual*, inc, change 1, march 28 2013 edition, February 2006.

Executive Office of the President. Safeguarding against and responding to the breach of personally identifiable information. Memorandum M-07-16, 22 May 2007.

The UK Cabinet Office. Security policy framework, April 2013.

Lukasz Olejnik, Claude Castelluccia, Artur Janc, et al. Why Johnny can't browse in peace: On the uniqueness of web browsing history patterns. In *5th Workshop on Hot Topics in Privacy Enhancing Technologies (HotPETs 2012)*, 2012.

Ian Oliver. An advertiser's paradise: An adventure in a dystopian post-'do not track world?'. In *W3C Workshop: Do Not Track and Beyond*, November 2012.

Ian Oliver and Ora Lassila. Integration in the large. In *W3C Workshop on Data and Services Integration*, October 2011.

United States. Congress. House. Committee on Commerce. *Child Online Protection Act: report (to accompany H.R. 3783) (including cost estimate of the Congressional Budget Office)*. Report. U.S. G.P.O., 1998.

Risk Taxonomy. The Open Group, 2009.

D L Parnas and P C Clements. A rational design process: How and why to fake it. *IEEE Transactions in Software Engineering*, 12(2):251–257, February 1986.

Payment Card Industry (PCI) Data Security Standard: Requirements and Security Assessment Procedures. PCI Security Standards Council, version 3.0 edition, November 2013.

Joe Peppard and John Ward. Unlocking sustained business value from it investments. 2005.

J.K. Petersen. *Understanding Surveillance Technologies: Spy Devices, Their Origins & Applications*. Taylor & Francis, 2000. ISBN 9781420038811.

Shari Lawrence Pfleeger. Risky business: what we have yet to learn about risk management. *Journal of Systems and Software*, 53(3):265–273, 2000.

Benjamin C. Pierce. Differential privacy in the programming languages community, October 2012. Invited tutorial at *DIMACS Workshop on Recent Work on Differential Privacy across Computer Science*.

R.M. Pirsig. *Zen and the Art of Motorcycle Maintenance: An Inquiry Into Values*. Bantam Books: Nonfiction. Vintage, 1974. ISBN 9780099786405.

Andrei Popescu. Geolocation API Specification. World Wide Web Consortium, Working Draft WD-geolocation-API-20081222, December 2008.

J. Postel. Transmission Control Protocol, September 1981. Updated by RFCs 1122, 3168.

Peter Pronovost, Dale Needham, Sean Berenholtz, David Sinopoli, Haitao Chu, Sara Cosgrove, Bryan Sexton, Robert Hyzy, Robert Welsh, Gary Roth, Joseph Bander, John Kepros, and Christine Goeschel. An Intervention to Decrease Catheter-Related Bloodstream Infections in the ICU. *New England Journal of Medicine*, 355(26):2725–2732, 2006.

P.S.Meilinger. When the fortress went down. *Air Force Magazine*, pages 78–82, 2004.

Zahid H. Qureshi. A review of accident modelling approaches for complex socio-technical systems. In *Proceedings of the Twelfth Australian Workshop on Safety Critical Systems and Software and Safety-related Programmable Systems - Volume 86*, SCS '07, pages 47–59. Australian Computer Society, Inc., 2007.

Zahid H. Qureshi. A review of accident modelling approaches for complex critical sociotechnical systems. Technical Report DSTO-TR-2094, Australian Government Dept. of Defence: Command, Control, Communications and Intelligence Division, January 2008.

James Reason. *Human Error*. Cambridge [England] ; New York : Cambridge University Press, 1990. xv, 302 p., 1990.

James Reason. Human error: models and management. *British Medical Journal*, 320(7237):768–770, March 2000. ISSN 0959-8138.

J.T. Reason. *Managing the risks of organizational accidents*. Ashgate, 1997. ISBN 9781840141054.

Jason Reed and Benjamin C. Pierce. Distance makes the types grow stronger: A calculus for differential privacy. In *ACM SIGPLAN International Conference on Functional Programming (ICFP), Baltimore, Maryland*, September 2010.

Jeff Reed. *Project Management with PRINCE2 Best Practice Handbook: Building, Running and Managing Effective Project Management - Ready to Use Supporting Documents Bringing PRINCE2 Theory into Practice*. Emereo Pty Ltd, London, UK, UK, 2008. ISBN 1921573104, 9781921573101.

Trilaterial Research and Consulting. *Privacy impact assessment and risk management*. Information Commissiner's Office, May 2013.

Neil M. Richards and Daniel J. Solove. Privacy's Other Path: Recovering the Law of Confidentiality. *The Georgetown Law Journal*, 96:123–182, 2007.

Sasha Romanosky, Alessandro Acquisti, Jason Hong, Lorrie Faith Cranor, and Batya Friedman. Privacy patterns for online interactions. In *Proceedings of the 2006 conference on Pattern languages of programs*, pages 1–9, Portland, Oregon, 2006. ACM. ISBN 978-1-60558-372-3.

Jennifer Rowley. The wisdom hierarchy: representations of the DIKW hierarchy. *J. Information Science*, 33(2):163–180, 2007.

Owen Sacco, Alexandre Passant, and Stefan Decker. An access control framework for the web of data. In *Trust, Security and Privacy in Computing and Communications (TrustCom), 2011 IEEE 10th International Conference on*, pages 456–463. IEEE, 2011.

Robert Schmitt and Carsten Scharrenberg. Approach for improved production process planning by the application of quality gates and DRBFM. In George Q. Huang, Kai-Ling Mak, and Paul G. Maropoulos, editors, *DET*, volume 66 of *Advances in Intelligent and Soft Computing*, pages 1089–1100. Springer, 2009. ISBN 978-3-642-10429-9.

Geri Schneider and Jason P. Winters. *Applying Use Cases: A Practical Guide*. Addison-Wesley Longman Publishing Co., Inc., 1998. ISBN 0-201-30981-5.

Bruce Schneier. *Applied Cryptography (2Nd Ed.): Protocols, Algorithms, and Source Code in C*. John Wiley & Sons, Inc., New York, NY, USA, 1995. ISBN 0-471-11709-9.

Bruce Schneier. *Beyond Fear: Thinking Sensibly about Security in an Uncertain World*. Copernicus, September 2003. ISBN 0387026207.

Bruce Schneier. Architecture of privacy. *IEEE Security & Privacy*, 7(1):88, 2009. ISSN 1540-7993.

PCI Security Standards Council Scoping SIG, Tokenization Taskforce. *Information Supplement: PCI DSS Tokenization Guidelines*, August 2011.

Shayak Sen, Saikat Guha, Anupam Datta, Sriram K Rajamani, Janice Tsai, and Jeannette M Wing. Bootstrapping privacy compliance in big data systems. In *Proceedings of the 35th IEEE Symposium on Security and Privacy (Oakland)*, 2014.

IBM Global Services. *Privacy Architecture Overview*. Government of Alberta, Canada, May 2003.

Claude E. Shannon. A mathematical theory of communication. *The Bell System Technical Journal*, 27:379–423, 623–656, July, October 1948.

Yuval Shavitt and Noa Zilberman. A study of geolocation databases. *CoRR*, abs/1005.5674, 2010.

A. Shostack. *Threat Modeling: Designing for Security*. Wiley, 2014. ISBN 9781118809990.

Adam Shostack. Experiences of threat modeling at Microsoft. In *Modeling Security Workshop. Dept. of Computing, Lancaster University, UK*, 2008.

Daniel Solove. Privacy Self-Management and the Consent Paradox. *Harvard Law Review*, 126, 2013.

Daniel J. Solove. Conceptualizing Privacy. *California Law Review*, 90(4):1087–1155, 2002.

Daniel J. Solove. A taxonomy of privacy. *University of Pennsylvania Law Review*, 154(3):477 pp., January 2006. GWU Law School Public Law Research Paper No. 129.

Ian Sommerville. *Software Engineering*. Addison-Wesley, 9 edition, 2010.

Sarah Spiekermann. The challenges of privacy by design. *Communications of the ACM*, 55(7):38–40, July 2012.

Sarah Spiekermann and Lorrie Faith Cranor. Engineering privacy. *Software Engineering, IEEE Transactions on*, 35(1):67–82, 2009.

Michael Stamatelatos, Homayoon Dezfuli, George Apostolakis, Chester Everline, Sergio Guarro, Donovan Mathias, Ali Mosleh, Todd Paulos, David Riha, Curtis Smith, et al. Probabilistic risk assessment procedures guide for NASA managers and practitioners. 2011.

D. Stuttard and M. Pinto. *The Web Application Hacker's Handbook: Finding and Exploiting Security Flaws*. Wiley, 2011.

JohnR. Suler. Identity management in cyberspace. *Journal of Applied Psychoanalytic Studies*, 4(4):455–459, 2002.

Latanya Sweeney. κ-anonymity: A model for protecting privacy. *Int. J. Uncertain. Fuzziness Knowl.-Based Syst.*, 10(5):557–570, October 2002. ISSN 0218-4885.

N.R. Tague. *The Quality Toolbox, Second Edition:*. ASQ Quality Press, 2005. ISBN 9780873896399.

Kuo-Chung Tai. A program complexity metric based on data flow information in control graphs. In *Proceedings of the 7th International Conference on Software Engineering*, pages 239–248. IEEE Press, 1984.

Andrew Tanenbaum. *Computer Networks*. Prentice Hall Professional Technical Reference, 4th edition, 2002. ISBN 0130661023.

Technical Standardization Committee on AV & IT Storage Systems and Equipment. Exchangeable image file format for digital still cameras: EXIF Version 2.2. Technical Report JEITA CP-3451, JEITA, April 2002.

Simon Thompson. *Type Theory and Functional Programming*. Addison-Wesley, 1991.

United States Code. Sarbanes-Oxley Act of 2002, PL 107-204, 116 Stat 745. Codified in Sections 11, 15, 18, 28, and 29 USC, July 2002.

Jennifer M. Urban, Chris J. Hoofnagle, and Su Li. Mobile phones and privacy. *Social Science Research Network Working Paper Series*, 12 July 2012.

Eduardo Ustaran, editor. *European Privacy: Law and Practice for Data Protection Professionals*. An IAPP Publication, 2012. 978-0-9795901-5-3.

Abhishek Vaish, Abhishek Kushwaha, Rahul Das, and Chandan Sharma. Data location verification in cloud computing. *International Journal of Computer Applications*, 68(12):23–27, April 2013. Published by Foundation of Computer Science, New York, USA.

Jeroen van Rest, Daniel Boonstra, Maarten Everts, Martin van Rijn, and Ron van Paassen. Designing privacy-by-design. In Bart Preneel and Demosthenes Ikonomou, editors, *Privacy*

Technologies and Policy, volume 8319 of *Lecture Notes in Computer Science*, pages 55–72. Springer Berlin Heidelberg, 2014.

Renata Vieira, Douglas da Silva, and Tomas Sander. Representation and inference of privacy risks using semantic web technologies. *CEP*, 90619:900, 2010.

T.M. Virtue. *Payment Card Industry Data Security Standard Handbook*. Wiley, 2008. ISBN 9780470260463.

M.V. Volkenstein, A. Shenitzer, and R.G. Burns. *Entropy and Information*. Progress in Mathematical Physics. Birkhäuser Basel, 2009. ISBN 9783034600774.

L. Von Bertalanffy. *General System Theory: Foundations, Development, Applications*. The international library of systems theory and philosophy. Braziller, 2003.

R. Wacks. *Privacy: A Very Short Introduction*. Very Short Introductions. OUP Oxford, 2010. ISBN 9780191609626.

Michael Wei, Laura M. Grupp, Frederick E. Spada, and Steven Swanson. Reliably erasing data from flash-based solid state drives. In *Proceedings of the 9th USENIX Conference on File and Storage Technologies*, FAST'11. USENIX Association, 2011.

R Wood. *Aviation Safety Programs*. Jeppsen, 3rd edition edition, 2003.

R.H. Wood and R.W. Sweginnis. *Aircraft Accident Investigation*. Endeavor Books/Mountain States Litho, 2006. ISBN 9781892944177.

Implementation manual WHO Surgical Safety Checklist. World Health Organization, 2008. WHO/IER/PSP/2008.05.

Jean Yang, Kuat Yessenov, and Armando Solar-Lezama. A language for automatically enforcing privacy policies. pages 85–96, 2012.

Chaim Zins. Conceptual approaches for defining data, information, and knowledge. *JASIST*, 58(4):479–493, 2007.

Dr Ian Oliver is a privacy officer and software engineer in the Security, Privacy and Continuity team at Here - a Nokia Company - with responsibility for auditing, mentoring and developing solutions for privacy in Here's information and mapping systems. He also holds a Research Fellow position at the University of Brighton working with the Visual Modelling Group on diagrammatic forms of reasoning and description logics and applying these technologies to understanding information systems.

Prior to that he worked for many years at Nokia Research Centre on Semantic Web and Big Data technologies, UML, formal methods and hardware-software co-design. He has also worked at Helsinki University of Technology and Aalto University teaching formal methods and modelling with UML. He holds 30 patents in areas including the Internet of Things, semantic technologies and privacy.

Printed in Poland
by Amazon Fulfillment
Poland Sp. z o.o., Wrocław